TWO BROTHERS

TWO BROTHERS

JONATHAN WILSON

Little, Brown

LITTLE, BROWN

First published in Great Britain in 2022 by Little, Brown

1 3 5 7 9 10 8 6 4 2

A CIP catalogue record for this book is available from the British Library.

Hardback ISBN 978-1-408-71449-2
Trade Paperback ISBN 978-1-408-71450-8

Typeset in Sabon by M Rules
Printed and bound in Great Britain by Clays Ltd, Elcograf S.p.A.

Papers used by Little, Brown are from well-managed forests
and other responsible sources.

MIX
Paper from
responsible sources
FSC® C104740

Little, Brown
An imprint of
Little, Brown Book Group
Carmelite House
50 Victoria Embankment
London EC4Y 0DZ

An Hachette UK Company
www.hachette.co.uk

www.littlebrown.co.uk

CONTENTS

Preface   1

Introduction   5

1 Home   9
2 Childhood   23
3 Doubts and Debuts   40
4 Years of Drift   53
5 Munich   64
6 The Rise of the Machines   82
7 Regeneration   96
8 Modernity and its Discontents   114
9 Their Finest Hour   129
10 Grail   161
11 Success and Superstition   173
12 A Farewell to Arms   187
13 Decline and Fall   194
14 Next Steps   220
15 The Long Good Wednesday   240
16 His Own Land   263
17 Another FAI Mess   277
18 Years of Glory   292
19 After the Party   310
20 Curtain   330

Acknowledgements   339
Endnotes   341
Bibliography   363
Index   367

PREFACE

First the boy ducked, then he was forced to crawl. He was fifteen years old and over six feet tall, shuffling on his knees in the dark. A blast of hot air hit him from a ventilation duct and he tasted coal dust in his mouth, felt grit in his eyes. There was an explosion, a great roar that shook the earth and reverberated through the narrow tunnels several hundred feet below the surface. The machinery clanked and banged. The boy was hunched over, he couldn't see and he couldn't hear. It was hell. And it was dangerous. Death stalked the pits.

Linton Colliery was fortunate. It never had a disaster – not like the nearby pit at Woodhorn, where thirteen men died in an underground explosion in 1916. But still, everybody knew somebody who had lost their life down there. The previous year, twenty-six-year-old Thomas Tait had been crushed by a fall of coal. Nine months before that, just before Christmas, Frederick Johnson, a coal-cutter, had perished from ruptured organs. A year earlier, Cyril Queen, a twenty-one-year-old drawer, had died six days after a heap of stone had fallen on him and been buried in St John's churchyard in Ashington. Between 1897 and 1961, Linton suffered fifty-three fatalities.[1]

And it wasn't just the danger. The pit was deeply unpleasant. It was dark and windy, hot and cold. When they fired the shots, it was deafening, even though everybody covered their ears.

Then they would stand where they were for five minutes while the dust settled before it became possible to see again. Food had to be hung from the roof in pails to protect it from mice. Most miners had scars down their spines from scraping against the roofs of the low tunnels. They spent their lives covered in coal dust. In the days before the baths were installed at the pits, many would have a permanent black square on their backs which they couldn't reach to wash – and besides, superstition suggested that washing a back made it weak. Their hands would seem permanently grubby, not from dirt itself but from nicks and scratches that were stained by the coal.

This was where the boy's father spent five and a half days a week throughout his working life, where he had sustained an injury that for weeks had left one side of his face swollen and bruised – not that he took a day off work. It was where his grandfather had laboured, where almost everybody he knew earned their meagre living. The boy had agitated to come down the pit. When he'd begun his apprenticeship, he'd been assigned to a conveyor belt on the surface, sorting coal from debris for eight hours a day. Patience did not come naturally to him, and he was bored. He begged for a move and was shifted to the weigh cabin, where he calculated the amount of coal in wagons leaving the shaft. He still found it dull, but at least there were breaks during which he could draw on the walls with a piece of stone or lay snares in the nearby fields. The boy had a natural sharpness with money – his grandfather was a notorious local bookmaker – and soon developed a side line selling the rabbits he had caught. But the surface wasn't real mining: eventually he would have to go down the pit itself.

His first day of a sixteen-week apprenticeship, though, was enough. His job was to be 'hanging on and knocking off'. He watched another miner perform the task, standing at the junction of two rail lines, grabbing the tubs as they approached, slowing them down, knocking off the haulage ropes, pulling the tubs round and hanging them on the ropes that took them off in the other direction. He would be standing there in a dark, draughty tunnel eight hours a day, five and a half days a week, alone but for the mice – and the ghosts who were widely believed to haunt the tunnels, heard in the grunts and sighs of the shifting earth. The mine, the boy decided, was not for him. He was a child of the outdoors. He fished and he hunted. He poached. He had been a tearaway, forever getting into scrapes as a child. From the moment he could walk, he'd roamed far and wide. He was not somebody who could be constrained.

Two weeks earlier, largely because he thought it was what tall people did, the boy had applied to join the police force. But there was another, far more enticing possibility. Shortly before his fifteenth birthday, after playing well for Ashington YMCA's under-eighteen side against Barkworth, the boy had been approached by a scout from Leeds United and offered a trial. The boy hadn't liked the idea of leaving home for the big city; what he loved were the fields and the rivers and the sea. And besides, everybody knew the footballer in the family was his younger brother, Robert. Even his mother thought the club must have confused the two of them. And, if he was honest with himself, the boy was worried by the possibility of failure. He may have seemed brash and self-confident, but he couldn't bear the thought of leaving Ashington only to return a few weeks later in humiliation.

But having experienced the pit, none of that seemed so significant any more. And so, Jack Charlton decided to become a footballer.

INTRODUCTION

Jack Charlton pushed himself up from the turf where he had collapsed in exhaustion. England had just won the 1966 World Cup and, as the final whistle blew at the end of extra time, he had summoned his final reserves of energy to run half the length of the pitch to celebrate with Geoff Hurst, who had scored a hat-trick. By the time he got there, Hurst had gone and Jack fell to his knees. But Bobby was there, two brothers united in England's greatest footballing triumph. 'We just put our arms round each other,' Jack said. 'He wasn't smiling at all, yet I know in my heart he was overjoyed.'[1]

Accounts vary as to what Bobby said to Jack as they embraced after the final whistle. According to Bobby he said, 'Our lives will never be the same.'[2] According to Jack he said, 'What is there to win now?'[3] If the latter is true, the answer was obvious: the European Cup with Manchester United. But what is striking, whatever Bobby's question was, is how ambivalent he seemed about success. Jack was shattered but ecstatic, perhaps still grateful to have been part of it; Bobby, by his own admission, felt relief alongside the joy. The pressure perhaps told more on the more talented brother, but that was very typical of him: he may have been a natural footballer, but he was not somebody to whom euphoria came readily. The emotions football inspired in him were always complicated.

That was a moment of achievement and family harmony, and the story was appealing: these two lads from the coalfield, very different in physique, temperament and style, who played for very different clubs, coming together for their country. There was Bobby, a player of extraordinary natural gifts, who had suffered the agonies of the Munich air crash, supported by the elder brother who was far less gifted but had dragged himself into the national side just over a year earlier.

Yet with hindsight there is a curious sense in which that image of the pair of them embracing marks a moment at which their relationship began to change, the first time perhaps that Jack could have been considered Bobby's equal. Bobby still had two more great triumphs to come, the second of them the almost unbearably emotional success of the European Cup final. But he was committed to an old style of football, one rooted in romance and individuality. Jack was more modern in his thinking, a tactician who saw the game as being about the team unit. His best years in club football were also still to come, but it was as a manager that he excelled. But here, in English football's greatest moment, they were united.

Jack and Bobby, in their contrasting ways, were vital to England's World Cup success. Their story has fascinated ever since. How could they look so similar – with their matching blond comb-overs – and yet be so different? The younger was more gifted, but also more withdrawn, more conservative; the elder was ebullient, often brusque and yet radical in outlook and open to new ideas – and not just in football. Yet it was Jack who became disillusioned with football and Bobby who, in his role as Manchester United director, perhaps only by failing to protest loudly enough, played a role in its growing commercialisation. That for several years they barely spoke only added to the wider intrigue. For a long time it was assumed that Bobby was the more clubbable but that image was overtaken by Ron Atkinson's line – supposedly originally formulated by

Jack – that Bobby had been the better player but he, Jack, was the better bloke.[4] That too is a simplification: both were complex and contradictory.

Both have written autobiographies and, although they are very different in tone – Bobby's measured and diplomatic, Jack's open and argumentative – both, like most sporting autobiographies, are as significant for what they omit as for what they contain. Bobby's is almost devoid of anything personal, controversies passed over; Jack's is full of score-settling and explaining why, actually, he was right all along. Neither offers much on the detail of games; perhaps when life becomes just one match after another, individual fixtures blur into each other. Memory is slippery and inevitably involves an element of wish-fulfilment. One of Jack's set pieces in his after-dinner speaking was to ask the audience what the greatest goal ever scored for England was and, when he'd got his audience to agree that it was Bobby's 25-yard drive into the top corner against Mexico in 1966, point out that it was he who had given Bobby the ball, a self-deprecating joke about the undervalued brother demanding his due. It was a good line and usually got a laugh, but it wasn't true: Bobby received the ball from Roger Hunt.

There have been other studies of the pair before, but *Two Brothers*, as well as examining their very different characters, considers also how they were shaped by and in their own small way shaped or were representative of much broader trends both in sport and the wider culture. They were contrasting figures in that regard, too. Bobby was a great footballer, probably the greatest England has ever produced but – perhaps in part because of his reaction to Munich – he seemed oddly out of time, a representation of a previous age of phlegmatic derring-do and duty, resistant to the youth movement and uneasy about the liberalisation of the sixties. When the FA wheeled him out to promote their various doomed bids to host the World Cup, it was partly because he seemed to represent an old England of fair play and gentlemanliness. Jack was far more voluble, showed his emotions and was more open to change, far more radical in his vision of football. As well as taking in their early years, successes as players, and Jack's remarkable time in charge of Ireland, this book looks in more detail than any previous work at their club management careers, which was when their profound differences really became clear.

This is about two remarkable men and their relationship, and about football, but it is also a story about England and Englishness (and Ireland and Irishness) in the second half of the twentieth century.

1

HOME

The Ashington in which Jack and Bobby grew up was a relatively prosperous place, the self-styled 'biggest mining village in the world',[1] with Station Road and its grand Co-op the largest shopping street between Newcastle and Edinburgh. Yet when the first lease for the sinking of a shaft at Felham Down ('Fell 'Em Doon', as it became known) was issued in 1847, Ashington was just a small collection of farmhouses with a population of around eighty. There is some evidence of earlier bell-shaped pits and monastic workings, but the area boomed as the Duke of Portland encouraged migrants fleeing the Irish famine to settle and work in his collieries. Within forty years there were four mines in the area and Ashington's population was 25,000.

The closure of Ashington Pit in 1988, seven years after Woodhorn Pit had shut down, caused mass unemployment. The town has never really recovered. Linton, where Jack and Bobby's father worked, had been exhausted by 1968. Ellington, the last colliery in the area, shut down in 2005.

Jack was vocal during the miners' strike of 1984–85 and on occasion campaigned with Arthur Scargill, but he subsequently acknowledged that, 'If you were to talk to some of them now, they would tell you that the closing of the mines was the best thing that ever happened to them. They have found a new life-style and, more importantly, new hope.'[2] But for many, that hope was to be found elsewhere.

The impact on Ashington has been dismal. The deprivation, the boarded-up shops, the vandalism, the sense of decline are obvious today. When Andy Haldane, the chief economist at the Bank of England, visited in 2018, he spoke of 'barren economic tundra, permanently leeched of nutrients.'[3] There's a reason for the sense for alienation and anger that led to a 56 per cent Leave vote in the Wansbeck constituency in the 2016 Brexit referendum and for the startling fall in MP Ian Lavery's majority to just 814 at the 2019 general election. It had traditionally been a Labour stronghold.

And yet to speak only of decay is to offer only half the picture. On a bright spring bank holiday, Ashington retains a sense of bustle. The market on Woodhorn Street is lively, the atmosphere on the terrace outside the Rohan Kanhai – the Wetherspoon's pub named after the great Guyanese batsman, who played for the local cricket club in the early sixties – convivial. But perhaps most striking are the occasional reminders of what Ashington used to be; less the pit sites that have become business centres or country parks than the glimpses of grandeur, of the time when there was enough wealth to build a basic public necessity with a sense of style, or at least solidity, the most notable of which, perhaps, are the toilets on Milburn Road.

Nobody should think life down the pit was anything other than brutal and terrifying or miners anything other than impoverished but there was some compensation in the sense of community around the collieries. The rivalry of the social clubs extended also to the welfare associations, maintained by a levy on miners' wages, which created the ideal environment for developing sporting talent. A selection from *Ashington Colliery Magazine* extracted in the historian Mike Kirkup's memoir of growing up in Ashington, *Coal Town*, gives some picture of what life was like: there are (lots of) results from sporting fixtures, details of musical accomplishments, jokes and the announcement of two deaths in mining accidents.[4]

Jack and Bobby aren't the only World Cup winners from Ashington; there's also Mark Wood, who won the cricket World Cup in 2019 (and even he is probably only the second-best fast bowler from Ashington, after Steve Harmison). They weren't the first professional footballers in their family and they weren't even the first players from Beatrice Street to be named footballer of the year, their neighbour Jimmy Adamson, the captain of Burnley, won it in 1962. That somebody of the stature of Rohan Kanhai (seventy-nine Tests in which he scored 6227 runs at 47.53) played for Ashington is indicative not only of the importance placed on sport in the area but the fact that in the sixties the club could afford his wages.

Beatrice Street was a typical colliery row, part of a block of terraces running roughly north-west to south-east between Woodhorn Road and Hirst Park. They have small front gardens, perhaps twenty feet square, before a pavement and then the front garden of the facing row. It seems impossible that the path outside could ever have been other than pedestrian-only, but a photograph from around 1960 in the Woodhorn Museum shows Jack, Bobby and their two brothers standing proudly with a car in front of their house. Most vehicular access, though, was via the back lanes, which is where Jack and Bobby first kicked a ball around. It remains much as it looks in old photographs – a few more cars now, and the tops of the walls spiked with broken glass – but essentially the same. No. 114 Beatrice Street, now clad in a toffee-coloured glaze, is unremarkable, almost poignantly so.

In 1971, Jack presented a Tyne Tees Television documentary about Ashington, *Big Jack's Other World*. It's notable for his charisma and his warmth, his comfort in front of the camera at a time when many sportsmen, including his brother, found it excruciatingly awkward, the easy way he involves the people around him. He goes back to the house in which he and his three brothers shared a bed through their childhood, barges in on the Kennedys, who'd moved in four years earlier, and pokes around, admiring the inside toilet and the oven (his mother had cooked over the fire), and demonstrating how he and Bobby used to play football in the back lane. He goes whippet-racing, visits his father's ramshackle pigeon cree and listens appreciatively to a brass band. He expresses some views on the role of women that are perhaps most generously described as traditional, and doggedly argues, long after it's apparent he's wrong, with his father about the species of the geese nesting on a nearby pond.

But the most telling moment comes after he's bought a round in a working men's club. He reflects on the golden age of such institutions, when they'd compete to have the best facilities and to attract the biggest stars and then, over a lingering shot of men laughing as they play bingo, claims that people in the North-East are the 'happiest' he's ever come across. That fits the general sentimental tone, but he then goes on, acknowledging that he 'wanted something more'. He was proud of his roots, celebrated them frequently and came home often, far more often than Bobby, but for a long time he found the North-East easier to love from afar. 'If you stay till you're nineteen,' he said, reflecting on his younger brother's reluctance to come and work for him in Leeds, 'I don't think you've any chance of getting away.'[5]

And that was when Ashington was thriving. In 1999, a syndicate of ten people living in Linton Colliery, the village that remains where the pit used to be, won £1.1 million on the National Lottery. The *Guardian* sent a journalist to investigate the impact on the tiny community. He watched a game of bowls at the 'Tute – the Village Hall Institute – where the syndicate was based, and asked if anybody would use the money to make a new life elsewhere. '"Leave Linton?"' he reported two spectators saying. '"Nobody leaves Linton."'[6]

Thanks to football, though, Jack and Bobby got away.

*

A man walks into a barber's in Ashington and sits down.

'Can I have a perm, please?' he asks.

'A perm? Aye, alreet,' the barber replies. 'Ah wander'd lurnly as a clood ... '

Even in the North-East, the Ashington accent is seen as a little strange, so much so that there's an entire sub-genre of jokes about it.

'I went to Ashington aquarium the other day but it was closed for training porpoises. Just as well, really. They were re-stocking when one of the tanks shattered. Turtle mayhem.'

Jack's accent softened a little, and Bobby's rather more so, as they got older. Both were widely regarded as speaking with a geordie intonation, but neither did, really. What they spoke was pitmatic, the blanket term for the varied dialect of the north-eastern coalfield, which, as the historian Dan Jackson puts it, is characterised by its 'combination of musicality and terminological exactitude'.[7] As the pits closed and life became more focused on the major cities, and with developments in transport and technology, there has been a process of consolidation but each community used to have its own distinctive patterns. Even as late as 1978–79, linguistic experts were able to pinpoint the 'Wearside Jack' tapes – the hoax communications supposedly from the Yorkshire Ripper to the police – to Castletown, a former pit village subsumed into the west of Sunderland.[*]

No version of pitmatic, though, is quite so distinctive as that of Ashington. Most obviously the 'oh' sound becomes an 'ur' but every vowel undergoes a shift (or, more accurately, has *not* undergone the shift that happened in most other English

---

[*] Peter Sutcliffe was arrested in January 1981 and subsequently convicted on thirteen counts of murder and seven of attempted murder. It turned out he had already been questioned nine times but eliminated because of his West Yorkshire accent. It wasn't until 2005 that the hoaxer, John Humble, was identified by DNA evidence. It turned out he was from Castletown. Whatever the many faults of the Ripper inquiry, the linguistic experts were absolutely right; the problem was not that the tape was not from Castletown, it was that it was not from the murderer.

between 1400 and 1700).[8] In *Big Jack's Other World*, there is a remarkable section in which his younger brother Tommy tells a story about the 'clivirist' dog he's ever known, a whippet cross who 'wakked ahl the way hyurm' with an 'igg' in his 'mooth'.[9] Even to those of us raised in the North-East, it borders on the incomprehensible.

Sporting prowess ran through Cissie Milburn's family. Her great-grandfather Jack had played in goal for various village teams in Northumberland. His son was also called Jack but was more generally known as 'Warhorse' – and you wonder quite how tough somebody must have been to acquire that nickname in the Northumberland coalfield in the late nineteenth century. He was a forceful full-back in village games, often turning up on a Saturday afternoon straight from his shift. He was a sinker, his job to open up new pits by digging and blasting shafts to seams often hundreds of feet underground. On his nose there was a blue scar – a typical 'miner's tattoo' – the result of coaldust getting into an open wound caused when a charge he had laid went off prematurely.

Cissie was the daughter of Warhorse's son Jack, who was known as 'Tanner' because when he was born he was half the size of his elder brother Bob – a tanner (sixpence) being half a bob (a shilling). When Cissie was two, Tanner left to fight in the First World War. He was taken prisoner on the Somme and, while he was away, her mother supplemented her allowance by working in a local chippy. They moved from a house in a colliery row on Hawthorne Road to a slightly larger one on Sycamore Street, something Tanner only discovered when he knocked on the wrong door after returning from his PoW camp in 1919.

Tanner was Ashington's goalkeeper during their brief period in Division Three (North) in the 1920s, noted as the best left-handed keeper at that level – a boast proudly repeated by various members of the family since, although it's not entirely clear why it should matter which hand he favoured. His real gift, though, was coaching sprinters and he had significant success at various athletics meetings across the region at a time when races drew large crowds and there were serious prizes on offer. All four of his sons played professional football: Jack for Leeds United and, briefly, Bradford City; George for Leeds and Chesterfield; Jim for Leeds and Bradford Park Avenue and Stan for Chesterfield, Leicester and Rochdale.

Stan was probably a better sprinter than footballer but one year at the Morpeth Olympics, Tanner agreed with the coach of Stan's main rival that they would split the twenty-pound prize whoever won. Stan was beaten by a fraction and his father took his ten pounds, refusing to give him anything on the grounds that he had lost and the money had been secured only by his own intelligence in hedging. Stan never ran competitively again. That was typical of Tanner who was, as Cissie put it, a 'rogue'.

The photograph taken of him when he became Prisoner of War No. 1749 shows a balding man with an extraordinary kiss-curl oozing over his forehead, a slight smirk playing on his lips. He was a bookie's runner and would involve his children and later his grandchildren in various scams; the young Cissie, for instance, had to deliver betting slips hidden in the little bucket she played with when they went to the beach at Newbiggin. In public, Tanner was generous, convivial and quick-witted. In private, he was mean and penny-pinching.

Cissie herself was a tomboy, forever getting into scrapes on the shale-strewn waste ground where children in Ashington played. She became school netball captain and would fight her sister Etty in a ring made from a washing line for a cash prize provided by their brothers.

But the family's greatest sportsman was Cissie's cousin,

Jackie. A self-effacing man who seemed never quite to get over his early fear of his father – who once clouted his son for what he took to be show-boating when he saw him collapse after winning a sprint at his school sports day, not realising it was the fourth event he'd won that afternoon – Jackie Milburn was Newcastle's all-time leading scorer until the advent of Alan Shearer. His bronze statue stands outside St James' Park, having been moved from its original position by the McDonald's on Northumberland Street in the centre of Newcastle. He remains, perhaps even more so than Shearer, the greatest of all Newcastle's sporting folk heroes, the origin of the fabled reverence of their fans for a number 9.

Milburn was quick and powerful and brought success. He scored both goals in the 1951 FA Cup final against Blackpool, the second of them a strike of legendary velocity and precision. He was part of the side that retained the Cup in 1952 and then scored the opener after forty-five seconds as Newcastle beat Manchester City 3–1 in the 1955 final. That was the earliest goal scored in a final until Roberto Di Matteo took the record in 1997, and that FA Cup remains the last domestic trophy won by Newcastle.

When Milburn was called up by England for a game against Northern Ireland in Belfast, the only way for Jack and Bobby to witness it was to go the cinema to watch the Pathé news reel that was showing before the Moira Shearer film *The Red Shoes*. So long were the queues though, that by the time they got in, the news was over and the film had been on for fifteen minutes. *The Red Shoes* may now be regarded as a classic, but the travails of a ballet dancer held little interest for them then and they sat bored through the two hours that remained to catch the next showing of the news. After the credits, an usherette tried to move them on and they were allowed to remain only when it was explained who they were and why they were so desperate to see the brief highlights of a 6–2 win in which Milburn marked his debut by scoring England's third.

But Jackie Milburn was more than just a great footballer. Fans could see in him one of their own, a miner employed at Woodhorn who'd attended a trial at St James' after being unimpressed by the level of play in a wartime friendly. When he first started playing for Newcastle, he would arrange it so that he worked the midnight to 7 a.m. shift on a Saturday morning, then take the number 3 bus from Ashington to St James' to play. Milburn retained an instinctive modesty, but as the lad from the coalfield who scored winning goals at Wembley, he came to symbolise something profound.

Woodhorn is the only one of the five pits that made up the Ashington coalfield that still exists, although it is now a heritage museum. Many of the outbuildings have gone but the pit wheel still stands, as do the stables and a section of narrow-gauge railway that used to transport coal to the coast. A series of videos give some sense of the darkness, noise and claustrophobic chaos of life in the mine, explaining how the coalface would first be undercut and then drilled before explosive charges were set. Hewers, those who actually worked at the coalface, were the most respected men in the colliery, hacking away with their pickaxes, often hunched and on their knees.

There is also a gallery in which seventy-five works by the so-called Pitman Painters are on display. There is an idea that football was the only creative outlet for the men of the coalfield,[10] but actually there was a remarkably fecund cultural life in Ashington, a powerful autodidactic drive.[11] The painters developed from the art appreciation class first put on by the Ashington Workers Educational Authority in 1934. Their tutor, Robert Lyon of King's College, quickly realised that his academic approach was having little impact and so encouraged his students to produce their own works, to learn about painting by painting. The results were remarkable, a depiction over fifty years of life in the coalfield, above and below ground, in a variety of styles. What is perhaps most striking is the way many of the early works pastiche the likes of Van Gogh or Cézanne; magazines and books had clearly been studied to give an idea of what great art was. An exhibition of the Pitman Painters' work was the first from the West to be held in China after the Cultural Revolution, regarded by Mao Zedong as a fine example of workers' art.[12]

In one painting, a middle-aged Jackie Milburn crouches with a whippet, and many others depict both the brutality of the job and the stark beauty of the surrounding landscape. Most affecting, though, is probably the final painting in the exhibition which, in loving pastels, shows a hewer, lying almost flat in a low tunnel, swinging at the coalface by the soft light of a lamp.

It wasn't just the Milburn side of Cissie's family that was athletically gifted. Her mother had been a Charlton – a lot of people were. Both the Charltons and the Milburns were reiver families – surnames, as the clans were known – who had made their living raiding across the border to rustle cattle. A map of the distribution of surnames in the 1580–90s, drawn from warden's reports and printed in Graham Robb's *The Debatable Land*, places the Milburns just north of Hadrian's Wall, about five miles southeast of Bewcastle, perhaps a quarter of the way from Carlisle to Newcastle, with the Charltons further north and east, around what is now the north edge of Kielder Water.*[13]

It's easy to forget now when, whether travelling by road or rail, the border slips by in a blur of gorse, but Northumberland used to be, as the historian Dan Jackson puts it, 'a dangerous

---

* The reservoir, northern Europe's largest man-made lake by volume, was completed in 1981; before that it was an area of farmland.

frontier zone which, after centuries of violence, transformed into a great crucible of the Industrial Revolution where the same qualities of endurance were relied upon and celebrated.'[14] Between 1040 and 1745, only three English monarchs did not either invade Scotland or fight off an invasion from Scotland, and that inevitably left its mark upon the people who, according to Robert Bowen in 1550 were 'wild and misdemeanoured ... much inclined to disorder'[15] and William Stukeley in 1776, were, 'old and hardy ... fierce in manners'.[16]

The Charltons were firmly in that tradition. The last man publicly executed in Carlisle was a Charlton, hanged in 1862 for murdering a widow with a pickaxe and hedge-slasher to steal the money she had saved for her funeral.[17]

Cissie's maternal grandfather, George, meanwhile, had been a champion Northumbrian sword-dancer and a keen quoits player. One night, returning drunk after winning a dancing competition, he had fallen asleep in a hedge. He reacted aggressively when a policeman woke him to move him on and, in the altercation that followed, George was struck on the head with a truncheon. He subsequently suffered mental health problems and was for a time held in an institution. After his release, he would go wandering and would often be found preaching to the moon and the stars. He began drinking heavily as well and became violent; Cissie remembered the nights when her grandmother would come to take refuge at their house.

When Cissie Milburn was fourteen, she took the overnight bus south from Newcastle and began work as a general maid at a house in Watford. She hated it, wasn't treated particularly well and was desperately homesick, but she stuck it out because she couldn't face returning home as a failure.

After two years, she secured a better position as a mother's help in Harrow-on-the-Hill and was beginning to settle to life there when she was summoned home. Her mother was ill and it was feared she had terminal cancer. As it turned out, it was a false alarm, so Cissie set off to find work once more, this time going to Leeds, where three of her brothers played football. She became a mother's help again. She got engaged, to a boy called Charlie Burton, but they were never committed and soon drifted apart.

She began to suffer problems with her throat and was diagnosed with quinsy, a serious complication of tonsillitis. When her mother visited and saw her, evidently unwell, cleaning windows with a flannel tied around her throat, she told her to come home: they weren't so poor, she told her daughter, they didn't need the money that badly.

Cissie got a job in a pork butcher's, filling pies and serving behind the counter. She met a lad called Joe Bennett and got engaged for a second time. This time it was serious and when he met somebody else, Cissie was 'heartbroken'.[18]

A couple of weeks later, Cissie went to the Princess dance hall to try to cheer herself up. But the sight of other couples only depressed her further and she sat against the wall feeling sorry for herself until 'a handsome lad with a big grin' wandered over and said, 'You've fallen out with your lad and I've fallen out with my lass – let's have this dance.'[19]

His name was Bob Charlton, he was a hewer at Linton and seven years earlier he'd been to the same school as her. Six months after that first meeting, they married at Morpeth registry office. Their wedding reception, for which they hired an accordion player, was held at Cissie's mother's house on Laburnum Terrace.

Bob, unusually in Ashington, didn't much care for football. Boxing was his sport and he was good at it. One night he took on a pro for a one-pound purse at a travelling boxing booth and won, spending 17s 6d of his prize on a wedding ring for

Cissie and the remainder on a fireside kerb. He was a quiet, reserved and naturally cautious man who liked the solitude of his allotment. That Cissie's volubility occasionally irritated him was no secret, but he also had a stubborn, difficult side.

'He embarrassed me, he annoyed me, he argued just for the sake of argument,' Cissie said, to the point that she threatened to leave him just as soon as their youngest had turned fifteen.[20] On Tommy's fifteenth, Bob asked her if she were going as she'd insisted. 'No,' she replied. 'You've mellowed since then.'

Cissie also acknowledged that her attitude to her husband changed after she took a trip down the mine at Woodhorn, which she described as 'terrible – dirty, dark and mouse-infested'. From that moment on, she vowed, she would never hear a word said against pitmen: 'they deserve all they earn and more just for going down that awful place.'[21]

On the allotment Bob grew potatoes and cabbages and kept pigeons, chickens, pigs and, briefly, a pit pony he'd rescued from the mine once it became too old to work. They would take it to Newbiggin to gather sea coal, which would wash up on the beach having been dislodged by shot-firing in the shafts that ran out under the sea bed or having been jettisoned by colliers putting out from Blyth if they ran into bad weather. He would bring wood home from the colliery for the fire, but before burning it would sort through it methodically, seeing if there were any screws or nails he could repurpose.

In *Big Jack's Other World*, Jack visits the allotment and pokes disdainfully at his father's homemade cree, fashioned from a seemingly random assortment of planks. He's forced to admit, though, that it's solid enough and does the job it's supposed to. Function, you suspect, always mattered far more to Bob than appearance.

After they'd married, Cissie and Bob stayed with his mother until they were able to rent a flat on the same street as her mother. During Second World War air-raids, the family would gather at Tanner's house as seemingly the sturdiest of any of the clan. As it turned out, only one bomb ever fell on Ashington and it missed both industry and residential property, landing on the ice rink.

When her mother died, at the age of fifty at Christmas 1943, Cissie and Bob moved in with Tanner on Laburnum Terrace, where Gordon was born a year later. They were offered a colliery house on Chestnut Street, and it was there that Tommy, the youngest of the four brothers, was born in 1946. Two years later, the colliery offered them a bigger house and they moved again, to 114 Beatrice Street, their home for the following eighteen years. There was no bathroom, just a scullery with a cold tap off the kitchen that, with the laying-up room reserved for best, doubled as a living room.

2

CHILDHOOD

Bobby had just been born and Cissie was lying in bed, recovering, when she heard a funeral procession approaching outside. From downstairs there came a shout from her cousin Nancy Fear. Cissie pulled herself up so she could see out of the window and there below, in the street, toddling behind the hearse and the Salvation Army band, was Jack, wearing just a nappy. 'From the moment he was born,' Cissie said, 'Jack was full of devilment.'[1]

She soon gave up trying to restrict his movement, deciding the best policy was to dress him in red so he could easily be seen. Jack wandered incessantly. When he was four he made it as far as the village of Guide Post, four miles away. Soon after, he stowed away in a bakery van and wasn't discovered until he'd travelled fifteen miles south to Gosforth. He liked exploring and had little sense of danger. When, years later, the family got a car and started to go out for drives, they realised they didn't need a map; Jack knew every road and every footpath. Bobby remembered how Jack would often overreach, dragging him out on long hikes that would leave them so exhausted that they would take it in turns to lean on the other as they walked back – although the brothers being who they were, Bobby would do far more supporting of Jack than the other way round.

Jack's wandering gradually developed a more precise focus as he would go bird nesting and gathering mushrooms. He would scramble around the soft clay of the old quarry or hang around the old church at Bothal, fascinated by the slit through which lepers had supposedly once watched services. But the place he really loved was the Sandy Desert, a boggy pond in winter that dried in summer into a dusty wasteland. People would dump rubbish there and that drew rats, which Jack would shoot with his catapult, using as ammunition metal pellets his father would bring home from the mine.

And then there was fishing. Three or four nights a week after school, Jack would head out to the coast and sit with as many as a hundred other fishermen, waiting for mackerel and casting with flies made from silver paper and pieces of goose feather. In autumn he would stay out all night and fish the storm beaches for cod, rotating around a brazier with the other fishermen, heading straight to school the following morning. From the age of twelve or thirteen, using just a string and a dropper with a worm attached, he would catch trout in the Wansbeck at Bothal, sometimes landing as many as ten in a night. Bobby occasionally joined him, and devised a means of catching tiddlers using a jam-jar baited with bread. He was too squeamish, though, to fix the worm on the hook himself.

Jack was always getting into scrapes. He was quick to anger and quick to forgive. He was big and tough and didn't mind getting into fights to defend his honour or that of his family. On one occasion he heard a boy call his great grandmother – 'Little Granny' – a witch, so he chased him and hit him on the head with a glass bottle. He broke a finger punching a wall after a far weaker boy who he had no intention of fighting started laying into him. There was a time when he became convinced his head was abnormally hard and began boasting about it; when challenged to prove it, he headbutted the pavement. Chaos and injury followed him around. He and his friends would climb to the top of a disused windmill; one day one of them fell and broke his arm. Another friend broke his leg after tripping over a hidden wire as they chased through a cornfield. He once fried his brother Gordon's goldfish to go with some chips he'd just cooked. Or at least, that's how the anecdote goes. But memories from childhood are distorted.

Everybody agrees that Jack got a fishhook stuck in his thumb and had to go to hospital to have it removed, but there are two distinct variants of the story. In one, he was fishing overnight at Newbiggin, calmly went for treatment and returned to resume his position on the rocks before dawn. In the other, he found himself unable to hold the plane properly during woodwork class and was in so much pain that, to his embarrassment, he began to cry. When he returned from hospital with his hand swathed in bandages, it was with a sense of vindication: he had had something to cry about.

More disturbing is the tale of the death on the railway line, which seems to surface for the first time in Norman Harris's biography of the two brothers. Jack, it's said, was part of a group of boys who would mess about by the tracks, laying coins on the rails to be flattened by passing trains. One night, one of them was struck by a passing engine and killed. Jack and the others laid the body by the side of the road, after which he returned home, covered in blood.[2] Yet the incident isn't mentioned in Jack's autobiography and Leo McKinstry, in *Jack & Bobby*, notes only that 'the event gradually faded from Jack's memory'.[3]

A search of local newspapers and the local records office* turns up one episode that seems to fit, from 22 February 1948, when Jack would have been twelve. Jack's presence is not mentioned in either the newspaper or the coroner's report, but two boys, Robert Graham and Ronald Witcombe, both from

---

* Thanks are due here to Dan Jackson, Anthea Lang and Charlie Pontoon for their help in tracking this down.

Newbiggin, were knocked down and killed by a train near Woodhorn Bridge. According to the account given by a fifteen-year-old witness, Edwin Young, they had been part of a group of boys walking along the railway track so as not to get their shoes muddy on the path. It had been a windy night and it had begun to hail, meaning they had all been walking with their heads down and that it had been difficult to hear.[4] But whether that is the incident in question, or what exactly happened, is impossible to be sure.

At school, Jack was good at metalwork, woodwork and nature studies, but didn't much care about anything else. He was easily distracted, prone to following his own interests. When a plane passed by, he would go to the window to watch it, even in the middle of class. To nobody's surprise, he failed his eleven-plus and so went to Hirst Park secondary modern.

As Jack got older, he began to poach and hunt. His uncle Buck taught him how to lay snares and in his teens Jack would set off before dawn with his father to sit in the dunes at Cresswell, waiting for ducks to come in off the sea to a pond so they could shoot them, or borrow whippets to chase rabbits.

His fishing became more sophisticated. Tanner used to have his sprinters wear lead weights in their shoes in the early rounds of big meetings, slowing them down just enough to lengthen their odds of winning the final, when they would run without the handicap. Jack found the weights one day and, not understanding what they were, stole them, melted them down and used them as sinkers.

Fishing ran in the family, and so did the capacity to get into trouble. Uncle Tommy was dressed up in his suit on his way to a wedding when his brother Dave decided they should go sea fishing and take Bobby with them. Tommy, unwisely, agreed. Their boat became grounded on a sandbank at the shallow mouth of the Wansbeck. They waited for a while, hoping the tide would free them, but as Tommy became increasingly frantic, Dave agreed to carry him back to the bank, keeping him – and, more importantly, his suit – clear of the water. The decreased weight in the boat, though, meant that it began to rise and his uncles had only gone a few yards when Bobby realised he was drifting out to sea. In a panic, Dave dropped Tommy and rushed back to grab the boat. Tommy's suit was ruined.

From somewhere, nobody seems quite sure where, Jack acquired his own air rifle and one day took it into school with him. He aimed a shot at a nearby church tower, only for the bullet to ricochet off a fence and graze a girl called Bernadette Reed near her eye. Cissie took Jack round to the Reeds that night to apologise and he had enough charm and liveliness that nobody seemed to find it possible to be angry with him. Mr Reed ended up simply showing Jack his own gun collection.

Similarly, when Jack stole a cauliflower from the back garden of some neighbours called Curtis and went round to the front door and tried to sell it to them, it was laughed off as Jack being Jack. He attempted a similar ruse at a shop, taking bottles from the backyard and claiming the deposit on them, and also took daffodils from gardens and parks to sell.

The scams were indicative both of an inherent sense of mischief and a canniness with money. By his early teens, Jack had a number of thriving businesses. He ran deliveries for a local grocer, had a morning milk round, sold spare firewood from the mine and collected slops to use as pigswill and traded the excess. What he was most proud of, though, was his Sunday paper round. Realising that the pre-existing patchwork of routes was highly inefficient, he plotted them out on a map and rationalised them, leading what was effectively a syndicate of paperboys for a job that took him five and a half hours and brought in fifteen shillings a week – early evidence both of his organisational brain and his leadership.

While Jack put together his business empire, Bobby's

money-making was more restrained: doing deliveries for Donaldson's grocery shop on a bike equipped with a big tray at the front. When Jack left Ashington aged fifteen, he was furious that Bobby not only failed to maintain his bike, a gold Hercules Kestrel with drop handlebars, but let the paper round fall apart.

Inevitably, Jack became wrapped up in some of Tanner's schemes. For a time it was his job to give the signal at race meetings for Tanner's agents simultaneously to place their bets with the various bookmakers to ensure the odds didn't shorten before he'd had the chance to maximise his stake.

Another ruse exploited the brief delay between a race at the greyhound track ending and the result being phoned through to the bookmaker. Tanner had Jack's uncle Buck stand on the toilet cistern at the working men's club with his head out of the window to listen for the tannoy at the track. He would then relay the information to Tanner who would pass pre-written betting slips to Jack to run down to the bookies and stuff in the collection box outside. The scheme was only uncovered when Buck slipped and became trapped in the window.

Bobby couldn't have been more different. Aside from what became known as 'our Bobby's mad half-hours', when he would impersonate Frankenstein's monster or put a sheet over his head and howl like a ghost, he was quiet and serious. He didn't care much for the outdoors, and when Cissie made Jack take him with him on his expeditions, Jack would give him a clout round the head before they got to the end of the street so he could be away without the hindrance of his younger brother.

He hated getting into trouble, or fuss of any kind. In that regard Bobby took after his father while Jack, in terms of temperament, was like their mother. Throughout his childhood, Cissie seems to have accepted Jack's behaviour as simply being part of his devilment; theft was the only offence she took seriously.[5] What worried her far more were 'Bobby's quiet ways';

it took her time to accept that 'he wasn't shy or reticent, just very self-contained.'[6]

On one occasion, while he was still young, Bobby was asked for an autograph and instinctively recoiled, only for his mother to force him to sign, clearly revelling in the attention. 'For her,' he said, 'life was a matter of going and getting what you could and not being too shy in celebrating your successes.'[7] He hated the way she would often discuss him and his career in front of others, something that made him cringe. 'I suspect, deep down, it was something of a regret for her that she wasn't born to play the game herself ... she was a Milburn and it was the most natural thing to be good at football.'[8]

'My mother,' said the youngest brother, Tommy, 'would talk about football all the time.'[9] On a Sunday there were often mass kickabouts in the park, and there were evening games that Cissie would come out and join, but Bobby would be there every night of the week, often kicking a ball around alone. On his way to school or when sent on errands, he would dribble a tennis ball, playing passes to himself off the walls and the kerbs. At home, he would fashion a ball out of rolled up socks and act out matches between Earth and Mars, commentating on the deft interplay between Stanley Matthews and Wilf Mannion using his mother's iron as a microphone.

Days out watching football were not just day trips but, Bobby said, 'pilgrimages'.[10] In various interviews and his autobiography, Bobby said he and Jack would go to Sunderland as well as Newcastle, and he seems to have been an admirer of the Sunderland inside-left Len Shackleton, but Jack always insisted they had only ever gone to St James' and it's those trips that Bobby described in more detail. They would pay two shillings on the bus to Haymarket, then either have pie and chips in the café at the bus station or go for the wider menu at the Civic restaurant, before walking up the hill to the stadium, where they would choose their stand according to the opponent: the relevant paddock if there was a winger they particularly wanted to see or one of the ends to watch a centre-forward or goalkeeper.

The expense restricted how often they could go, so most of the brothers' early spectating experience was watching Ashington playing in the North Eastern League at Portland Park. Crowds would always be comfortably in four figures, and an FA Cup second-round tie against Rochdale in 1950 drew twelve thousand.

Football occupied Bobby's thoughts almost all the time. One day at school they were told to draw something they knew well from the local environment, such as a pithead. Bobby did draw a pithead, but it was in the background, with a football match in the foreground. For another exercise the class was asked to design an advert for National Savings. Bobby drew 'A Goalkeeper Making a Great Save'.

After Tanner fell ill and moved in with his daughter, it was Bobby's job on a Saturday evening to read out the *Evening Chronicle*'s sports edition to him. Tanner would then quiz him on what he had read, fuelling Bobby's fascination and knowledge. A teacher who accompanied Bobby on the train from Newcastle to London for an England schoolboy international recalled asking him to name all ninety-two league clubs. Bobby fell three or four short; on the return journey, he got them all.[11]

Too young really to understand his grandfather's skulduggery and ruthlessness, Bobby loved Tanner and the competitiveness of his world. He was fascinated by the miners' galas at which there would be contests to untangle impossible knots, races to break out of tied sacks and the sprints in which his uncle Stan was a champion despite often giving up eight or nine yards' handicap in the 110-yard dash.

Having seen four of his sons have professional careers, Tanner had little doubt of Bobby's ability. When Bobby played in the schoolyard, he would stand behind the railings in his habitual brown striped suit, flat cap and white muffler, watching and offering advice, always urging him to work harder. He would encourage Bobby to join in as he was training his sprinters, even if it meant giving Bobby an 80-yard start so he stood a chance.

Bobby had always played football, had always been obsessed by football. He'd devoured the *Stanley Matthews' Football Annual*, he kicked a ball wherever he went and he'd loved hearing his uncles discuss the game. He'd even loved it when they took him to the club and left him at the door with a glass of squash, imagining the great football conversations they were having over their pints inside. He had always known he was good at football, but the first public acknowledgement of that came when he was at North Hirst primary school.

The headmaster, James Hamilton, came into the classroom and summoned Bobby to join him. That was usually a bad sign, but Bobby couldn't think of anything for which he might be in trouble. They stopped at a display table of mining equipment: picks, shovels and a helmet. Hamilton unwrapped a crimson football shirt and handed it to him to put it on, then told him to pick up the helmet and carry it as though it were a ball. As Hamilton hummed the *Sports Report* theme tune, Bobby ran back into his classroom, now designated school captain. Another teacher, Miss Houston, made satin shorts for the team from blackout curtains left over from the war, while the boys were instructed to source red-and-white socks as best they could. From that moment, Bobby never really doubted football would be his life; he never felt the looming threat of the pit as Jack had.

Bobby's first boots, a pair of Playfair Pigskins, were bought by Uncle Tommy, his father's brother, and he remembered lovingly soaking them before putting them on for the first time so they would mould themselves to his feet. Jack's first boots were second-hand. When he was seven, during the war, Cissie saw an ad offering a pair of Mansfield Hotspurs for ten shillings. She sent Jack with the money to collect them; he managed to negotiate the price down to eight shillings.

Bobby had been looking forward to the game at St Aloysius Roman Catholic school in Newcastle. They were one of the places that gave both sides a hot meal and a drink afterwards, a rare luxury. Often, he found playing games for Bedlington grammar very easy and there had been plenty of occasions on which the teacher who ran the team, Mr McGuinness, told him to hang back to as not to embarrass the opposition. But St Aloysius were gifted and they were tough. Bedlington were in danger of defeat. For almost the first time in his life, Bobby felt under pressure. This was down to him. There could be no easing back here.

Gradually he began to assert himself on the game. He was surprised by how influential he was, surprised by the way he discovered a new level. He remembered Tanner's line, that if you tried hard enough anything was possible. Bedlington equalised, then Bobby scored the winner. He knew that St Aloysius were good, and knew that he had turned that game: how good then, he wondered, might he actually be?

Bobby was only at Bedlington thanks to the efforts of his mother. He had passed his eleven-plus at the second attempt, winning a place at King Edward VI grammar, Morpeth. It was, though, a school that played rugby rather than football and so was wholly unsuitable for him. Cissie petitioned the local education authority and they agreed to move him to Bedlington. Even then, though, the school was weirdly reluctant to assist his football career, refusing to allow him to leave early to catch the train to London to play for England Schoolboys. As it was, the games master George Benson solved the problem by giving him a lift to the station in his car. Bobby scored twice in a 3–3 draw against Wales, the first with the sort of long-range drive that would become his trademark.

By that point, Bobby said, 'I was sure both of my talent and my ambition.'[12] He suffered few of the doubts that so beset Jack. Cissie went out of her way to be supportive, and admitted that, from the time he was nine, she made sure he had what he needed.[13] That in turn had an impact on Jack. In terms of personality, he may have been far more similar to his mother than Bobby was, but 'I always knew I was not her favourite'.[14] That is not, though, how Tommy Charlton, remembers it. 'Jack's relationship with mother,' he said, 'was special. He was the apple of mother's eye.'[15] Perhaps Jack was speaking with the resentment of an eldest child towards those who come after or perhaps Tommy, who was born a decade after Jack, was remembering how things were after the two elder brothers had left home.

When Leeds United, for whom three of his uncles had played, approached the family to ask if Jack might be interested in a trial, Cissie laughed them off, thinking they had the wrong brother. Her eldest boy wasn't fascinated by football in the way Bobby was. He would play in the big kickabouts in the park on a Sunday but didn't obsessively follow the scores or practise his skills. 'Although Jack enjoyed his game of football,' she said, 'he just wasn't the same calibre of player as Bobby.'[16]

It was something of a surprise to everybody when, at the age of thirteen, Jack was selected for Hirst Park school's under-fifteen side. He already had the gangling frame that would later characterise him, although nobody quite knew where it had come from – he had a very tall great-great grandfather but none of the rest of his family had anything like his height. But still his talent was far from obvious. He went to a trial for Ashington Juniors at Portland Park and was turned down.

Bob left the football to Cissie. She'd taken the boys in their prams to the Welfare Ground and Portland Park. Boxing was the only sport he cared about. He trained his sons, sometimes punching them with a fist wrapped in a towel, and took Jack to a boxing club on the other side of Ashington, showing far more interest in that than he ever did in his sons' football. Jack soon left, though, when he sensed the reluctance of other boys to spar with him, although he never knew whether it was because he was from the wrong part of town or because he was bigger and stronger than everybody else. Both he and Bobby had some success in boxing, but neither seriously pursued it. Football exercised a far greater allure.

In one of his early games, Jack was playing for Park school against the East, the big derby on the main pitch at the Miners Welfare, the one that had nets on the goalframes, while Bobby was playing on a different pitch for Hirst Juniors. Bobby's game finished just in time for him to see Jack concede a penalty in the last minute that was converted to give the East a 1–0 win. 'What did you give that away for?' Bobby asked later that evening. To which Jack 'cracked' him around the head, knocking him off the sofa.[17]

Jack started out as a full-back and impressed enough to be selected for East Northumberland, although he could struggle against nippy wingers. On one occasion, after he responded to a winger darting past him by staring after him in confusion, Jack was dropped by the games master Mr Harvey for several games. He was recalled for a County Cup tie at Portland Park when he was told half an hour before kick-off that if he had time to get home and get his boots he could play. He raced home and collected them, excelled, and was never dropped at that level again.

At fifteen he and Bobby, then thirteen, played together in an under-eighteen league for the YMCA, a terrible side that was regularly thrashed by double figures. When they managed a 2–2 draw once against Backworth, it was regarded as a great triumph. And yet it was in one of those games that Jack was spotted by a scout from Leeds – although he was self-aware enough to admit that he probably wouldn't have been given the opportunity had his uncle, Jim Milburn, not still been playing for the club.[18]

Once the club had persuaded Cissie that they knew which of her sons they were talking about, he turned them down. He came from a region that produced huge numbers of talented footballers and, knowing he was nowhere near as gifted as many of his peers, Jack was haunted by the prospect of going away, only to have to return. He may have been fearless in many respects, but the possibility of failure scared him. Cissie had felt something similar when she went away to be a servant; Jack saw the anxiety as football-specific, but it was perhaps more universal than that, the suspicion directed towards those who left that helped bind the community together.

Jack's experience at the mine sharpened his focus. Better to risk the embarrassment of being rejected as a footballer, he reasoned, than to live life underground. The day after he'd been down the pit, Jack went to the manager's office and resigned. It was a difficult conversation. Jack had been one of twenty trainees selected for further education and had done two days a week at college. The mining company had invested in his development and was furious that would be wasted. Jack was told he would never work again in a pit in the North-East. He didn't care.

Leeds asked him for another trial in a game against Newcastle's youth team. But that gave Jack a problem. The game was in Leeds on a Saturday morning and his interview for the police force was in Newcastle on the Friday afternoon. He looked at whether it would be possible to attend the interview and still travel the hundred miles down to Leeds to arrive on time and concluded it wasn't. He could attend only one; he cancelled the police interview.

He went into town with Cissie and she used some savings to buy him a Burberry overcoat and blue pin-striped suit, the first long trousers he had ever owned. More nervous than he had ever been, he took the train to Leeds for a game that would shape the rest of his life.

It was anti-climactic. It snowed. It was not a particularly good game. Nobody stood out; Jack felt he had played decently but not brilliantly. Was that enough? It seemed it was: they asked him to come back and join the ground staff for five pounds a week. 'Life seemed good to me at that time ... ' he said. 'It was a far cry from the pit.'[19]

For Bobby the game had been largely unremarkable: East Northumberland away at Jarrow & Hebburn on a frosty pitch on a chilly day in January. He hadn't played brilliantly, but he felt he had done all right on a hard and slippery surface. As he left the pitch, he was approached by a short, wizened, grey-haired man. He was Joe Armstrong and he'd been told of Bobby's talents by the headmaster at Jack's school, Stuart Hemingway. He knew what he'd seen, noting immediately how, despite the conditions, Bobby used the ball intelligently with both feet and had the spatial awareness to hang deep, biding his time before making a burst into the box. He recommended Bobby to Manchester United without hesitation.

At the beginning of March 1953, Bobby was invited to Maine Road for a trial ahead of the England Schoolboys game against Wales later that month. It was then that Matt Busby first saw him. He was immediately impressed by how 'he did everything with care, almost as if he were sitting at a piano'.[20] Bobby played well enough to be selected but what stayed with him was less his own performance than what he saw from the bus window as he returned to the station afterwards – thousands and thousands of fans making their way to Old

Trafford for United's game against Preston. He knew most of the Manchester-based boys from the trial would be there and he desperately wished he could have joined them to witness United beating Preston 5–1, with their new centre-forward Tommy Taylor, a British record signing at £29,999, scoring twice on his debut.

Bobby was already well-disposed to Manchester United. The FA Cup final in 1948 had fallen on the birthday of one of Bobby's friends. He went round to his house for tea and, as they kicked a ball around in the street, they kept the doors open and the radio on. All the other boys wanted Blackpool to win because of Stanley Matthews, but Bobby was taken by United's comeback and developed a soft spot for them, one that grew over the following few years as he began to understand the club's focus on youth and Matt Busby's attempts to develop a fluent, attacking style.

Other scouts made their pitches. According to Cissie, a total of eighteen clubs courted Bobby, many offering (illegal) financial inducements. At one point she was shuttling between a scout in the laying-in room and another in the kitchen. Sunderland were keen, but Bobby had been disappointed in the way their scout had ignored him in that game at Jarrow, instead approaching his friend, the goalkeeper Ron Routledge; with that, thoughts of emulating Len Shackleton faded. He briefly considered Arsenal, but Armstrong remained a constant pres- ence, to the point of pretending to be an uncle when the local education authority decided scouts had become a distraction and banned them from games.

The case for Newcastle United was half-heartedly made by Jackie Milburn. Although the club had promised to secure him a placement at the *Evening Chronicle*, allowing him to pursue the idea of being a journalist (it was never entirely clear how serious Bobby was; his apparent interest seems largely to have been based on journalists getting into games for free), Milburn made sure Bobby was aware that there was no real development programme at Newcastle, that training was essentially a kick-about on Tuesday and Thursday evenings, and that he would almost certainly be better off elsewhere. When Bobby did opt for Old Trafford, his mother received letters from outraged fans, condemning her and Bobby for 'betraying' his home.

Bobby had always known his path lay in football and, since 1948, his dream had been United. But just because he had been mentally preparing to leave for years did not mean that his departure, aged fifteen, was not a wrench. He left a girlfriend, Norma Outhwaite, but what seems to have troubled him most was the change in his relationship with his parents – mainly with his mother – as he became more independent and began to take control of his own life. His headmaster at Bedlington told him he was wasting his education, while Bobby said, 'I felt very guilty for my parents' sake, after being at a grammar school for four years to give it all up.'[21]

The psychology requires some unpacking. Bobby must have known that there was nothing Cissie wanted more than for him to become a footballer. And yet he seems also to have felt that the safe path was to stay on at school – that was what sensible boys did – and that, by turning away, he was breaching some sort of familial or social contract, as represented by the formidable figure of his mother. Quite how academically gifted Bobby was is unclear. Jack often spoke of Bobby's brightness, but there is little evidence of that, either from his school reports or the recollections of teachers or schoolmates. That he took two attempts to pass his eleven-plus may be telling. But then a mind already committed to football perhaps didn't have much space for anything else.

Bobby didn't abandon his education immediately. Cissie seemingly had no problems with Jack serving on the ground staff at Elland Road, but she was adamant Bobby would not be sweeping terraces and cleaning toilets at United. He was transferred instead to Stretford grammar school, Manchester, for what he later described as 'the most terrible three weeks of my life'.[22]

He would get up at 7.30 a.m., be in class by 9 a.m., then attend training for three hours in the evening before getting in at 9 p.m., only then settling down to his homework. To make a difficult situation worse, Stretford followed a different curriculum from Bedlington, meaning he often had very little idea what was going on. He toiled away, often working until after midnight, worried about what his mother would say about his poor grades.

Finally, when the school demanded he should play for their team rather than United on a Saturday, Bobby plucked up the courage to tell the headmaster he wanted to leave. He became an apprentice electrical engineer at Switch Gear, where he made the tea, ran errands and occasionally filed metal. It was so boring that there were times when he would go to the toilet just so he could gaze out of the window at the clock on Stretford town hall and watch the seconds passing before he could go training. His reward for the tedium was two pounds a week, half what the ground staff were on.

But it was a start. Jack and Bobby had begun the journey to becoming professional footballers.

3

DOUBTS AND DEBUTS

Fear of failure haunted Jack. He had no idea whether he was good enough to make it as a footballer, or whether he would be packed back off to the North-East to re-apply to the police or beg for another job at the pit. The crucial date would be 8 May 1952, when he turned seventeen and Leeds either would or would not offer him a professional contract.

Jack may have had two uncles in Leeds but he stayed in a boarding house on Beeston Hill run by the seventy-six-year-old Mary Crowther and her daughter, Laura. Having a bed to himself he regarded as a great luxury. Mrs Crowther was, in her own way, just as formidable as Cissie and Jack lived there happily for seven years, despite a misunderstanding when she mistook a comb-case she found in his bed for a condom and thought he'd breached her prohibition on 'hankie-pankie'.[1] She liked to drink a bottle of milk stout in the evening, and after being persuaded to buy a television, took to pouring the ale into a mug and hiding it behind the chair so the people in the box couldn't see her indulging.

At the club, Jack swept the terraces, oiled the turnstiles, cleaned and painted the toilets, kept the boots of older players in good shape and pumped the balls. Occasionally, he was even allowed to train. Of his five pounds a week, two pounds and ten shillings went on board and he sent a pound back to his mother. Although he became good friends with the midfielder Mel Charles, at least until his departure for Swansea, Jack barely left Beeston, saving his money and focusing on his football.

He worked ferociously hard. He trained five days a week and on a Saturday morning would play for the youth team in the Northern Intermediate League. On a Saturday afternoon he would often travel as a reserve with the third team – even though there were no substitutes – just in case an opportunity to play came up. At sixteen, he played for the West Riding as they beat Northumberland at St James' Park, which brought a sense of personal vindication. He had returned to the North-East – and had done it triumphantly.

Yet a sense of disillusionment lingered. 'Frankly,' Jack said, 'I don't know just what I expected but it did not come up to the standard I had envisaged as a youngster … the terracing in those days was made from ashes and not concrete and there was more than a liberal sprinkling of weeds sprouting around the ground and from the terraces.'[2]

And Jack didn't know whether Major Frank Buckley, the eccentric manager, rated him. Buckley was one of the great characters of English football. Born in Urmston in Greater Manchester, he was educated in Liverpool and signed up to the King's Regiment, expecting to fight in the Boer War. When he was instead sent to Ireland, he bought himself out of the army and joined Aston Villa. He pursued a peripatetic career and had just left Derby for Bradford when the First World War broke out. He joined the 17th Middlesex Regiment, commanding the Football Battalion, was wounded in the shoulder and lung at the Somme and rose to the rank of major before joining Norwich as secretary-manager at the end of the war.

Financial problems led to his departure in 1920 and, after four years at Blackpool that demonstrated hints of his unorthodox thinking, he was appointed manager of Wolves in 1927. It was there that he flourished, taking the club to promotion to the First Division, where they twice finished as runners up, and to the 1938 FA Cup final. He also established the youth system and direct approach that would bring the great successes of the fifties, when they were managed by his captain and protégé, Stan Cullis. Buckley was also one of football's first great manipulators of the press, claiming he was giving his squad a serum derived from monkey glands in the build-up to the Cup final, while actually having them snort neat Bovril. Whether this was because he believed it would have a beneficial physical effect or because he saw a psychological advantage in having his players think they had additional energy was never clear.

Buckley left Wolves towards the end of the war and after brief spells at Notts County and Hull City was appointed Leeds manager in 1948. The club he took over was short of money but, after a successful scouting trip to south Wales in September 1948, had one huge asset: the emerging talent of John Charles – Mel's brother – who was physically imposing, deft of touch, almost unbeatable in the air and equally at home at centre-half or centre-forward.

With Buckley came his array of gimmicks. He would play dance tunes over the tannoy during training to try to improve his players' rhythm and took to sitting in the stand, barking orders through a megaphone, until complaints about his language by local residents forced the club to silence him.

For Jack, Buckley was an unpredictable figure of baffling mood swings. Once, seeing Jack's ragged shoes, he bought him a new set of brogues, but on another occasion he set Jack and another trainee to collecting weeds, promising them a shilling for every bucket they gathered, only to renege on the deal when they came to collect their earnings on the grounds they were club employees and already drawing a wage.

Approaching his seventeenth birthday, Jack still had no idea whether he was any good or not. He went to see Arthur Crowther, the club secretary, to ask if he were being offered a professional contract. Crowther told him he didn't know and, as the first team were away on a post-season tour of the Netherlands, he would have to wait. When Buckley returned, he authorised Crowther to offer a contract worth eighteen pounds a week during the season (probably something like five hundred pounds in 2022 or, to put it another way, roughly double the average weekly wage for the time[3]) and fourteen pounds a week in the summer. Jack delightedly signed. He then wandered over the road to a newsagent, where he learned that a number of First Division scouts had been hanging around waiting to see whether he would commit to Leeds.

He was soon captaining the under-eighteens, but he was still playing at full-back. Then, in a practice game, presumably because of his height, Jack was set to marking the great John Charles. Jack had played centre-back for the YMCA side, but this was his first serious game at the heart of the defence. He did well enough to be moved into the middle for the reserves. After six further games, on the Friday morning before the final weekend of the season, he checked the team sheets posted in the dressing room and saw he had been included for the match away at Doncaster Rovers. Only four years had passed since he had played his first match for Park school; he would, remarkably, make his league debut at a younger age than Bobby. It was a disorienting experience.

'The manager never came near me that day,' Jack said, 'never told me why he had put me in his team, nothing. And when I climbed aboard the first-team bus taking us to Doncaster the next day, I was left completely alone, without as much as a word from my new teammates. I mean, nobody told me what I was expected to do, no tactical talk, nothing.'

Eventually the wing-half Eric Kerfoot, seeing Jack's bewilderment, came over to him. 'Son,' he said, 'they've picked you because they think you're good enough. Now, go and prove them right.'[4]

By the standards of the day, Bobby was used to travelling, having taken the train from the age of ten or eleven to go and visit his uncle George in Chesterfield and having made regular trips to play for various representative sides. He went to Manchester alone, proudly wearing a full-length sea-green mackintosh. He met Busby's assistant Jimmy Murphy at the station and the two took a taxi to his digs, run by a Mrs Watson, near Old Trafford cricket ground. As he gazed out of the windows, observing just how smoky the air in Manchester seemed, how blackened the buildings, Murphy described another young player who lived with Mrs Watson, a giant two years Bobby's senior who had every footballing gift imaginable: Duncan Edwards.

He could have been an intimidating presence, but Edwards took Bobby under his wing. Seeing how little Bobby had, he gave him one of his shirts, which was far too big, but the gesture made Bobby feel welcome, and it established an almost fraternal relationship between the pair. And this big brother didn't get impatient with him or knock him around.

Bobby settled in quickly. His roommate at Mrs Watson's was Mark Jones, a commanding central defender from a mining village near Barnsley. He had been born four years before Bobby, but the gap seemed even bigger. Jones smoked a pipe and was a natural leader, taking his housemates on long marches into Manchester to go to the cinema. After Jones moved out to marry June and fulfil his dream of owning an aviary – which at any given time would house around fifty birds – Bobby shared with Billy Whelan. Born in Dublin, Whelan was two years older than Bobby and a devout Catholic. On the pitch, he was languid and skilful; off it, he was quiet and diffident. 'If you weren't such a great player,' Murphy used to say, 'you'd make a smashing priest.'⁵

The centre of Bobby's group of contemporaries was the diminutive wing-half Eddie Colman, a figure unlike any that Bobby had ever encountered. He was streetwise and a snappy dresser, the first person Bobby had ever seen in drainpipe jeans. He lived with his parents on Archie Street near the docks in Ordsall, which was used in the original opening credits of *Coronation Street*. Saturdays would typically begin in the parlour at the Colmans' with a jug of beer ordered in by Eddie's parents from the off-licence on the corner. His grandfather would stop by and tell jokes. The family of Wilf McGuinness also helped to look after Bobby.

After a couple of years, Bobby and his friends took to meeting at the Bridge Inn in Sale before moving on to the Plaza, owned by Jimmy Savile, the Locarno or perhaps the bar at the Café Royal opposite the Midland hotel. There was a time when they preferred the Sportsman's on Market Street, or the Bodega jazz club or the Zanzibar coffee bar. All of which is absent from Bobby's autobiography, which depicts the pre-Munich years as being about education and improvement and the thrill of playing with the likes of Duncan Edwards, Eddie Colman and David Pegg, as though he can't quite bring himself to allow the outside world to intrude on that footballing paradise.

In later life Bobby developed a reputation for standoffishness. George Best repeatedly suggested that he had no idea how to have fun. But in those days Bobby had plenty of friends and seems to have socialised as much as any teenager. He would take Pegg and Colman up to stay at the family home in

Ashington. He was not an especially big drinker but neither was he abstemious. He organised crib competitions and was a decent impressionist. His reserved manner made Bobby a far better poker player than his elder brother; few ever had much doubt whether the hand Jack held was any good.

'In the right company,' said John Giles, who joined United's youth ranks in 1956, 'with people he trusted, he was one of the lads, enjoyed a drink, a game of cards, a song – he loved Frank Sinatra and he had a good voice.'[6]

In December 1954, Mrs Watson caught her husband in bed with a maid. She expelled him and, raging at the world, served only Spam for Christmas dinner, at which the club decided to move its players out. The gang was split up, and Bobby ended up in new digs at Gorse Hill with David Pegg, who became his new roommate, Tommy Taylor and Jackie Blanchflower.

Knowing what was to come, there is a sense of those days as some prelapsarian idyll, all lads together, joking around, having fun, getting into scrapes, while at the same time being moulded into perhaps the most exciting football team in the country. From November 1953 that team had a nickname that was almost universally applied, despite Matt Busby's disapproval. It was bestowed by the headline of the *Manchester Evening Chronicle* after a 0–0 draw against Huddersfield in 1953: 'Busby's Bouncing "Babes" Keep All Town Awake'.[7]

As soon as he turned seventeen, Bobby left Switch Gear and signed a professional contract at United. There had never been any doubt that one would be offered, but when he arrived at Old Trafford in October 1954 as a pro, the first person he met was the trainer Tom Curry, who had been a wing-half for Newcastle. He asked what Bobby was doing there and when he explained, called him a fool, telling him football was a hard game and that he should have stuck to his trade.

And it wasn't easy. Bobby had been used to being the best player in any team he played for but at United he was just one good player among many. He had fallen into bad habits, relying too much on his instincts – and he was always somebody who chafed against tactical restrictions. That was where Jimmy Murphy came in.

Murphy had been born in the Rhondda in 1910 and had played more than two hundred times at wing-half for West Brom. He had been working as a PT instructor in the army when Busby spotted him, offering him a job after he was appointed United manager in 1946. Murphy was good on the practicalities of football, the little details that made a differ- ence. If you're putting the ball out of play, he would say, don't just knock it over the line, belt it deep into the stand to give your team a few extra seconds to reorganise. He set about turn- ing Bobby into a professional, trying to encourage him to pass shorter and always be on the move. Bobby had a habit of shout- ing at himself when he made a mistake: Murphy demanded he stop, seeing that as an indication of immaturity and insecurity. Bobby never stopped shouting at others, though: some saw him as a leader who demanded high standards, others as a terrible moaner, but everybody agreed he was extremely vocal on the pitch.

Murphy taught Bobby how to mark, how to create half a yard of space with a touch, and how and when to call. He saw his job as being to toughen players up. He had Eddie Colman repeatedly kick Bobby in his first training session and, in prac- tice matches, would mark those he really rated, staying tight to them, tripping them and obstructing them. He could be hard – cruel, even – regularly reducing players to tears and yet those who worked with him seem to have adored him. 'Bobby was loaded with talent, but needed hardening,' he said. 'He was one of the hardest pupils I ever had to work on. He had so much going for him, perhaps too much. We had to bully him.'[8]

Every Sunday, Murphy, in his shorts and a tracksuit top that did little to disguise his booze-induced pot-belly, would take Bobby for special one-on-one training involving him kicking balls for Bobby to chase until he was exhausted. They would then repair to the pub, where Bobby tried to chat about the great players of the past, just to stem the flow of his drinking. Murphy encouraged Bobby to kick with both feet and had him practise for hours, drilling a ball against a wall at Old Trafford, looking to keep it below a line Murphy drew three feet above the ground. He believed there was no need ever to take precise aim: keeping the ball under the bar and hitting it hard in the general direction of the net was enough.

The team would train by the Ship Canal, on a pitch surrounded by factories, so implanted in the heart of local industry that they could smell whatever was being served for lunch in the canteen at the Metro-Vicks plant. Many youth games were played at Old Trafford, occasions Bobby relished. Two huge dark warehouses stood next to the ground, one with a pale chimney and one with a dark. In time, Bobby came to feel that, while their gloom intimidated opposing teams, their size and solidity became comforting for home players, emblematic of the 'dark but vital sprawl' of Manchester.[9]

Bobby was always worried; that's just who he was. But at the beginning of September 1956, he was worried about something new. Football, for a long time, had been the one thing he didn't worry about. He was good at it; it came naturally to him. But for the first time, his career seemed to be stalling.

He'd served his time in the fifth team, playing in the Altrincham League, in which United would regularly win games by twenty goals. He'd played for the third team in the Manchester Amateur League, competing against the hard, physical sides from the docks and the factories. He'd played in

the youth team, which attracted huge crowds as it won the FA
Youth Cup five years in a row between 1953 and 1957. Murphy
would tell his players when Busby was coming to watch, knowing that would provide an additional determination to impress.

'His presence seemed to electrify all of us,' Bobby said. 'We
would tear into the game like lions. It was the only way, in a
sense, that we could communicate with him at that time. We
would all have run ourselves into the ground for him.'[10] True
as that may have been for the Babes, though, and true as it
perhaps remained for Bobby, it was not true of those players
who would later dine with Busby at the Crompton Club, or
those who played golf with him at Davyhulme. There's a sense
in which Bobby needed that remote figure of authority and was
reluctant always to get close enough to risk a change in their
relationship.

Bobby never suffered the doubts about his career that Jack
had but, as his brother began to make his way in the game, he
started to wonder when he would get his chance. There was
a spell in 1955–56 in which Bobby scored fifty-six goals in
forty-seven games for the youth and reserve sides, but still he
didn't make the breakthrough to the first team. Cissie was so
outraged that she approached Busby and, with a typical lack
of tact, asked if her boy was being left out because he wasn't –
as Busby, Murphy and many of Busby's closest allies were – a
Catholic. Bobby, of course, was mortified.

But other than scoring goals and playing well, what could
Bobby do? United had just won the league title. How could
he hope to force his way into the senior side? Bobby looked
at the other attacking options United had, at John Doherty,
Billy Whelan and Eddie Lewis, and wondered if he would ever
make it. But what was the alternative? He had no desire to leave
Manchester United.

He played in a reserve game against Manchester City and
went in for a 50–50 with Keith Marsden. Bobby was not a

good tackler, despite Murphy's best efforts. Marsden was properly set, Bobby wasn't, and he took the full impact on his right ankle, which rapidly swelled up. Ted Dalton, the club physio, applied a kaolin poultice and told him to rest while nature took its course. So Bobby did, but that only gave him more time to think.

The injury was another reminder of just how fragile a foot-balling career could be. Doherty was a fine player and had played sixteen games the previous season, earning a championship medal. He was twenty-one but already was struggling with knee injuries. A circular scar showed where a portion of cartilage had been removed. As it turned out, Doherty's career was already almost over. He played only three times in 1956–57 and in October 1957 he was transferred to Leicester City, where he lasted only a year before winding down his career at Rugby and Altrincham.

After three weeks, Bobby began training again. The ankle was still sore. He couldn't put pressure on it and every time he kicked with his right foot, he felt a twinge of real pain. It was then that, on the first Friday of October 1956, just under a week before his nineteenth birthday, he was summoned to Busby's office. That could mean one of only two things: he was either going to get a bollocking, or he was playing the following afternoon against Charlton Athletic. He couldn't think what he might have done wrong, and he knew that Roger Byrne, Edwards and Taylor were away playing for England against Northern Ireland, so he prepared to lie.

Sure enough, Busby asked how his ankle was. Never been better, Bobby replied. And he was told he was in the team against the side that were bottom of the league. There was a flash of exhilaration and then, Bobby being Bobby, more worrying.

That night he lay, sleepless, staring at the ceiling, waiting for dawn. He imagined what might go right, the glory he could achieve; but also what could go wrong. Dunc, he told himself, had done this when he had been almost two years younger. Surely he could cope. But Dunc was Dunc, a different order altogether.

He walked to the ground, having to resist the urge to blurt out to every passerby that he was about to play for Manchester United. At 11.30 a.m., the bus took the team to Davyhulme Golf Club, where they had their pre-match meal of steak and poached eggs. The players wandered for a while on the course. Bobby would become a notorious chatterbox before games, dealing with his nerves by trying to talk himself into self-belief, but that day he was too in awe of his teammates to say anything. Remembering something Allenby Chilton, the great centre-half of the immediate post-war era, had told him, Bobby had a nip of sherry, believing that would give him renewed energy in the later stages of the game.

He walked out before a crowd of 41,439. This was the stage he had always imagined. This was the fulfilment of a dream. And then United fell behind. It didn't matter, though. Johnny Berry soon equalised. Then, on thirty-two minutes, Bobby turned with the ball on his right foot. He remembered everything Jimmy Murphy had told him, kept his head down and hit it early, ignoring the pain that flashed through his right foot: 2–1. Five minutes later the ball dropped to him on the volley. He anticipated the pain before he struck the shot, but still made clean contact: 3–1.

Bobby missed a straightforward chance for his hat-trick in the second half, but nobody other than him worried about that. His debut meant that every member of the reserve team that had won the championship the previous season had been blooded at senior level.

United won 4–2, maintaining their unbeaten start to the season, remaining comfortably top of the table. But more than that, Bobby was a first-teamer, a 'golden asset', as the

Manchester Evening News had it, 'in an Old Trafford nursery that has become the envy of the club soccer world'.[11] A threshold had been crossed. He had become a Manchester United player.

4

YEARS OF DRIFT

As it turned out, Jack's debut for Leeds had been Major Buckley's final game. Repeatedly, he had taken Leeds close to promotion but, over-reliant on John Charles and without the resources to strengthen the side, never quite achieved it. It was indicative of the financial restrictions placed on him that, when Buckley quit in the summer of 1953, it was to take over at lowly Walsall.

Leeds knew immediately who they wanted to replace him. They had tried to appoint Raich Carter before approaching Buckley in 1948, but he had been reluctant to accept a three-year deal and had gone to Hull City instead. It was never entirely clear why they were so keen. Carter had been a great player, a clever and clinical inside-forward who, at just twenty-two, had captained Sunderland to the 1935–36 league title, following that up with the Cup a year later. When Sunderland didn't renew his contract after the war, he moved to Derby and won the Cup with them in 1946. As player-manager of Hull, he had inspired promotion out of Third Division North at the first attempt but, just after the start of his fourth season in charge, he had resigned for reasons there were never adequately explained to run a tobacconist's. He returned as a player a few months later to help the club battle relegation. He retired again at the end of that season, before accepting an offer of fifty pounds a game to play for Cork City for the final three months of 1952–53, helping them to the Irish Cup.

Carter was still only thirty-nine when Leeds appointed him in June 1953. That summer, as he looked for a house in Leeds and completed the sale of his tobacconist's, his wife, Rosa, died from heart disease. She was thirty-eight.

It's impossible, of course, to know precisely what impact that had on Carter. There are those who suggest the loss made him colder and more remote, calcifying the self-possession that had characterised him as a player into arrogance as a manager. But Carter had always been a man apart, a trait that made him a young leader and that was perhaps exaggerated by him always being in charge.

On his first day at Leeds, Carter showed his squad photographs of himself in his playing days. It might not quite have been Brian Clough arriving twenty-one years later and telling everybody to throw their medals in the bin because they'd won them by cheating, but it didn't go down well. 'I loved the man,' said John Charles, 'but I always felt he was a bit of a bighead. He was never happier than when talking about himself and he often took the credit for other's achievements. I always felt he was in love with himself.'[1]

Carter had a picture of himself hung on the wall of his office and during pay negotiations would jab a thumb over his shoulder at it, saying, 'You'll not get a rise till you start playing like him.'[2] Leeds described him as a tracksuit manager, but the only tracksuit Carter wore was to join in the unruly games on the gravel pitch behind the stand that made up the bulk of training. Coaching was not something in which he believed. 'You're either a player or you're not,' the *Guardian* columnist Frank Keating recalled him saying.[3]

Leeds remained inconsistent, and almost entirely reliant on Charles. In October 1953, when it became known that he was suffering from tonsillitis and so would not be able to play against Bristol Rovers, the crowd dropped by nine thousand, around a third. A lack of height at the back was a major problem and, although Leeds scored eighty-nine goals, they conceded eighty-one, finishing tenth. The following season, the captain, Tommy Burden, submitted a transfer request, disgusted by the way Carter had blamed the goalkeeper, Jack Scott, for a goal conceded in a 5–3 reverse against Bury amid a run of five defeats in a row. Carter made Charles captain and restored him to the defence. Leeds rallied to finish fourth, a point off promotion.

Jack missed it all.

A couple of months after making his first-team debut, Jack was called up for national service, which he performed with the Royal Horse Guards in Windsor. Army life didn't begin well, as he was put in a cell for a few hours for going absent without leave, having missed a message to report to Catterick to play for the Northern Command, but after that he rapidly took to the service. Although opportunities to play for Leeds were limited, he had plenty of football. Jack was the first private to captain the Horse Guards team – an early sign of his willingness to take responsibility – leading them to victory in the Cavalry Cup in West Germany.

Cissie always said it was the army that had given Jack discipline[4] but, if anything, his life in Windsor seems to have been rather less restrained than it had been in his early years in Leeds, almost as though he needed authority to rebel against. For the first time in his life, he became interested in women and cigarettes. Army regulations, meanwhile, were just another opportunity for his entrepreneurial genius. He realised there was money to be made by dealing in soldiers' chits to travel to see their families. He would buy them for two shillings from those who lived in the Windsor or London area and use them to go up to Leeds, claiming four or five pounds each time from the club, even though he was restricted largely to playing for the reserves. That enabled him to make £25–£30 a month rather than the twenty-five shillings a week that was standard army pay and that, along with the occasional ten-bob note from his mother, enabled him to lend money at interest. By the end of his time in the army, Jack had more than four hundred pounds in the bank – near enough twelve thousand pounds in 2022.

But he wasn't just richer. Jack had changed. 'I went to the army a boy of eighteen,' he said, 'and came back a man of twenty.'[5] The doubts about his footballing ability had vanished and he had become somebody who wasn't going to be pushed around. 'Maybe,' he later acknowledged, 'I was a bit too full of myself.'[6]

His third senior start came towards the end of September 1955, in the ninth match of the season, at home to Rotherham. Carter had retained Charles at centre-half, but when Archie Gibson was injured, Jack replaced him and Charles moved to right-half, from where he could talk Jack through games. He offered the only real coaching Jack had experienced to that point, explaining the benefits of turning slightly side-on when facing an oncoming centre-forward and how headers could best be directed.

It was the return of Charles to the forward line after a 4–0 defeat at Sheffield Wednesday three weeks later that proved pivotal – and gave some sense of how well Jack fitted in. Not that Jack's relationship with Charles was entirely straightforward. When Charles decided to drop back for the final ten minutes to defend a one-goal lead against Fulham, for instance, Jack told him to 'fuck off back up field'.[7] Charles ignored him, then held Jack's head under the water in the bath afterwards. Leeds remained inconsistent, particularly away from home, but a run of six straight victories at the end of the season carried them to promotion in second place.

Arnold Price, whose daughter was married to the Leeds full-back Jimmy Dunn, owned a fish-and-chips shop just over the road from the main gate at Elland Road. For his business and the team, autumn 1956 seemed a time of great promise. Although there was a 5–1 defeat at Tottenham, Leeds had begun their first season back in the top flight exceptionally well. They had won six of their first nine games and lay second in the table. And then, in the early hours of 16 September, Price woke to an intense smell of smoke. Fire, he soon realised, was raging in the West Stand, the roof of which had already collapsed onto the seats below. Barefoot and in his pyjamas, Price rushed down the street to find a telephone to raise the alarm, but it was already too late. The stand was ruined, the pitch scorched by the intensity of the blaze. A subsequent investigation blamed an electrical fault.

By the time the fire was put out, as *The Times* described it, 'The charred remains of it stood in the sunlight, a ring of metal girders looking for all the world like the dark skeleton of a whale.'[8] It wasn't just the spectators' accommodation that had been destroyed, but also the club offices and records, the dressing rooms, directors' facilities and press box, as well as the team kit, boots and a load of physiotherapy equipment. Damage was estimated at over a hundred thousand pounds and the club was woefully under-insured. The financial problems that had nagged at them since the war suddenly reached crisis point.

Carter was determined momentum should not be lost and insisted that Saturday's game against Aston Villa should go ahead as scheduled. He bought forty pairs of new boots and had them soaked, ordering the players to wear them as much

as possible that week to try to break them in. Leeds and Villa
changed at the Whitehall Printeries sports ground in Lowfields
Road, then boarded a coach to the game, walking on to the
pitch through the shell of the stand. Charles got the only goal
to keep Leeds second but, as the season went on, form began to
drift and it became apparent the real struggle was off the pitch.

With assistance from the council, the board launched an
appeal that raised sixty thousand pounds, but a new stand
was going to cost more than double that. There was only one
possible outcome: at the end of the season, John Charles was
sold to Juventus for sixty-five thousand pounds.

The absence of Charles cemented Jack's place in the team –
or rather, it should have done. But Jack was wild and
ill-disciplined. By his own admission, he found it hard to concentrate, stayed out too late and too often, drank too much
and let himself be distracted by women. Training, which was
little more than some running and a kickabout, bored him. In
those days, he wasn't even a particularly good header of the
ball, struggling to direct his clearances.

Among his teammates, he was notorious for his financial
canniness. It wasn't just that he never bought a packet of
cigarettes – justifying his tightness by claiming that cadging
cigarettes was a good ice-breaker – it was that he was always
looking for ways of supplementing his income. In pre-season,
for instance, he bought large bottles of pop from a local newsagent and then sold it to players at tuppence a glass. He also
had a short fuse, making him a regular target of dressing-
room banter. Over Christmas 1957, Leeds played away at
Sunderland, staying in the Seaburn hotel on the seafront. Jack
was known as 'Turkey' because of his long neck, a nickname
he hated. During the meal on the day before the game, Bobby
Forrest went into the kitchens, helped himself to a turkey's

head and, knowing Jack would be last down to the restaurant, left it in his place. When Jack arrived, he erupted, grabbing a plate and hurling it against the wall.

His temper formed part of a wider sense of unease at the club, in which Jack played a central role. Having finished eighth in their first season back in the First Division, Leeds slipped to seventeenth without Charles. Carter's five-year contract was up and, despite his protestations that he hadn't been given any money to replace Charles, it was not renewed. Having decided Carter was not the answer, though, the club had little idea who might be and after dithering till December, they ended up appointing Bill Lambton, a coach who been brought in by Carter the previous November and had been caretaker since the end of the previous season. He was, Jack said, 'a nice enough man but he wasn't a player, he wasn't a coach, he wasn't anything'.[9] The winger Jackie Overfield saw him as 'a sergeant-major type who thought he could run a football club like you would the army'.[10]

Lambton had no authority and gimmicks such as having the players train in running spikes did little to change that. When he did try to impose himself, it only made matters worse. Players complained at one training session that the balls had been pumped too hard, to which Lambton replied that footballers with good technique should be able to play with any sort of ball, barefoot. Jack challenged him to do so and Lambton doggedly did, refusing to admit he was in obvious pain.

He seemed to have no sense of which battles were worth fighting. Lambton made little attempt to stop players drinking before games, yet dug his heels in over food at a hotel restaurant before one match, insisting Jack couldn't have both soup and melon. Jack was hungry and wanted two starters, but what really enraged him was the impression Lambton gave that he knew how to behave in a civilised restaurant and Jack did not. They had a furious, public row.

It wasn't just Jack who was frustrated. Grenville Hair, having submitted a transfer request in September 1958, submitted another after Lambton was given a contract, saying the stress of the team's poor form was damaging his health. Chris Crowe and Jackie Overfield also asked to go and then, in mid-January 1959, Wilbur Cush resigned the captaincy.

Then Jack's request to give a couple of his relatives a lift on the team bus was turned down on the grounds it was for club personnel only. Just weeks later, Lambton invited four waiters from the team hotel to join them on board. It was the final straw. Jack, awkward and quick to anger as ever, got off the bus and got back on only after directors had ordered the waiters off. Whatever credibility Lambton had left disappeared.

A 6–2 defeat at Wolves on Valentine's Day was the beginning of the end. The following four games yielded a single point, which came in a home game against Portsmouth for which only 14,900 fans turned out. In early March, the directors called a crisis meeting with the manager, his staff and the squad. With the players in full revolt, Lambton offered a fresh start but it was too late. He resigned at the board's request later that day.

Lambton's assistant, the sixty-two-year-old physio Bob Roxburgh, took over as caretaker and Leeds stayed up, but the search for a new leader was no better thought through than it had been after Carter's departure. Arthur Turner was announced but decided to stay with non-league Headington – who he would soon lead into the league after they became Oxford United. A string of other candidates turned the job down, including the former captain Tommy Burden, who was by then at Bristol City. Leeds may have been in the First Division, but the manager's role was simply not an attractive job, and in the end they settled for QPR's Jack Taylor, who had played for Buckley at Wolves and for Carter at Hull. He brought with him his brother Frank, an FA-qualified coach.

For the first time, training at Leeds began to focus on

technique and on playing different types of pass. Frank Taylor would set up a ball between a pair of bricks to encourage players to focus properly when kicking. Jack liked the brothers, but there was a sense that Jack Taylor was simply too nice and too indecisive to be a successful manager. They never recovered from a dismal November in which they lost four in a row, conceding fifteen goals. After a 3–0 defeat to Wolves at the beginning of April, a headline in the *Guardian* lamented that their 'Play Conforms to No Logic'.[11] They were relegated a couple of weeks later.

That could, perhaps, have been an opportunity to clear out some of the dead-wood and reset but Eric Smith, who joined that summer from Celtic for ten thousand pounds, spoke of a regime in which players wandered in, after what were supposed to be long training runs in pre-season, licking lollies. The club was not just ill-disciplined, but unlucky; Smith broke his leg in the second game of the season.

Leeds won just three of their first fifteen games and, when another crisis meeting was called just before Christmas, players amused themselves – and showed up Taylor's lack of authority – by throwing streamers around as he tried to speak. With a sense of inevitability, he resigned in March 1961.

One night in 1957, Jack had gone to the cinema with a couple of teammates. After the film, he popped upstairs into the Majestic Ballroom, not really intending to stay. There, he saw a young woman called Pat Kemp and introduced himself. Pat hadn't really wanted to go out that night but had been persuaded by her sister and was with her mother when Jack approached. She had no interest in football and doubted this gangling smoker actually played for Leeds as he claimed, but she liked the look of him. 'He was really clean ...' she said. 'He just looked shiny and clean and neat.'[12] Only when he was called up on stage to present an award was she convinced that Jack really was a footballer.

They married on 6 January 1958 at St Peter's church in Bramley, Leeds. It was a characteristically chaotic affair. Jack had borrowed a car, but it got a flat tyre which he changed himself and he was flustered and sweating when he arrived at the church. Bobby was best man – at the time, the two were close – and Tommy Taylor, Billy Whelan and David Pegg were all guests; a month later all three would be dead.

Jack and Pat went to Scarborough for their honeymoon, which lasted just two days because Jack wanted to watch a Cup game between York and Birmingham. That was indicative of two things: most obviously, of Jack's uncompromising nature and his tendency always to do things to suit himself, but also of his increasing interest in football in general and how it was played.

It was a former Leeds player called George Ainsley who had stimulated his fascination with coaching. Ainsley led sessions at local schools and one day took Jack with him to Batley grammar. With the pupils gathered around in the school gym, Ainsley asked them how many successive headers they thought he could do without the ball touching the ground. One boy said five, at which Ainsley performed a hundred and immediately had the group's attention. Jack understood the lesson: 'You must entertain, you must be a showman.'[13]

Jack studied for his preliminary coaching badge and then went to Lilleshall, Shropshire, for the FA's summer course. He returned the following summer to complete his full badge and became a regular visitor. The likes of Bill Shankly and Brian Clough were sceptical of the value of coaching and classes but Jack was open to new ideas, loved discussing the mechanics of football and read widely. His brother, who had been the keener on football as a boy, did not.

Before one game between the aspiring coaches, a counsellor

came round and gave them each a word to remember. At half-time, everybody had forgotten it and the counsellor gave them the word again, but at full-time, again, nobody could remember what their word had been. The lesson was that playing football was all-consuming; players couldn't even remember a word, never mind a complicated schema. Instructions, Jack realised, had to be kept as simple as possible: 'The less choice you give a player, the more likely he is to make the right decision.'[14]

And so, partly because of his new-found fascination with coaching and partly because of the responsibilities of marriage, Jack began to settle down. And, of course, there was a financial benefit: as an FA-approved coach, working at schools in Leeds and Castleford, Jack earned thirty shillings an hour, meaning he might make sixty or seventy pounds a month to go with the twenty pounds he earned as a player.

Jack's wedding was one of two vital moments in the development of Leeds that took place that year. The other was the arrival in November of Don Revie, signed for fourteen thousand pounds from Sunderland.

5

MUNICH

Harry Gregg got up in the early hours of 1 February 1958 to go to the toilet. In the corridor of the Lancaster Gate hotel, he passed two policemen, but it was only when he awoke later that morning that he discovered why they had been there: George Whittaker, a director of Manchester United, had died overnight. As a result, for the last game they played in England before the tragedy at Munich, United wore black armbands, as did their opponents, Arsenal. United were in tremendous form, unbeaten since Bobby had returned to the side in December. In their previous league game, he'd scored a hat-trick in a 7–2 win over Bolton, and he'd then got both goals against Ipswich in the fourth round of the Cup.

United were ahead within ten minutes at Highbury, Edwards firing in a Dennis Viollet lay-off, and Bobby then smashed in an Albert Scanlon cross on the half-hour. 'Charlton,' the *Guardian* noted, 'has grown from a limited left-sided player of little pace into a brilliant inside-forward.'[1] By February 1958 he was established in the side and his goal at Highbury was his eleventh in eleven games.

Taylor made it 3–0 before half-time. Arsenal fought back, scoring three goals in a little under three minutes in the second half, but United came again, Bobby and Scanlon combining to set up the fourth for Viollet before Taylor made it 5–3 from a tight angle. Derek Tapscott got a fourth for Arsenal to threaten another fightback, but United held out. 'The thermometer was doing a war dance,' Geoffrey Green wrote in *The Times*. 'There was no breath left in anyone. The players came off arm in arm. They knew they had fashioned something of which to be proud.'[2] United had already established themselves as a very good side but, with youth and momentum, there was a sense they were on the cusp of something truly extraordinary. 'We were a group of young men with everything to play for,' said Harry Gregg.[3]

It had been a genuinely great game, one that might have been remembered whatever had happened next. But it became more than that; it became the Babes' epitaph.

Scoring two goals on his debut had not made Bobby an automatic starter, although he did play fourteen league games, scoring ten goals, as United retained the league title in 1956–57. He had fallen out of favour by the end of the season, though, and was named in the side for the 1957 FA Cup final against Aston Villa only because Dennis Viollet had a groin strain. The day turned out to be a huge disappointment for Bobby. United's goalkeeper Ray Wood was knocked unconscious and suffered a fractured cheekbone after a late challenge from Villa's Peter McParland and, with Jackie Blanchflower taking over in goal, United lost 2–1. So averse was Bobby to conflict or controversy that even a decade later he was referring to the incident as 'an unfortunate clashing of heads'.[4]

As his playing career was beginning, Bobby was also performing his national service. Called up in 1956, he was told by Busby to apply for the Royal Army Ordnance Corps at Donnington near Shrewsbury. After five weeks of training in Portsmouth, he received the notice that he was to be posted to Malaya, where guerrilla forces were fighting British rule. In a panic, Bobby rang the club, and the next day found himself redeployed to the Nesscliffe Barracks, Shropshire, where Edwards had already been posted. Edwards immediately took charge of his teammate. He showed him to his billet and, on noticing a spring poking through the mattress, he picked up the entire bed frame and carried it away to find a replacement.

Bobby worked in the ammunition shed, moving shells and crates of bullets about. He didn't seem particularly to have minded the work: in *Forward for England* he suggests that had it not been for football, he might have been interested in a career in the army.[5] A very clear structure of command, perhaps, suited his temperament.

Bobby's first season of first-team football was also United's first season of European competition. They hammered Anderlecht 10–0 in the preliminary round in a game played at Maine Road because the floodlights were still being installed at Old Trafford. Bobby was still at Shrewsbury and got a lift to the game with Sergeant-Major White. The margin of victory was so huge as to obscure how well United had played; the following day, Bobby found himself in the mess having to convince others that Anderlecht were a decent side and that United had been exceptional. Whatever the doubts, seventy thousand fans turned out at Maine Road to see United go 3–0 up against Borussia Dortmund in the first round. They then conceded twice, but a 0–0 draw in Germany saw them through to a quarter-final against the Spanish champions, Athletic of Bilbao.

Athletic were a step up in quality from Dortmund. By half-time in the first leg at San Mamés, Athletic led 3–0 but goals from Taylor and Viollet in the first ten minutes of the second half got United back into it. Athletic, though, came again and by the seventy-eighth minute had restored their three-goal advantage. But with five minutes remaining, Billy Whelan picked the ball up deep, languidly evaded two challengers and brought it back to 5–3, giving United hope in the second leg.

This was the game that woke England up to the glories of European football: the foreign travel, the largely unknown opponents magnified by their unfamiliarity, the possibility of epic comebacks in a two-legged tie, the passion of a surging crowd in the dark stands around the iridescent pitch. 'The Greatest Victory in Soccer History',[6] roared the *Daily Express*'s headline, as United, having pulled level on aggregate with Tommy Taylor's seventieth-minute goal, won the tie through Johnny Berry five minutes from time.

This was new and it was thrilling and Britain loved it, even if United were comprehensively beaten by the perennial champions Real Madrid in the semi-final. And yet within the romance, there was a dark foreshadowing. There had been a snowstorm in Bilbao but United, wary of angering an already disapproving league by postponing their Saturday fixture against Sheffield Wednesday, were adamant they had to return. Players leant a hand, brushing snow from the wings, helping to shovel slush from the runway. Even then, strong headwinds on the return flight meant an unscheduled stop in Jersey to refuel. At the time it was all done in good humour, lads mucking in together, but just over a year later many would look back on that trip and wonder how close they had come.

As United won at Highbury, Wolves were hammering Leicester 5–1 to retain a six-point lead, with the two sides scheduled to meet the following Saturday. Win that and, with thirteen league games remaining, the title race would be very much open. But first there was the trip to Belgrade to defend a 2–1 first-leg lead against Crvena Zvezda in the European Cup quarter-final.

Foreign travel was still an event and a mark of status. Every summer, a 12-foot-by-12-foot sign would be erected outside the Plaza in Manchester, bearing the message, 'Jimmy Savile is going to the south of France, leaving your entertainment in the very capable hands of good friends.'[7] The carrier Aviogenex had begun flying direct from the UK to the Dalmatian coast in 1957, although Yugotours – which did much to popularise the package holiday – wasn't founded until the following year and didn't really take off until the sixties. The players were unsure what they would find in Yugoslavia. Eddie Colman's mother made up a parcel containing apples, oranges and loose-leaf tea. A wrap of newspaper, the tea leaves still inside, was later found beside his body. Bobby took sweets, chocolates and biscuits, although as the food was far better than he'd feared, he ended up giving it to the maid in the hotel.

Colin Webster didn't travel because he had flu. The chairman, Harold Hardman, and two other directors stayed in Manchester to attend George Whittaker's funeral. Alex Dawson was left behind because a slight doubt over Roger Byrne's fitness meant Geoff Bent was taken as cover instead. Jimmy Murphy had to go to Cardiff to manage Wales in the second leg of a World Cup qualifying play-off against Israel. Trivial details that made the difference between life and death. Mark Jones overslept, having been up late tending to a sick budgerigar. What if he'd been even later?

The Zvezda game itself prompted tantalising possibilities of other timetables, other outcomes. Dennis Viollet put United ahead after two minutes and two strikes in quick succession from Bobby seemed to have settled the game before half-time. But Zvezda came back with three goals in the first quarter-hour of the second half, leaving United to cling on for the final half-hour. 'I had a big chance,' said the Zvezda playmaker Dragoslav Šekularac, one of the greatest of all Yugoslav players. 'I was to blame, maybe, that we didn't win the game. I curse myself for that. I was three or four yards from the goal and I put it over the crossbar. I wanted to put extra power on it and it didn't work out right.'[8]

It was almost sixty years later when I went to his flat in Belgrade to talk to him about the game. He was clearly ill, his skin sallow, his voice weak, although it would be another two years before he finally succumbed to his cancer. His sheets lay tangled on his bed and he had fairly evidently just got up for the interview. Across the road was the Majestic hotel, where the post-match banquet had been held in 1958. There had been beer, *slivovitz* – plum brandy – dancers and cabaret acts and, when the official festivities were over, a number of players carried on drinking with embassy officials. The game had been tough, but the players clearly got on well with each other.

There was no football memorabilia in Šekularac's flat, apart from one plaque commemorating that game against Manchester United. He was haunted by what had happened, and particularly by his miss. 'It could have been 4–3,' he said. 'Then we would have played a third game and they would not have travelled on that day.'

In fact, that is almost certainly not true. With no away goals rule, a 4–3 win for Zvezda would have meant a replay, but with the league insisting its fixture list was sacrosanct, a third game would probably have been played the following week: even if Šekularac had scored, United would still have been on the same plane.

United landed in Munich in a blizzard. It was cold, the sky was dark and there was a covering of snow on the runway. The players disembarked while the plane refuelled, heading into the terminal where they wandered idly round the shops and drank coffee. Duncan Edwards sent a telegram to his landlady saying that all flights were cancelled and he wouldn't be home until

the following day. There was the listlessness that comes with a
return journey, a desire to be home.

The players trooped out again, feeling their hangovers, but
still largely ebullient. They were in the European Cup semi-
final. They were playing Wolves that Saturday in a game that
would go a long way to deciding the destination of the title.
Just one more leg and they'd be back in Manchester for a meal
and a sleep in their own beds before getting down to training
again. Bill Foulkes, Pegg, Kenny Morgans and Scanlon started
playing cards again at one of the plane's tables. Across the aisle,
Byrne, Whelan, Wood and Blanchflower had their own game
going. Bobby and Dennis Viollet chatted, trying to work out
what had gone wrong in the second half in Belgrade.

The first attempt at a take-off was aborted. So too was a
second. Frank Swift, the former Manchester City goalkeeper
who had become a journalist with the *News of the World*,
angrily demanded to know what was going on. There was a
technical fault, they were told. Everybody had to return to the
terminal while it was fixed. Coffee was ordered, but before it
arrived, they were ready to attempt a third take-off. There was
grumbling, and some doubts: how could the fault have been
remedied so quickly?

Everybody returned to the plane. The mood had subtly
changed. The players were quieter, more reflective. The card
schools didn't start up this time. Morgans and Pegg went to the
rear of the plane where Jones, Edwards, Taylor and Colman
sat with the journalists, seemingly in the belief it was safer
back there.

There was a pause. They were one short. Alf Clarke, it
turned out, was phoning through the story of the delay to the
Manchester Evening Chronicle. He boarded to ironic cheers
and good-natured mockery. Bobby, for reasons he could never
subsequently explain, didn't take his overcoat off before buck-
ling himself in next to Dennis Viollet.

A mood of apprehension settled over the plane. 'Now or never,' said Roger Byrne. Mark Jones, who hated flying, was noticeably pale. Bill Foulkes took his shoes off and tucked himself down, reasoning that if his head was below the level of the seat it wouldn't be crushed by the bulkhead should anything go wrong.[9] 'If this is it,' said the devoutly Catholic Billy Whelan, 'I'm ready.' Earlier in the day, Harry Gregg had been reading Roger McDonald's erotic novel *The Whip*; he wondered whether, if this was it, that might be enough to send him straight to hell.

Bobby turned away from Viollet and stared out of the window. He saw the snow-covered airfield bounce by. It occurred to him that it all seemed to be taking a very long time, but then he'd noticed that about Elizabethans – as Airspeed Ambassadors were known – before. Not that he knew it, but the plane reached V1, the speed at which it was unsafe to abort. It continued, briefly, to accelerate, but before it reached V2, the velocity required for take-off, it began to slow. There was a terrible thump and then 'the grind of metal on metal'[10] and then, nothing.

Bobby awoke on his back in the snow, still strapped into his seat, around forty yards from the plane. Everything ached, but his head most of all. He was bleeding, aware of the smoke and the grit in the air. At first all he could hear was the howling of the wind. The plane had crashed through the perimeter fence and smashed into a house, before spinning into a hut in which was parked a truck filled with fuel. The port wing had sheared off and the rear of the plane was on fire.

He saw a teammate nearby, obviously dead. Some deep-rooted sense of decency and discretion meant he never revealed who. Strapped in the seat next to him, Dennis Viollet was in a bad way, covered in blood, still unconscious. A few yards away lay Matt Busby, conscious and groaning in pain. Everywhere, sirens wailed. Leading from the plane was a curiously straight line of bodies, some moving, many not.

Viollet came round and asked him what was going on. 'Dennis,' he replied, 'it's dreadful.'[11] It was an honesty he would always regret. Bobby stumbled over to Busby, took off his overcoat and draped it around his manager's shoulders. Somebody told him Roger Byrne was dead. Bill Foulkes was nearby, dazed in his stocking feet. Harry Gregg, having already pulled a baby from the wreckage and dragged Bobby and Viollet out of range of a possible explosion, was using his tie as a tourniquet to try to staunch the bleeding from Jackie Blanchflower's arm. Much later, after suffering crippling headaches and anxiety, Gregg found he had done it all with a hairline fracture of the skull.

A truck pulled up beside them. Busby was loaded on a stretcher into the back, Foulkes and Gregg sat in the middle, Bobby and Viollet at the front. They set off, then stopped to pick up the courier, a Mrs Miklos, who had been badly burned. Off they went again, too fast for Foulkes's liking and he began to punch the driver on the back of the head. He paid no attention, and eventually Foulkes settled to trying to keep Busby's stretcher steady.

They got to the Rechts der Isar hospital in Munich. The scene was confused. Nobody seemed certain about anything. Abruptly, Bobby snapped, screaming abuse at an orderly. He felt a sharp prick in his neck as a doctor gave him an injection and then, again, nothing.

The young forward Alex Dawson was playing snooker. In the corridor outside, he heard running footsteps, and recognised the short-legged stride pattern of his teammate Mark Pearson. He looked up from the table as Pearson rushed in and knew immediately something was very, very wrong.

*

Cissie Charlton had a premonition. She had felt unsettled all day and in the early afternoon had trudged through thick snow in Ashington to see a neighbour with whom she discussed her sense of anxiety. She had just got home when the local newsagent, Ted Cockburn, called round. Before he'd said anything, Cissie knew. 'It's Bobby, isn't it?' she asked.

Cockburn had wanted to warn her before putting out the placards saying that Bobby had been involved in a crash. He told her that the early reports suggested there had been no survivors. Cissie rushed out to the public phone box to call Old Trafford. The snow, though, had brought the lines down. There was no further information to be had.

The secretary of Leeds United, Arthur Crowther, burst into the dressing room. The players had finished their post-training baths and Jack was standing naked in the middle of the floor, towelling himself dry and joking with the forward Bobby Forrest. There was no opportunity, Crowther decided, for delicacy. He announced the news of the crash and said that nobody knew how many had died. The laughter stopped and the room fell silent.

Jack dressed quickly and went to the office, but Crowther couldn't get through to Old Trafford. Jack rang Pat to ask her to meet him at the station so they could go up to Ashington. As he was explaining, he broke down and wept as he had never wept before.

The train journey was awful. Other passengers blithely discussed the details of the crash. To somebody as naturally impatient as Jack, it seemed to take an eternity. At Haymarket bus station in Newcastle, Jack picked up a late edition of the *Evening Chronicle*. It carried the news that Bobby was among the survivors.

'Bloody hell!' Jack shouted. 'He's OK!' He grabbed Pat and danced a jig of relief.

By the time he got to Beatrice Street, Cissie had received
a telegram from the British consul in Munich, acting on Bill
Foulkes's instructions: 'Alive and well. See you later, Bobby.'
What Bob Charlton made of it all is unknown: Jack, Bobby
and Cissie have all given their accounts of that day; he is never
mentioned.

Mid-afternoon in the Manchester office of the *Daily Express*
tended to be calm before the evening rush but on the sports
desk there was always work to do. Long before the print dead-
lines there were statistics to be logged and racing results to be
compiled. Then came the emergency flash: 'Manchester United
aircraft crashed on take-off.' There was silence. A few minutes
later came a second flash: 'Heavy loss of life feared.'

Professional instincts kicked in. Accounts were sought,
details checked, pages prepared. The deputy sports editor,
David Nicholls, cancelled a day off. The sports editor, Eric
Cooper, wept. The *Express* had lost one of its own: Henry
Rose, the larger-than-life Manchester-based football correspondent, one of eight journalists who died. A photo arrived
and they could see him, white-shirted, lying dead in the snow.

Finally, at 2 a.m., the last edition was sent and they could
go home. But nobody did. Nobody could face being alone,
nobody could sleep. And so they went to the Press Club or the
Cromford Club and drank. But they were back the following
day for the grim aftermath of the crash, reporting how those
in hospital were getting on, how many would survive and how
many would not.

Nobby Stiles had finished for the day. He waited with the
other ground staff in the reserve team's dressing room to be
told they could go home. Arthur Powell and Bill Inglis came in

and announced they had bad news: the plane had crashed. But nobody knew how bad, nobody thought much of it. 'Maybe we'll get a game now,' somebody joked.

Stiles took the 112 bus up Rochdale Road towards his home in Collyhurst. When he got off, he bought a newspaper. Only then did he realise the scale of the tragedy. He went into the church and, sobbing, prayed for the injured and the dead.

A few days later, the skip containing the kit the team had worn in Belgrade arrived back at Old Trafford. Stiles was set to cleaning the boots. When he'd finished, he asked if he could keep those belonging to his hero, Tommy Taylor. He held onto them for several years before donating them to the club museum.

The heavily pregnant June Jones was in the supermarket buying food for that evening. As she walked down an aisle she heard two other shoppers mention a crash and was gripped by a terrible fear. Her husband, Mark, never made it home for dinner.

Jimmy Murphy was buoyant. His Wales side had beaten Israel to secure qualification to the World Cup for the first time – and United were through to the European Cup semi-final. He took the train from Cardiff to Manchester to await the triumphant return of the squad, carrying with him a large box of oranges he'd been given by the Israelis. He was struck by how quiet everything seemed at Old Trafford. He left the oranges inside the main entrance and went into the boardroom where, weary from the journey, he poured himself a scotch.

Busby's secretary, Alma George, came in and told him about the crash. He couldn't take it in. His only response was to offer her a sherry. She told him again and still the words didn't register. Only when she told him a third time, breaking down as she did so, did Murphy understand. He took the scotch to his office and wept. But then the phones began to ring. Murphy answered. He kept drinking and got on with the business of informing the families of the victims, working out what had happened and what needed to be done. By the time he went to bed, the bottle of scotch was empty, but the rebirth of the club had begun.

The next day, he flew to Germany.

'Keep the flag flying, Jimmy,' Busby said to him, and he did. In public, he remained foul-mouthed and furious, the same unyielding coach he had always been. But Harry Gregg never forgot the moment he had turned a corner on the stairs in their Munich hotel and found him hunched over, sobbing.

In the Zemun district of Belgrade, Dragoslav Šekularac left a cinema. As he walked down the steps outside, a boy ran up to him. At first he assumed he was after an autograph, but he quickly realised this was something else, something far more serious. Manchester United's plane had crashed, the boy told him. Šekularac couldn't believe it, didn't want to believe it. He hurried home and turned on the radio.[12]

The annual press ball had been scheduled for the Plaza that night. As the horror of what had happened began to become clear, Jimmy Savile put a 'cancelled' sign up outside and sat on the floor with his staff, surrounded by decorations and trestle tables loaded with food, listening to updates on the radio.

John Arlott, the great cricket commentator, had begun writing the regular Friday football lead for the *Guardian* and covered United's 5–4 win at Highbury. He was fascinated by the growing appeal of European competition and when it seemed that Donny Davies, 'Old International', the regular football correspondent, would not be able to travel, he was excited by the prospect of a trip to Belgrade. In the end, Davies was able to make the journey. Arlott made his disappointment clear. 'No use swearing,' said the sports editor, Larry Montague, 'Donny is the soccer correspondent, and it is his choice.'[13]

Annoyed with the *Guardian* and unable to settle, Arlott went on a trawl of London's bookshops. He was in Bertram Rota's on Savile Row when an assistant told him there was a phone call for him. It was Valerie, his wife. She'd been doggedly tracking his progress south through his familiar haunts. He was to call Montague immediately: he had to write Donny Davies's obituary.

When Bobby regained consciousness, he was in a hospital bed, his head stitched and bandaged. A German patient lay in a nearby bed with a newspaper. From the photographs, Bobby knew he was reading about the crash. Noticing he was awake, the German said gently, 'I'm sorry.'

Bobby had seen the bodies. He knew there had been fatalities. He asked the German who had made it and who hadn't. Reading remorselessly from the newspaper, the German went through a grim roll call:

'Roger Byrne – dead.

'David Pegg – dead.

'Eddie Colman – dead.

'Tommy Taylor – dead.

'Billy Whelan – dead.

'Mark Jones – dead.

'Geoff Bent – dead.'

Also dead were the club secretary Walter Crickmer, the trainer Tom Curry and the coach Bert Whalley, the journalists Alf Clarke, Don Davies, George Follows, Tom Jackson, Archie Ledbrooke, Henry Rose, Frank Swift and Eric Thompson, the steward Tom Cable, the travel agent Bela Miklos and Willie Satinoff, a friend of Busby who might have become a director.

And so too, from their injuries, would later die the co-pilot Kenneth Rayment and the player Bobby always believed was the greatest he had ever seen, Duncan Edwards.

The days in the hospital were brutally lonely. Other survivors were visited by members of their family, but Bobby had nobody. He was single, his father was unable to get away from the pit, Jack had his commitment to Leeds and his mother, who underwent surgery for breast cancer three months earlier, had been advised not to travel unless it was absolutely necessary.

Bobby's injuries were not serious and, after a few days, he was able to return home. Before he left the hospital he went upstairs to visit Busby and Edwards. Both lay in oxygen tents in a critical condition. Busby's left lung had collapsed and he came so close to death that he was twice given the last rites. Edwards had sustained multiple fractures to his legs and ribs and had suffered such serious damage to his kidneys that an artificial organ was installed. That, though, reduced his blood's capacity to clot, leading to internal bleeding. He died in the early hours of 21 February.

The morning after the crash, with the buses cancelled because of the snow, Cissie hitched a lift into Newcastle on a delivery van and took the train to Manchester. On learning that Bobby was not seriously hurt, she threw herself with customary vigour into helping out in the office at Old Trafford – something by which Bobby was seemingly subsequently embarrassed.

Bobby returned to England by train and was met by Cissie and Jack at Liverpool Street station. Jack drove up the M1 to

Leeds and then Cissie and Bobby continued to Newcastle by train. He barely spoke throughout the journey.

In Ashington, he began to take some walks. Ron Routledge took him to the park to kick a ball around. To get the press to leave him alone, Bobby was persuaded by Cissie to allow himself to be photographed drinking a cup of tea, hugging his mother and playing in the back lane with some local kids. For hours on end, he would listen to Frank Sinatra records, particularly 'Only the Lonely'. He learned of Duncan Edwards's death after he realised his mother had hidden a newspaper that contained the story.

Bobby went to see Dr McPherson, the family GP in Ashington, to have his stitches removed. The doctor told him of his own experiences in the RAF, of seeing comrades killed and having to fly again later the same day. The tendency in modern accounts of the disaster is to regard his words as heartless, even to blame him in part for Bobby's suffering. But that perhaps is to misunderstand the context. Jimmy Murphy, similarly, spoke to the survivors of his experiences in the war, of the experience of losing comrades and of the need to fight on in their memory. This was thirteen years after the war had ended, in a mining community in which accidental death and injury were accepted as an inevitable part of working life. Everybody had lost somebody and everybody had just had to get on with it. 'I expect to see you at Wembley,' said the doctor, words that, three months later and, even more so, ten years later, would come to seem strikingly prophetic.[14]

Manchester United games scheduled for the two Saturdays after the crash were called off, but football was and is remorseless. United had to restart sometime, and it was decided they would begin again with their FA Cup fifth-round tie against Sheffield Wednesday on Wednesday 19 February, two weeks

after the game in Belgrade. The space on the back of the programme for the line-up was notoriously left blank given the
uncertainty over who might be available. Gregg and Foulkes,
remarkably, were able to play, and there were two new signings, Ernie Taylor and Stan Crowther, picked up after the FA
relaxed its regulations on playing for more than one side in the
Cup in the same season.

The match took on a vital, symbolic role. This was the
beginning of the club rising again and that it could was thanks
largely to Murphy who, as Foulkes put it, 'showed almost
superhuman strength and resilience'[15] to put a team together.
For much of the rest of that season, the squad was based at
Norbreck Hydro near Blackpool to spare them the sight of the
coffins being lined up in the gymnasium and other, less tangible
associations.

Bobby felt that he had to be at Old Trafford for United's
return and asked the only member of his family with a car, his
uncle Tommy Skinner, to drive him. He went into the dressing
room before kick-off and hugged everybody, including kids
such as Bobby Harrop, Reg Hunter and Reg Holland who were
in the squad but didn't play. He experienced a profound sense
of togetherness and commitment. United won 3–0 against
opponents who seemed very aware of their responsibility not
to upset the mood of recovery.

A couple of days later, Bobby returned to Manchester on a
more permanent basis. He still had three months of his national
service left to run, but the army bowed to public pressure and
released him early. Football was a relief, the sense of momentum provided by the Cup run carrying him forward. He had
missed the funerals of his friends, but he didn't understand
how he could possibly have coped with a public expression of
grief. As it was, he would spend plenty of the rest of his life
attending memorials.

No day went by when he didn't think about the crash, a

point he makes on the first page of his autobiography.[16] 'David Pegg and Tommy Taylor were really close to me,' he later told the journalist Hunter Davies, 'I think because they came from a mining background, like me.'[17] They had escaped the pit, and its constant spectre of premature death, but they had died anyway.

Others noticed 'a material difference' in Bobby after the crash. 'Though never by any means an extrovert, now his happy-go-lucky days had truly gone,' said Foulkes. 'He was quieter, more withdrawn, apparently less able to express himself.'[18] There were some days when it seemed Bobby was almost unaware of those around him, unable to hear, unable to respond.

On the field, at least in the short term, Bobby excelled, as though playing football offered some relief from his thoughts. The reality of a patched together squad meant United won only one league game after Munich that season, but the Cup offered the possibility of something remarkable. After a 2–2 draw away to West Brom in the sixth round, United won the replay, Colin Webster scoring a late winner after Bobby had burst through three challenges to cross. Bobby then scored both United goals in a 2–2 draw in the semi-final against Fulham and again in the replay as United won 5–3.

That left just Bolton between United and a Cup success that, given what United had been through, would have ranked as probably the most emotional in the competition's history. Yet football rarely hands out sentimental favours. Bobby hit the post early on, but felt shattered. United were drained and Bolton won 2–0. Eleven days later they lost 4–0 away to AC Milan in the European Cup semi-final and their season, at last, was over.

6

THE RISE OF
THE MACHINES

By the time he left English football in 1977, Don Revie was the most controversial coach in a generation of highly controversial coaches. Worse, he came to be seen as a traitor, as somebody who had abandoned his country for the riches available in the UAE. Yet, unlike many of his peers, he was never somebody who wilfully provoked controversy, while his decision to walk away from England came after three years of spluttering form and consistent complaint. Having spent months calling for Revie to be ousted, much of the media were then outraged when he chose to leave on his own terms. When he quit, England, having failed to qualify for the last four of the 1976 European Championship, trailed Italy in World Cup qualification by three points with two games remaining.

'I sat down with my wife, Elsie, one night and we agreed that the England job was no longer worth the aggravation,' Revie said. 'It was bringing too much heartache to those nearest to us. Nearly everyone in the country wants me out. So, I am giving them what they want. I know people will accuse me of running away and it does sicken me that I cannot finish the job by taking England to the World Cup finals in Argentina next year, but the situation has become impossible.'[1] It might be easier to have sympathy with Revie if his decision to quit hadn't coincided with a lucrative offer from the UAE, but money had always been the greatest of Revie's many insecurities. He was a man overtly shaped by the difficulties of his childhood.

Revie was born in Middlesbrough in July 1927. His father was a joiner, his mother a washerwoman who died from cancer when Revie was twelve. Against the backdrop of the Depression and mass unemployment, his childhood was tough and desperately poor. Brian Clough, who was born a mile and a half south-east of Revie eight years later, liked to speak of his humble origins and reflect of how far he had risen, opening his first autobiography by describing his mother's mangle as a symbol of his supposedly straightforward family values.[2] He was by no means wealthy, but his origins were far more comfortable than those of the manager who would become his great rival. Both men were driven by a desire to provide security for themselves and their families and both were shaped by what they felt they had missed as children. After failing his eleven-plus, Clough was haunted by a sense of intellectual inferiority;[3] what Revie wanted most of all was the sense of a family.

And yet at the same time, in his early days, Revie's football career came before his family: aged fourteen he turned out for Swifts – a very talented local club in Middlesbrough – rather than attend his sister Jean's wedding.[4] His dedication paid off and in 1944 Revie was signed by Leicester City, where he was taken under the wing of his fellow north-easterner, the Whitburn-born half-back Septimus Smith.

Smith was a brilliant passer of the ball, but he was also a keen thinker about the game, which he believed could be boiled down to four basic principles:

'1. When not in possession, get into position.

'2. Never beat a man by dribbling if you can beat him more easily with a pass.

'3. It's not the man on the ball but the man running into position to take the pass who constitutes the danger.

'4. The aim is to have a man spare in a passing move, then soccer becomes easy.'[5]

Smith was tough, and so unsparing in his analysis that Revie would often go home and cry after training. But it made Revie a player.

Revie made his Leicester debut as league football returned after the war in 1946–47 and within a year had established himself as the creative hub of the team, despite a broken ankle reducing what little pace he had. But he was clever. He noticed things, encouraged by Smith, who kept notes on opponents and would produce dossiers before key games, which proved especially useful during Leicester's run to the FA Cup final in 1949, when they were a struggling Second Division side. Smith had realised that their fourth-round opponents, Preston North End, built up almost entirely through their wingers; Leicester closed them down and won 2–0.

In the semi-final, Leicester faced Portsmouth, who would claim the First Division title the following month. Smith, thirty-seven by then and largely a reserve, pointed out to Revie that the Portsmouth keeper Ernie Butler had a habit of gathering crosses by palming the ball over the head of the oncoming forward and gathering the rebound. Revie accordingly hung back and, having scored the opening goal, added his second by beating Butler to a loose ball after he'd patted away a cross to make it 3–1 with twelve minutes remaining.

Those final weeks of the 1948–49 season oddly foreshadow what was to come. As a player, Revie would make his name by dropping deeper, playing as a withdrawn centre-forward. As a manager, his research and dossiers on opponents would become notorious. But there were two other trends. A week before the

FA Cup final, Revie suffered a nasal haemorrhage and fell seriously ill. He missed the game as a result and Leicester lost 3–1 to Wolves. Misfortune seemed always to stalk him.

A week later came the final league game of the season. Leicester, for all their giant-killing, had struggled and, playing away to Cardiff, needed a point to be sure of avoiding relegation. They drew 1–1, but relief at survival was tainted by allegations of match-fixing. Revie, still recovering, didn't play and there is no suggestion at all that he was involved, but similar suspicions would pursue him throughout his career.

Smith retired that summer and Revie was named captain. But results were poor and when Revie married Elsie Duncan, the niece of Leicester's manager, Johnny Duncan, he was concerned by possible allegations of nepotism. He asked for a transfer which Duncan would reluctantly have granted had he not been ousted, apparently a scapegoat after a number of the club's allocation of FA Cup final tickets ended up on the black market. The incident only confirmed Revie's desire to leave.

Having effectively lost two father figures in a matter of months, he sought a third, and joined Hull, who were led by another intelligent former inside-forward from the North-East, Raich Carter. Carter, though, was nothing like Sep Smith, had few theoretical thoughts about how the game should be played and was broadly uninterested in or unconvinced by the possibility of improving his players. At Hull, Revie was a moderate success. The right-back Andy Davidson spoke of him as 'a fine player', whose passing was 'second to none' and his control exceptional. 'The problem,' he went on, 'was Don was not a hard player ... and the rest of the team were unable to offer the protection he needed.'[6] It was not a mistake his own teams would ever make.

Revie left Hull soon after Carter in 1951, joining Manchester City. Although he was successful there, being named footballer of the year in 1955 and becoming noted for the 'Revie

Plan' – by which he operated as a withdrawn centre-forward, much as Nándor Hidegkuti had for Hungary when they had beaten England 6-3 at Wembley in 1953 – he was rarely entirely happy.

After City lost to Newcastle in the 1955 FA Cup final, Revie went on holiday to Blackpool with Elsie. In six years of marriage they had never been away together and had been forced to cancel a holiday the previous summer after the players had been called back to training two weeks early. Revie had spoken to the trainer Laurie Barnett and they'd agreed a fitness programme while he was away. But on his return, he found he'd been suspended for two weeks without pay by the manager Les McDowell for going absent without permission. Outraged, he demanded a transfer.

Revie was persuaded to stay but played only occasionally that season and had made just one Cup appearance when he was brought into the side for the final, against Birmingham. That game is famous now for Bert Trautmann's heroics, playing for the last seventeen minutes with a broken neck, but Revie was superb in a 3–1 win, setting up the opening goal and being named man of the match.

He had only found out he was playing three hours before kick-off and responded by instinctively touching two pieces of wood he was carrying in his suit pocket. He told teammate Roy Paul they had been given to him by a Roma woman and that he believed they brought good luck. Superstition was another theme that would run throughout his career. So too was his tactical acumen: at half-time, Revie told the right-half Ken Barnes to ignore his manager and play a little deeper. City had more control in the second half, but McDowell, who distrusted Revie anyway, never forgave him. The following season, he deployed Revie largely at right-half where he was less effective, leading him to seek a move.

Revie joined Sunderland in 1956, but what could have been

a golden return to the North East, the home of two of his mentors, was quickly soured when Sunderland were caught up in an illegal payments scandal that led to the resignation of the manager who had signed him, Bill Murray, and the appointment of the ruthless Alan Brown. He was a visionary in his own way and a significant influence on Brian Clough, but somebody who had no time for what he saw as Revie's ponderousness.

And so, in November 1958, aged thirty-one, Revie moved to Leeds.

In the summer of 1958, Scotland Schoolboys played England Schoolboys at Wembley. The second half was broadcast live by the BBC. Watching in Leeds, Bill Lambton and the prominent director Harry Reynolds were so impressed by the performance of a fifteen-year-old Scottish midfielder that they drove to Stirling to sign him. Billy Bremner had already attracted the interest of the two big Glasgow clubs, but his father wanted him to steer clear of the religious tensions. Arsenal, Chelsea and Sheffield Wednesday were also keen, but Reynolds was passionate and persuasive and Bremner opted for Elland Road.

He made his debut at outside-right in a 3–1 win over Chelsea at Stamford Bridge in January 1960, forty-seven days after his seventeenth birthday. He was talked through the game by Revie, who was playing at inside-right. His talent was obvious, but his youth made him vulnerable, particularly amid the disillusionment of the Leeds dressing room of the time. Revie, aware of the dangers, promptly made himself Bremner's roommate. Revie was fifteen years older than Bremner and soon became a guiding presence. Amid the anger and the frustration, he was calm and professional, a natural leader with a profound sense of responsibility. Bremner would become his representative on the pitch.

But Bremner was more than that. He was a symbol of a new

focus. Frank Buckley and Raich Carter had allowed youth development to decay, but Harry Reynolds, who would become chairman in December 1961, was clear that the only way to solve Leeds's seemingly perennial financial crises was for them to develop their own talent.

Revie turned thirty-three in the summer of 1960. He knew his body was beginning to creak and decided that the following season would be his last as a player. He also surrendered the captaincy, worried he had brought the club misfortune. Coaching seemed an obvious route to follow and, with his reputation as an intelligent player, Chester and Tranmere both approached him about becoming player-manager. It was an offer from Bournemouth & Boscombe, though, that focused minds.

That autumn, Revie had missed a number of games though injury and had taken to accompanying Harry Reynolds on scouting trips. Reynolds was an important background figure in the development of the club. Born in Holbeck with nothing, he had worked on the railways before becoming an on-course bookmaker and then a dealer in second-hand cars and scrap metal. He made his fortune selling steel during the Second World War and used his wealth to join the local hunt, buying polo ponies and breeding pigs. He'd become a director in 1955, but it was in the early sixties, as he stepped back from the business, that he began to devote more time to the club.

Reynolds and Revie got on well and, when Revie asked for a reference for the Bournemouth job, Reynolds realised he would make a good manager. Or that, at least, is the romanticised version of the story. The truth seems just as much to have been that Bournemouth, put off by the six thousand pounds compensation they would have had to pay, didn't pursue their interest, and Leeds turned to Revie in part as a cheap and convenient option.

Revie inherited a club that was sinking. For the final home game of the 1960–61 season, a 2–2 draw against Scunthorpe, the crowd numbered just 6,975. 'The club was fifth-rate,' said Eric Smith, 'and the players were undisciplined.'[7] That same year, Leeds won the Rugby League Championship while Yorkshire finished runners-up in cricket's County Championship. Football was the city's third sport – and a distant third at that. The whole place seemed mired in despair. To change the mood, Revie replaced Leeds's blue-and-yellow stripes with an all-white kit that mimicked Real Madrid's – although he claimed that he made the change not as a conscious homage, but because white is the easiest colour to pick out in peripheral vision. Either way, turning Leeds round required more than a change of shirt.

One of his biggest problems was Jack. 'I was a real one-man awkward squad,' Jack subsequently admitted.[8] Where others had been hesitant, Revie was direct, telling him he had to lose the chip from his shoulder because his attitude was undermining the club. As a player, Revie had been critical of Jack, who lacked positional discipline and would surge forward in the manner of an old-school centre-half. The crowd loved it, but it often rendered Leeds defensively vulnerable and neither Lambton nor Taylor were ever able to rein him in. 'I was amazed,' Revie said, 'to find how undisciplined a player he was.'[9] He was blunt: if he were manager and Jack played like that, Revie said, he would drop him.[10]

When Revie did become manager, there was predictable friction. Senior players would simply refuse to do circuit training, throwing weights and benches down the bank at Fullerton Park. Long runs were generally unpopular. 'Cross-country for Jack,' said Peter Lorimer, 'meant being in last position, getting a lift in a passing truck and smoking a fag.'[11]

Revie was determined to create a proper structure rather than lurching from one crisis to the next as Leeds had done in the past. He was a manager who wanted to manage and would come in to work every day impeccably dressed in blazer and tie, while his office was habitually neat. He set standards he expected others to follow.

Revie had felt homesick in his early days at Leicester and had been fortunate that his relationship with Elsie had presented him with a manager in Johnnie Duncan who was also a father-in-law in waiting. He wanted to ensure that all players were part of a family at Leeds; he was determined to look after them, to ensure they felt at home. And also, perhaps, to ensure he felt at home. His son Duncan would regularly be the first to arrive at Leeds grammar each morning because his father, who dropped him off on the way to Elland Road, hurried into work whistling with happiness.

He would talk to everybody – not just the players, but the ground staff, the secretaries and the laundry staff. He ended the practice by which a reserve-team player would have to vacate the pool table if a first-teamer wanted a game: a trivial detail, but emblematic of his determination to break the divide. At Manchester United, by contrast, the first-team dressing room was out-of-bounds to everybody else.

The night before games, players would stay in comfortable hotels to help them relax, with games of carpet bowls and bingo. Following Septimus Smith's lead, Revie took reams of notes on opponents and used them to compile dossiers for the players. 'Looking back,' Norman Hunter said, 'they were a bit boring and tedious.'[12] Some players admitted they never looked at them, but the point was that the information was there if they wanted it and, even if they didn't, there was at least a sense of confidence to be derived from the knowledge that their manager had done the necessary preparatory work.

Revie appointed Maurice Lindsay, who had been chief scout, as his assistant and Les Cocker as his trainer. Cocker had played more than three hundred games for Accrington Stanley and Stockport before becoming one of the first to pass the FA's coaching certificate. Having served in the Reconnaissance Regiment during the war, he was seen as a fitness specialist. The strident Syd Owen, voted footballer of the year in 1959 after inspiring Luton to the FA Cup final, had been brought in by Taylor and remained as coach.

For the first time, there was proper tactical training. For Jack, this was a moment of internal conflict. On the one hand, he supported what Revie was doing. He knew that a few laps and a bit of seven-a-side was no preparation for modern football. He appreciated the work on defensive structure. But he didn't much like being told to adapt his own game, and he certainly didn't like being shouted at by Syd Owen. He became difficult and argumentative and, for a time in the early sixties, there was a sense of his career stalling.

Crisis point was reached in January 1962 as Leeds lost 2–1 to Rotherham, the opening goal coming after the Leeds keeper, Tommy Younger, dived over a header from the edge of the box. At half-time, Revie blamed Jack, saying that if he'd picked up his man properly there would never have been a header on goal in the first place. Furious, Jack hurled a teacup at his manager. It missed, narrowly, and shattered against the wall. This was the kind of row that had undermined Lambton and Taylor but Revie remained calm. He walked out and said he would discuss the issue on Monday when everybody had calmed down.

A few weeks later there was another row after Leeds had conceded with Jack caught upfield having gone forward for a corner. Jack truculently then refused to go up for any set plays, despite his height and heading ability. Revie responded by moving him to centre-forward, with Freddie Goodwin replacing him at centre-half. But Goodwin insisted – to the horror of Jack, who had been won over by emergent thinking on the value of zonal organisation – on man-marking. Leeds struggled badly and by March were bottom of the table, facing relegation to the Third Division.

Don Revie sat in his car in a suburban street in Aintree and waited. The possibility was too great to go home without giving it one more try. The day before a journalist had called him and passed on a rumour that Everton might be willing to sell the Scottish midfielder Bobby Collins. He'd rung Everton's manager, Harry Catterick, who had confirmed that to be true. Collins had turned thirty-one the previous month, but Revie wasn't worried by that, nor by the fact that Collins was 5 feet 3 inches. He was a fine reader of the game, a good passer and he had a will to win that bordered on the pathological: he was just the man to build a young team around; somebody who could provide tactical intelligence and a winner's steel.

And Revie, at last, had money to spend. Reynolds had put in fifty thousand pounds when he became chairman, while two new directors, Manny Cussins and Albert Morris, both provided interest-free loans of ten thousand pounds. But when Revie had spoken to Collins after training, he'd been dismissive. He had no real desire to leave and believed he still had a lot to offer in Division One. Why would he want to drop down to play for a club who, at the time, were battling relegation to Division Three? For an hour, Revie had tried to persuade him, but with no success. He drove to Collins' house, arriving at around 2 p.m. Collins didn't get home until 7.30 p.m., but Revie was still there. They talked some more, Revie laying out his plans for the future. By the time Revie left, at 2.30 a.m., Collins had agreed to join.

The next morning Revie negotiated a fee of £24,000 with Catterick, who also wanted Billy Bremner. Revie, though, told him Leeds had a heavy run of fixtures coming up and asked if they could hold on to Bremner until the end of the season. Catterick agreed, but in the end had to make do with only the cash.

Later that day, Bill Shankly, who had heard the same rumour Revie had but twenty-four hours later, got in touch with Collins. Would he fancy a move to Liverpool? He might have done, Collins replied, especially as it would have meant he didn't have to leave Aintree, but he'd already agreed a deal with Leeds.

Revie later described Collins as the most important signing he ever made[13] and he was also the player who, more than anybody, earned Leeds a reputation for being dirty. Even Jack, who relished the physical side of the game, would try to avoid facing him in five-a-sides in training.[14] The tradition of England v Scotland games in training had to be stopped because Collins took them so seriously; even after retiring, he was so ferocious that he was quickly banned from the Ex-Players XI.

But Collins made an immediate impact. Leeds lost only one of their final ten games of the season, a 3–0 win at Newcastle on the final day ensuring they stayed up.

When Eddie Gray was fourteen, he travelled from Glasgow for a trial with Leeds. 'It was Christmas 1962,' he said, 'and traditionally that's the time that lots of trialists go all over the country for trials at football clubs, not like it is now. When I got there with all the trialists, Don came to me and he said to me, "You're training with me, with the first team." Nineteen-sixty-two was a terrible winter, the place was covered with ice and snow and my first recollection of Big Jack was getting the ball, going up to him and going by him and Big Jack booting me up in the air and me lying there in the snow and him saying, "Don't do that to me again, you little b ..."'[15]

*

In the summer of 1962, as Revie accelerated the reshaping of the squad – twenty-seven players left the club in his first two years in charge – he told Jack he was willing to let him go. Jack replied that it would be absurd to make any judgement when he'd spent much of the season operating at centre-forward. When Revie then said he was happy for Goodwin to continue at centre-half, Jack walked out.

He began playing with the reserves and, although he was never formally transfer-listed, started looking for a new club. Bill Shankly expressed an interest, but Liverpool could not afford thirty-thousand pounds. Jack was told that Manchester United were keen, but would not be able to act until they returned from a tour of the US. He refused to sign a new contract at Leeds. When Matt Busby returned, though, he said he had a young centre-half in his squad he wanted properly to assess before committing to a signing. Jack, feeling he'd been strung along, was outraged, went back to Elland Road, apologised and signed a new deal.

Revie, quietly, was delighted and told Jack that 'if he buckled down' he would not merely secure his place in the Leeds side but that 'he would become England's centre-half too'. This, Revie insisted, was not 'idle chatter ... but it needed a big change on Jack's part.'[16] He got it.

Eddie Gray was just old enough to see the change in Jack, saying he could 'remember Big Jack when he didnae like to do a circuit and he would throw the stuff down the steps' at the training ground. But as the sixties went on, 'He thought, If I knuckle down here, I've got a chance to be the best centre-half in the country, which he was. It might have just hit him a bit later on. Maybe it was because of the brilliance of Bobby and the plaudits he got, he might have thought, "I can do that," but I think a lot of it was down to Don and Don actually saying to him, "You can be the best centre-half in the world." Big Jack was very strong, strong-minded as well.'[17]

Briefly, John Charles returned, but he was not the player who had left and Leeds were fortunate to be able to offload him to Roma for seventy-thousand pounds. More generally, the focus was on youth. When he'd taken the job, Revie had consulted Busby about the best way to develop a youth structure and integrate young players into the side. That meant both being willing to trust young players and also to support them.

In late September 1962, for instance, Billy Bremner, feeling homesick and missing his girlfriend, Vicky, returned to Scotland. Revie followed him to Stirling, where he spoke to Vicky, explaining to her how much Leeds needed Bremner, and how significant a future he could have at the club. Bremner later married her. At the same time, Revie had to put a team out to face Southampton at home. It included six teenagers, among them Peter Lorimer, who was just fifteen years and 289 days old. Leeds drew 1–1, but more important was the sense of a squad growing together.

Leeds finished the season fifth and Revie's methods were clearly beginning to have an effect. John Giles arrived from Manchester United early the following season, with the centre-forward Alan Peacock offering an additional attacking option for the run-in. He was twenty-six and had played more than two hundred games for Middlesbrough, but he was startled by what he found. 'I thought, Wow, I've wasted years at Boro,' he said. 'Revie had everything mapped out, his methods were clear and innovative and the side responded exactly to the way he wanted them to play.'[18]

Eight wins and two draws in the final ten games of the season carried Leeds to promotion. Jack was in the First Division.

7

REGENERATION

The Manchester United team bus pulled into the car park at Leicester's Filbert Street. Matt Busby disembarked and made his way into the dressing room. But not all his team followed. The card school stayed behind, continuing their game of brag for stakes of a week's wages. Only when Busby sent out his assistant Jack Crompton did they finally put the cards away and begin to prepare for the game.

United were dreadful. They had a seventeen-year-old debutant, Ronnie Briggs, in goal, but he was not the problem. Rather the two wingers, Albert Quixall and Bobby, were unable to get into the game and, according to the *Daily Mirror*, 'the defence cracked too'.[1] Leicester City won 6–0. Busby was furious. When the card school started up again on the journey back, he strode up the bus, seized the cards and threw them out of a window.[2] The high-stakes gambling stopped, but, almost three years after Munich, there was very little suggestion that United were growing again.

The initial surge of adrenaline that had carried United to the FA Cup final had worn off. Busby thought it would take three-to-five years to have a side that could again challenge for honours[3] but he was also aware that was a compressed time frame. He had turned fifty the year after Munich; he was tired and his health uncertain. There was no guarantee he had a decade left in management – and so he resolved to buy. It wasn't his preference, which would have been to develop his own talent, but it had taken a decade to produce the Babes, even if he had managed to win the FA Cup in 1948 and the league in 1952.

He was making a major modification to his approach. Although Busby was ruthless in discarding players he felt had somehow stepped out of line, he usually signed very few – none at all between Tommy Taylor in March 1953 and Harry Gregg in November 1957. That, he felt, helped maintain the values of the club. Those were behavioural – the red passbooks that secured players admittance to the ground also included a code of conduct – but also to do with playing the 'Manchester United way' which, as Busby defined it, meant 'constructive football, attacking football, team football but with scope for spontaneous moves of surprise'.[4]

Busby's daughter, Sheena, had married the Sheffield Wednesday right-half Don Gibson a year after he'd left United. He was a regular visitor to the Busby house and would rave about the inside-forward Albert Quixall, which had helped to persuade Busby to sign him for £45,000, stretching United's finances to the limit. He was the first post-Munich signing and was followed by the left-back Noel Cantwell from West Ham, the forward David Herd from Arsenal and then, in 1962, Denis Law, liberated from a miserable spell at Torino for a British record fee of £115,000.

Change, though, meant compromise and that was particularly hard for the Munich survivors to process. 'For me,' said Bobby, 'the football of the late 1950s was the best it has ever been and, from a selfish, football point of view, that United team could not have been lost at a worse time. The difference after Munich was the commitment of the side. The team that played before the crash had nothing to prove. Those players knew they were great. Afterwards we had everything to prove.'[5] Playing with Duncan Edwards, Tommy Taylor and Eddie Colman had been the dream and, for Bobby, nothing ever quite lived up to it. It was only natural if, at times, he resented those who had replaced his mates, feeling they failed to live up to an impossible ideal of his youth. Certainly, he never seemed to have the same rapport with those who followed. His friends in the squad remained those from before Munich, the likes of McGuinness and Shay Brennan, while Cantwell said there were times he made those who had joined later feel like 'intruders'.[6]

But that is understandable enough. There are plenty of people in all kinds of professions who feel awkward when asked for support or advice because they cannot quite believe what they have achieved, or because their elevated position feels somehow contingent or as though it cannot last. Bobby didn't turn twenty-one until October 1958: if his response to younger players or new arrivals was bewilderment – Why are you asking? What do I know? – it would hardly have been unreasonable even if he hadn't been processing the loss of several close friends. 'If my demeanour was a little cool,' Bobby said, 'maybe it was because, despite the goals and the upward profile of my career, I too was in the position of just feeling my way forward.'[7]

Munich had transformed Bobby's status within the squad. He was, as Busby said, a 'boy who became a man overnight'[8] and that's quite apart from the more obvious trauma and the feelings of grief, uncertainty and guilt that provoked. 'There was very little wrong with me physically, but I could not stop thinking about the accident ...' Bobby said. 'I couldn't accept it for a long time and I felt drained of all emotion. I kept asking myself, "Why me? Why should I be left?"'[9]

The rules said that Bobby Charlton had to go in the box. That was how the long-running ITV quiz show *Double Your Money* worked. Contestants answered the presenter Hughie Green's questions on their chosen theme with the prize money doubling from a pound up to thirty-two pounds with each correct answer; one wrong answer, though, and everything was lost. At thirty-two Bobby had a choice: take the money or embark upon the treasure trail, on which the prizes rose to a maximum of a thousand pounds. The additional stipulation, though, was that contestants had to sit in a soundproof box for each question to prevent the audience shouting out help.

Bobby's first appearance had been on a special edition with other sporting celebrities: the sprinters June Paul and Roy Sandstrom, who'd chosen questions on cookery and geography respectively, and the Middlesex seamer John Warr, who went for classical music. After the first week, to general surprise, Bobby was the only one left. Even his choice of pop music had been greeted by a level of scepticism in the media – football and pop music were not then part of the same realm. Bobby, though, in his reserved, anxious way, was – unwittingly and unwillingly – at the forefront of a coming wave. His courtship of Hughie Green's assistant, Jean Clarke, the 'Wiggle Girl', was followed with startled fascination by the popular press.

Answering a series of questions on the Everly Brothers, the Kalin Twins and Connie Francis B-sides, Bobby progressed. At first, the box didn't bother him. 'Not such an ordeal as the Cup Final,' he said. But gradually his claustrophobia became worse and worse. By the time he got to the thousand-pound question, filmed exactly a year after Munich – in the same week in 1959 that a plane went down in a frozen cornfield five miles north-west of Mason City, Iowa, killing Buddy Holly, Ritchie Valens and the Big Bopper – Bobby couldn't face the confinement. He would only answer the thousand-pound question, he said, if he could do it from the studio stage. 'I start to shake as soon as I get inside that box,' he said. 'I can hardly put on the earphones. Last week I nearly failed over the five-hundred-pound question which was pretty simple. It wasn't so bad when I answered the first question but it has got progressively worse each time I have gone in the box.'[10]

Hughie Green, the presenter, stopped the recording and sought advice from the bosses of Rediffusion, who made the show. 'This guy takes a bigger beating than anyone else ever had on the programme,' he told the press. 'He really gets me worried because he is so nervous in there.' [11] Television quizzes were under scrutiny after revelations of collusion on a Granada show but it was decided that on this occasion, the rules could be bent.

ITV made the most of the drama. Bobby's refusal to enter the box was shown one week. The following week, the question was screened: 'Which group sang "To Know Him is to Love Him?", which was No. 1 in the US for three weeks in late 1958 and top five in the UK in January 1959?' Only in week three did they broadcast Bobby getting the answer right: The Teddy Bears. (Even in that, Bobby was unable to escape connotations of mortality. The song was written by The Teddy Bears' front man, Phil Spector, taking the title from a line chiselled on the gravestone of his father, who had killed himself in 1949. Spector himself was later convicted of the murder of the actress Lana Clarkson.)

Bobby used the prize money to buy his father an Austin.

Bobby had become as near as footballers came in those days to a celebrity, idealised by the media as a golden-haired young hero rising again from tragedy. That brought attention and pressure, a feeling that 'every move I made was watched'.[12] The shifting sense of a footballer's role was part of the wider changes just beginning to reshape society. As the world changed, so Busby's paternalism began to seem increasingly outdated. Paddy Crerand wasn't the only one of the new recruits to find the rules in the red passbook 'pompous'.[13] Players began increasingly to assert themselves, leading in 1961 to the abolition of the maximum wage, which prompted a round of pay talks.

That in turn brought insecurity, frustration and jealousy. Whereas previously the majority of senior players at First Division clubs had been on the maximum of twenty pounds a week, suddenly they had to negotiate. United offered a standard twenty-five pounds a week plus a five-pound appearance bonus and, while their higher-profile players ended up with thirty pounds plus ten pounds,[14] everybody knew Johnny Haynes had been granted a hundred pounds a week by Fulham. John Giles, at the time a twenty-year-old midfielder who was just beginning to establish himself at United, called his Ireland teammate Charlie Hurley at Second Division Sunderland and found he had rejected sixty pounds a week.[15] Even schoolboy players – or perhaps more accurately, their families – were becoming increasingly aware of their value. There was widespread dissatisfaction among the United squad but, one-by-one, the players went to see Busby in his office and, faced with his immense charisma and gravitas, found their objections melting away as they signed the revised contracts.

It later turned out that Busby had met the Liverpool manager Bill Shankly who, like him, had played in the days when a maximum wage was taken for granted, and agreed on an offer to make to players at both clubs, even though Liverpool were still in the Second Division. Understandably that led to anger. 'They were as exploitative as those who had exploited them,' as Giles put it.[16]

Many would claim Busby was merely doing what was best for the club, spending United's money as though it were his own, but the reality was more complicated. Eamon Dunphy is certain that he was sold to Third Division York City for four thousand pounds rather than First Division Birmingham City for eight thousand pounds because it enabled Busby to take 'a chunk for himself. That's how it was in those days'.[17] The Busby he portrays in *A Strange Kind of Glory* is not the benevolent patrician of myth, but a much colder, harder, more conniving figure, shaped as much by the General Strike of 1926, when he was a seventeen-year-old living in the Lanarkshire coalfield, as by the two world wars.

Even if Busby had never quite been such a man of unbending principle as he liked to pretend – part of United's allure for Duncan Edwards, for instance, was the washing machine the club provided for his mother[18] – as he sought to restock the club's youth section, he found himself having to offer ever more frequent and ever larger under-the-table inducements. Society was changing and Busby had to change with it, just as he was dealing with his injuries and the trauma of Munich. 'There were times,' Bobby said, 'when the struggle was desperate and you knew he was suffering doubts he had never known before ... he doubted himself, his calling as the messiah of a great football club and ... even doubted the deep faith in God that had carried him through so many difficult days.'[19]

At the same time, Busby was offloading many of those who had been at the club before Munich, some of whom had been injured in the crash. Football is a game awash with sentiment, and there was plenty of it behind United, but even in extremis, it rarely affects the relationship between clubs and their players. Colin Webster and Kenny Morgans were sold to Swansea Town and Albert Scanlon to Newcastle United. Jackie Blanchflower, forced to retire after suffering a broken pelvis and kidney damage at Munich, was offered a job loading meat pies into vans by the United director Louis Edwards. Johnny Berry, who was left with a fractured skull, worked briefly as a labourer at Trafford Park before being forced to move out of the accommodation provided by the club to make way for Maurice Setters, signed from West Bromwich Albion to bolster the midfield.

That, inevitably, led to bitterness from those discarded, and insecurity among those left behind.

Bobby was walking past the ice rink on Derby Street when he saw Norma Ball for the first time. The attraction was instant. He got her number and asked if he could take her out. She turned him down. So he asked again. And a few weeks later, again. Eventually, she agreed. She was struck later by how out of character the repeated phone calls had been. He was not habitually pushy, quite the reverse. What she warmed to in him was his gentlemanly shyness, even if that diffidence meant she wasn't aware of how serious he was about her. 'I knew straight away that she was what I wanted, what I needed,' Bobby said. 'And it wasn't just that she was beautiful. I felt good around her.'[20]

He also described her as 'sensational'[21] – a slightly old-fashioned word that rarely seems to be used these days outside of football punditry. Indeed, it's the adjective Bobby used as a co-commentator to describe England's performance in the first half of the 1990 World Cup semi-final. But that shouldn't diminish how heartfelt the sentiment clearly was.

Bobby had come to be seen as distinctly eligible, with his blond hair and quiet dignity. On his twenty-first birthday, he received more than two hundred letters, many of them from girls and young women – the Bobby-soxers, as they were slightly unconvincingly known. He was not George Best, far from it, but eight years before Best dragged football into the celebrity age, something was stirring.

Earlier in 1958, Bobby had attended a dance organised by Manchester's Jewish community and he been struck by the winner of 'personality girl of the year', Marlene Shapiro. The following year he met her again at the same event and asked her out. For five weeks they pursued a very intense relationship before her parents told her to break it off, due to the difference of religion. Both were clearly hurt by the experience and, by late 1959, Shapiro was regretting her decision. By then, though, Bobby had met Norma.

Norma was smart, clever and forthright and made demands on him. 'She can be very tough,' Bobby said. 'She doesn't mess around if she disagrees with me – or anyone else.'[22] They split up for a while because Bobby remained a little reticent about the depth of his feeling. Then one day he was having lunch with a couple of friends near the Queen's hotel when Norma walked past. Without a word, he stood up, left the table and followed her, determined not to mess it up a second time. From then on, he changed, not dramatically, but in ways that were clear to those who knew him.

Bobby had never previously been much concerned about his appearance. He could rarely be bothered to get his hair cut and would wear the same pair of shoes until they fell apart. On one occasion, he went to the shoe shop, bought a new pair and walked out in them, leaving his wrecked old pair behind – a story that, in terms of their later images, sounds far more like Jack than Bobby. After he met Norma, he stopped gambling, cut out the Wednesday visits to the Continental nightclub, became better organised, began polishing his shoes and took to wearing the club blazer he'd always previously neglected, not liking the attention it brought. The impressionist Mike Yarwood used to see him waiting outside Norma's office on Lever Street 'looking like a top toff'.[23]

They married in June 1961 in St Gabriel's Church, Middleton. A few United fans, wearing scarves and wielding rattles, turned up to wish the couple well, something that made Bobby deeply uncomfortable: for him, private life was private. He had asked Wilf McGuinness to be his best man and when it became apparent his Catholicism would be a problem, he turned to Maurice Setters – later Jack's assistant manager. He didn't ask Jack, although Bobby had been his brother's best man. Perhaps there was no great significance. Circumstances change. But Jack never entirely warmed to Norma, and she never warmed to him.

Football was also changing. The 6–3 humiliation against Hungary in 1953, which brought to an end England's unbeaten record at Wembley, had obliterated any sense of superiority that lingered because of England's status as the mother of the game. Suddenly, English football was forced to confront the reality that the style of football it had complacently practised since the change in the offside law in 1925 had been surpassed. The result was a flurry of innovation.[24]

Even Busby, an instinctive conservative, began to experiment. 'By a combination of short and long passes,' *The Times*'s football correspondent Geoffrey Green had written of the Babes, '[they] have discarded a static, conventional forward shape and, with the basic essential of a well-ordered defence, have found success by the sudden switching and masking of the final attacking thrust by their fluid approach. This aims at producing a spare man – or "man over" – at the height of the attack.'[25]

But as the old orthodoxies fell away after England's 6–3 and 7–1 defeats to Hungary in 1953 and 1954, football was changing rapidly, more radically than at any previous stage of its evolution.[26] The W-M formation, on which English football had been based for a quarter of a century, suddenly seemed outmoded. Burnley, captained by Jimmy Adamson, who had grown up on the same street as the Charltons, played a prototype back four in winning the league in 1960.[27] The Spurs double-winners of 1960–61 were strikingly modern with their push-and-run approach. When Ipswich Town won the 1961–62 title under Alf Ramsey in their first season after promotion, it was largely because their use of a back four with a withdrawn left-winger baffled opponents.[28]

Football, generally, was becoming more systems driven, more defensively aware. Structure and planning were taken increasingly seriously: it was no longer sufficient simply to expect teams to improvise their way to victory. Busby, though, remained wedded to the old principles. Training consisted of a few weights, a bit of head tennis, some running and then a game which, depending who was available, could be anything from five- to twenty-a-side on a hard pitch littered with cinders bordered on one side by the railway fence and on the other by the concrete wall of the stand. 'People kicked the fuck out of each other,' said Cantwell.[29] Dunphy described Bill Foulkes as 'a bully',[30] while Harry Gregg liked to play out of goal and would clatter opponents through frustration at his relative lack of technical ability. On one occasion he bit Shay Brennan for failing to pass him the ball.[31]

When Cantwell had been at West Ham, he had been part of a group of players led by Malcolm Allison and including the future United managers Frank O'Farrell and Dave Sexton, who met after training at Cassatarri's café near Upton Park to discuss football and how the ideas emerging on the continent could be implemented in the English game.[32] Allison had effectively led training, and players had begun to wear lighter shirts and boots. At United there was no such modernity. Training kit was old jumpers and mismatched socks with boots like cut-off Wellingtons, and there was very little conversation about the game. While Cantwell, Crerand and Gregg would travel to watch other teams in the North-West,[33] other players, Bobby included, seemed almost bored by football, or at least by discussions of it.

'If you talked about the match,' Gregg remembered, 'Bobby would pick up his pint and say, "I'm off if you're going to talk about football." '[34] This was a radical change for somebody who, as a child, would hang around outside the bar, imagining the conversations about football his uncles were having within. The difference, presumably, was the way the game was discussed: the technical and tactical aspects that fascinated Cantwell and Gregg left Bobby cold; he preferred a simple world of heroes and glory. And at Busby's United, he was not the only one. On one occasion, Cantwell recalled, Denis Law asked him not to say anything at a team meeting because he needed to get away.[35] When Giles moved to Leeds in 1963, he said it was like entering 'a new world'[36] as far as training and match preparation went.

There were questions too about United's medical practices. Perhaps the technology didn't exist that could have diagnosed the stress fracture that led to Wilf McGuinness snapping a bone in a challenge in a reserve game, but there were other examples. Giles left when his form deteriorated after he was asked to play while he was recovering from a virus[37] and when Jimmy Nicholson was sold to Huddersfield, they were able to diagnose and rectify a back problem that had gone undetected at United.[38]

Although the injuries Busby had sustained at Munich meant he was less involved in training than he been, at sessions led by Jack Crompton, assisted by John Aston – another stalwart of Busby's first great United side – it was he who set the philosophy. Which was, essentially, that there was no rigorous plan, only a 'pattern ... formed by individuals who are all different.'

In *Soccer at the Top*, published in 1973, Busby outlines what that means, position by position. Goalkeepers have to be 'in charge' and have 'an understanding' with their defenders. Full-backs 'require strength, pace and need to be quick on the turn'. The defenders as a whole 'need to have command in the air, have to be able to read situations'. It's not entirely clear what formation Busby is envisioning, whether it is a back three or a back four (the signing of Setters in 1960 allowed him to use something approaching four at the back), but he wants 'a smeller of danger' in midfield, 'taking up positions to counter situations when the ball is at the other end of the park ... The one thing to be avoided is giving the ball away.'

'The middle men,' he goes on, 'the creators, are the ones who really shape the game ... They have to have vision, imagination to hold the ball or pass if passing is "on", and ability to beat a man ... the middle man has also to be able to *win* the ball, so he has to be able to tackle, read, or smell when an interception is going to present itself.' As to how many there should be, Busby advocates two or three: 'four is the policy of fear'. Forwards, meanwhile, have to be able to play with their backs to goal and to find space and 'must obviously have great skill ... compared with twenty years ago, wingers are a rarity, but still most goals come from crosses from the flanks ... a bonus ... is the genius in the ranks.'

What's striking is that this isn't a systemic philosophy at all. His tactical thought consists of some vague outlines of the attributes needed in each position. As he acknowledged, 'the pattern over the years will gradually change' as the players change: 'it is *understanding* that makes the pattern from the individuals in it.'[39] Compared to the thinking of contemporaries like Revie, Ramsey and Shankly, it all seems very simplistic. Or as Cantwell put it, 'Give it to a fucking red shirt? You don't need a manager for that. How do you find a red shirt if you haven't worked on it and talked about it?'[40]

Cantwell wasn't the only one frustrated and that inevitably led to friction. Wilf McGuinness had become a coach after breaking his leg in 1959 and functioned as a useful liaison between the management and the players – or as a spy in the dressing room, depending on your view. 'Newcomers such as Noel Cantwell and Maurice Setters loved to talk exhaustively,' wrote McGuinness, 'and sometimes their views, particularly on modern coaching methods, would contrast radically with mine, which had been inculcated through growing up at Old Trafford.[41]

The humiliation at Leicester in January 1961 was only the most obvious manifestation of a deeper malaise. There were cliques in the dressing room. Foulkes and Gregg hated each other. Gregg accused Foulkes of cowardice on the runway, while Foulkes resented the way Gregg, having been at the club only a few weeks before the crash, presented himself as a keeper of the pre-Munich flame.[42] New players struggled to integrate with those who had been at the club before the tragedy. There was a spate of thieving in the dressing room, while Gregg was certain United had been involved in the match-fixing scandal of the early sixties that led to three Sheffield Wednesday players being jailed, although no charges were ever brought against any of their players.[43] Dunphy agreed, suggesting three games he thought had been thrown.[44] In short, United in the early sixties was, Dunphy said, a 'divided, unhappy place'.[45]

Busby struggled to maintain discipline. On the coach to one away game, a sheet of paper was passed around on which had been drawn a crude caricature of Busby with a penis for a nose and testicles for cheeks. It was captioned, 'Bollock Chops'.[46]

This was not a club that appeared on the brink of greatness.

For Bobby, it was the signing of Denis Law in 1962 that instigated the revival. He acknowledged there had been 'a touch of panic in United's attempts to rebuild'[47] but said that with Law 'a lot of the magic and the aura' returned.[48] Not that there was much sign of it in 1962–63. United won only three of their first fourteen games of the season and narrowly avoided relegation. They might not have survived but for a draw against Manchester City, who finished bottom, three points behind

United, in the third-last game of the season. Not only was it secured thanks to a controversial penalty with twenty minutes remaining but Crerand escaped dismissal despite punching City's David Wagstaffe in the tunnel at half-time. Nicholson, who left the club that summer, suggested there was simply a lack of quality in the squad.[49]

Questions were being asked even of Bobby. In 1958–59, playing as an inside-left, he had scored twenty-nine goals in thirty-eight games as United finished second, although there was a general sense that their position flattered them. After the sale of Scanlon the following season, though, United were short of an outside-left and Bobby was shifted into the wider role. He hated it, saying he felt like he was playing in a 'straitjacket'.[50] Only Denis Law seemed to think it was a position that really suited him. 'Playing in midfield,' Law said, 'he would inevitably hit long, raking passes out to the flanks, which was fine from the spectator point of view because it looked spectacular. But it was also terrific for the opposition because it gave defenders time to reorganise.' As a winger, though, 'he had phenomenal speed which could take him past any full-back. He could get to the byline and either chip balls back or across with that magical left foot, and cause all sorts of problems.'[51]

There was a familiar criticism of Bobby at that time. 'As a young player,' said Harry Gregg, 'Bobby was blessed with fantastic skill, balance, the most incredible change of pace and a rocket shot. The brain and the feet, however, did not work as one.'[52] Jimmy Murphy regularly 'bollocked him for "glory balls"[53] but even that 'lesson in professionalism',[54] as Bobby described it, couldn't entirely temper his instincts.

Cantwell saw Bobby as a superb player with a fierce shot in either foot, somebody of great courage who could take a kicking and come back for more, but he also described him as 'a right moaner on the field … he would sulk if things went wrong.' More than that, where Bobby Moore was always looking to improve, 'Charlton never searched. He just had a wonderful gift and went out and did it'.[55] Even as late as 1966, when the goalkeeper Alex Stepney joined the club, Cantwell told him not to throw the ball to Bobby because he 'could be a liability ... when he came back into defensive positions.'[56]

Dunphy even wondered whether Bobby retained his place in the team only because Busby was worried about a potential backlash from fans if he dropped him.[57]

The story may be apocryphal, but it was told often enough and believed by so many people that, even if not literally true, it clearly encapsulated an emotional truth. The great Celtic manager Jock Stein, it's said, was asked whether he ever discussed football and tactics with his fellow Scot, Matt Busby. 'Och no,' he is supposed to have replied. 'I wouldnae want to embarrass the man.'

Matters came to a head in the harsh winter of 1962–63. Between a 1–0 win over Fulham on Boxing Day 1962 and a 1–1 draw against Blackpool on 23 February, the weather made it impossible for United to play a single fixture. With no matches to focus on, tensions inflated, fights in the games behind the stand became increasingly frequent and frustration with the standard of coaching intensified. Eventually, Gregg went to Busby to complain, placing the blame firmly on Crompton.

Busby called a meeting to clear the air. Cantwell, Gregg and Setters laid out their complaints. Most stuttered through some pet theory of how they believed the club should train – more speed work, more ball work, more weights. Bobby remained characteristically quiet; the episode goes unmentioned in either of his autobiographies. For all his on-field moaning, his instinct off it was to avoid confrontation. Law said he hadn't been at the club long enough to express an opinion and avoids the issue in all three of his autobiographies. Crerand had been kicked out of Celtic for criticising the coaching so kept quiet, despite fairly obvious reservations.[58] Giles thought the whole thing was a waste of time and that the real problem was Busby's lack of authority and the way Crompton was left to take the blame.[59]

Crompton was given his right of reply. He accused Cantwell of spreading discontent. But Busby already knew what the issues were: he had McGuinness to keep him informed. For Dunphy, the meeting was less about thrashing through the issues than about testing how far certain players were prepared to go in their public criticism – the oddity being that Busby presumably had a good idea of what Cantwell, Setters and Crerand thought, given that he would sometimes dine at the Cromford Club with them (Bobby, notably, preferred to maintain a distance from his manager). Ten years later, in *Soccer at the Top*, Busby even refers to Cantwell as 'a straight-shooting intermediary'[60] – although his book is at least as notable for its self-justificatory and condescending tone as for its substance.

League results would suggest the meeting changed little. But Busby claimed that he could see the pattern for which he was searching beginning to develop; it was just that results continued to elude them. Where there was clear development was in the Cup. Huddersfield, Aston Villa, Chelsea and Coventry were seen off in March. A Law goal was enough to win the semi-final against Southampton, setting up a final against Leicester City. They had finished fourth in the league, beating United at home and drawing at Old Trafford, yet Busby still seems to have been put out that Leicester were widely considered as favourites.[61] It didn't matter. United were excellent, particularly in the first hour, and won 3–1, their first trophy since 1957. At last there was tangible evidence that Busby's attempts to rebuild the club were working; United were recovering.

But was Bobby? That was harder to say. At the final whistle, he found himself looking at Bill Foulkes. Both had thought instinctively of Munich and the lads who weren't there. Neither could say anything and both would later slip away early from the celebrations. It was the first of three great triumphs for Bobby at Wembley in five years. None of them brought him unconditional joy.

8

MODERNITY AND ITS DISCONTENTS

'Moment of soccer shame' roared the *Mirror*.[1] In the *People*, Jack Archer said he expected the referee's report to be 'spine-chilling'.[2] 'Managements, players and a few unruly spectators are, between them, killing the game,' the *Sun* insisted in a leader column.[3] The secretary of the Football Association, Denis Follows, admitted the problems were widespread. 'We must make soccer fit for people to watch,' he said.[4]

There are few things quite so preposterous as the British football press in one of its moments of sanctimonious hysteria, but Leeds's 1–0 win away to Everton in November 1964 was the culmination of a trend. A Bremner foul on Fred Pickering in the first minute set the tone and tackles flew from both sides. When the Everton left-back Sandy Brown was sent off after four minutes for punching John Giles in the pit of the stomach, he already had a set of stud marks on his own belly. Leeds then took the lead, Willie Bell heading in a cross from Bobby Collins – who was, predictably, at the heart of the aggression against his former club.

But it was after the Everton winger Derek Temple was knocked unconscious in a collision with Bell nine minutes before half-time that things got really serious. Temple was carried off the pitch but, as he received treatment, the Leeds physio Les Cocker was pelted with coins by fans chanting, 'dirty Leeds, dirty Leeds'. The referee Ken Stokes – an electrician at a pit in Newark – took drastic action, leading both sides off the pitch for ten minutes to let tempers cool. Leeds held on to win 1–0, remaining fourth in the table, four points behind the leaders, Manchester United. That should have been seen as a great achievement for a newly promoted side, but attention by then was firmly focused on their methods.

There was a sense that football that season had been becoming increasingly violent on and off the field. In the first twelve weeks of league action, an unprecedented twenty-six players had been sent off. The *Daily Mail* had taken to awarding teams marks for fair play that supposedly represented the percentage of players on either side who 'did their best to play the game honestly'[5] and scored this game 25–20 in Leeds's favour, the lowest marks it had awarded.

The blame, the *Telegraph* insisted, was the end of the maximum wage in 1961: 'It is anything but coincidence,' Bryon Butler wrote, 'that sportsmanship has counted for less in soccer since the wage ceiling was removed and crowd and position bonuses were introduced.'[6]

It was a characteristic *Telegraph* stance – of course all decency collapses when the working classes are allowed to raise their heads from grovelling penury – and there was far more to the outbreak of aggressive play than the lure of a win bonus. Crowd violence, for the first time, was beginning to become a serious issue. The *Sun*'s leader was illustrated not only with a photograph of Stokes at Goodison, but also of another referee, Ernie Crawford, looking despairingly at a pile of beer cans that had been hurled on to the field during Preston's game against Manchester City. That suggested this was part of a wider societal shift, the first signs in football, perhaps, of the declining respect for authority that supposedly characterised the sixties.

The *Guardian* thought Stokes was at fault. 'The early refereeing was not firm enough,' said Brian Crowther, which may seem slightly odd, given there was a sending-off after four minutes but that, he insisted, 'hardly could have been avoided'. Nobody, after all, was booked before the walk-off, nor were the players called together for a general warning. When they returned to the pitch, 'Rough play continued, little abated. The refereeing was permissive, presumably in the cause of finishing the game. The only player who had his name taken – Hunter for a foul on Vernon – none the less seemed unlucky to be singled out.'[7]

The players, society, the referee ... the only other possible culprits were the managers, and the *Sun* turned on them, painting an apocalyptic vision of football being led into perdition by a new breed of pragmatic coaches. 'There are plenty of things for people to do on Saturday afternoons,' it said. 'The drift away from watching soccer will not be ended unless a much more attractive and skilful spectacle is provided. And the biggest enemy of skill is the ruthless boot designed to put the skilful player out of action.'[8]

And perhaps there was something in that. Football in the sixties did become more physical and some of that was cynical. But the sense of despair seemed to conflate or confuse a number of issues. There was more physical contact because players were closer to each other more often than they had been previously, and that was the result both of improving fitness and of zonal systems of marking that reduced the space for attacking players. Of course, it's entirely reasonable to be appalled by punches or tackles that left stud marks on opponents' stomachs, but for many columnists that became entwined with the way the game was changing, leaving the old individualism behind, to become more structured and thoughtful. Others, notably Eamon Dunphy, saw 1964–65 as the first year of English football's decade-long Golden Age: 'Conflict was rendered vigorous *and* beautiful by a historical convergence of talent, contrasting philosophy and distinct personalities,' he wrote. 'What once sufficed to lay hands on the Championship and the FA Cup was no longer enough. English football required more of its pretenders during those years than had ever been demanded before.'[9]

Were Leeds dirty? Revie insisted his team were blamed for doing what every other club in the league did, pointing out that only twelve of the thirty-two fouls in the Everton game had been committed by his side and that Hunter had been the only player booked. Leeds had only had one player sent off in the previous forty years. Yet true as that was, nobody thought the reason three players had been sent off against Leeds already that season was that they were innocent victims opponents were trying to bully.

When Leeds followed up the win at Everton with a poor performance that nonetheless brought a 3–1 win over Arsenal, Revie sniped, 'Anybody who came expecting a punch-up went away disappointed.' Leeds, he insisted, were just quicker and more determined than other teams. 'When I was a player,' he told Ken Jones of the *Mirror*, 'I would have been nothing if there hadn't been players around who could get the ball for me. Unless you get the ball you can't do anything with it. And you don't have to be dirty to do it ... My team is fit and strong ... Our football is open and quick. I see it as part of the answer to problems of retreating defences. We go in at them, forcing defenders into errors and exposing them ... It means a lot of physical contact. But what is the game without that?'[10]

Leeds were tough; that much at least was clear. The previous season, as they had battled their way to promotion, there had been concerns about how far they were prepared to go. The two games against Sunderland, who had been promoted with them, were particularly rugged. Sunderland's 2–0 win at Roker Park on 28 December came in a game of thirty-nine fouls, twenty-three of them committed by Leeds.

'It was as brutal as a sickening ring bout ...' wrote Charles Summerbell in the *Mirror*, 'a raw tangle in which skill was abandoned and only revenge counted. It was the most violent brawl I have ever witnessed.'[11]

Even the *Yorkshire Evening Post*, which could usually be relied upon to be supportive, seemed uneasy, Eric Sanger writing of the 'spite and malice' of a game that had 'overstepped the bounds'.[12]

The following August, an editorial in *FA News*, the FA's official magazine, referred to Leeds having the worst record of any league club when it came to players cautioned by referees, suspended, censured or fined by the disciplinary committee in 1963–64.[13] It was a passing mention in a much broader piece about declining standards of behaviour that acknowledged statistics could be misleading; nowhere in the article, despite subsequent claims, did the word 'dirty' appear. But Leeds were outraged. Cyril Williamson, Leeds's general-manager secretary, pointed out that eighteen of the offences were 'small cautions' for junior players and noted that when Leeds were playing 'under men who are regarded as good referees' they had not had a single caution.[14]

Revie raged at the injustice of the allegation, realising how such a reputation could hurt his side, offering opposing fans and players an easy line of attack and perhaps conditioning referees against them. He pointed out that the first team hadn't had a single player sent off the previous season while only Bremner had been suspended.

But the 'dirty' tag never shifted. Jack always maintained that he and Norman Hunter, his regular partner at the heart of the defence, were hard but fair, and recalled berating Jimmy Lumsden for exulting in forcing an opponent off, injured, with an over-the-top challenge in a reserve game. But he also

acknowledged that while Revie 'wasn't a hard man himself ...
he was very protective of his players and maybe that led him to
turn a blind eye to some of the things that were happening on
the field ... We all looked after each other, so that if you kicked
me, I wouldn't kick you back, but somebody else would.'[15]

That Revie had not been a physically imposing player was
part of the issue, giving him a perhaps exaggerated respect for
those who were. 'I'd always felt if I'd been harder,' he said, 'I
would have been a better player.'[16]

Revie made Leeds a family – 'After the lack of togetherness
at United,' said Giles, 'I loved this atmosphere'[17] – but the consequence was often an 'us against the world' dynamic.

'Leeds,' said Lord Harewood, president of both Leeds and
the FA, 'were not at all the hardest club ... People liked to tell it
that way, as did the press, and quite a lot of Leeds fans liked it
because they liked to be behind a club that was feared as much
as a club that was loved.'[18]

The victory over Everton brought matters to a head. Leeds
fought back against the criticism. 'Our conscience is clear,' the
chairman, Harry Reynolds, insisted. Phil Brown, who covered
Leeds for the *Yorkshire Evening Post*, pointed out that what
had happened at Goodison had been 'nothing like as bad' as
the two games against Sunderland the previous season. Revie
maintained that the problem was other teams getting their
retaliation in first because of Leeds's reputation – a reputation
that he still blamed on the FA.

'Any inquiry into our Everton match or the game generally
will only be welcomed by us,' he said. 'There is no excuse for
the Everton spectators, but I do think that they were helped
into their shocking state by the fact that the FA labelled us the
dirtiest team of last season. Like everyone here at Elland Road
I resent that description and it has given crowds anywhere a
readymade excuse to attack our play at the slightest offence
by our lads.

'Our players play hard – I order them to – but they do not, I repeat, play dirty. They inevitably commit some offences, all players do, but whatever they do is now, because of that FA label, being seized on and exaggerated. Our players are sometimes getting such crowd-whipped-up treatment by opposing sides that they cannot play their best football – and they can play just as skilfully as most sides.'[19]

The club released details of the letter they had sent to the FA after the article in *FA News* protesting that 'the "dirty team" tag, which was blown up by the press, could prejudice not only the general public but the officials controlling the game.'[20] Denis Follows, after consultation with both disciplinary and publications committees, dismissed the protest. In the aftermath of the Everton game, Leeds called for the issue to be discussed by the FA council, but Follows again dismissed their complaint and attacked Leeds for releasing details of private correspondence.

With hindsight, the editorial in *FA News* looks trivial, and Leeds's protests appear an attempt to deflect the blame from their own robust play. Their sensitivity to the implied criticism hints perhaps at an awareness that it was not unjustified. But the furore probably made matters worse and Revie's fears came almost to justify themselves; however hard Leeds were in 1964–65, other teams – and their fans – were ready for them.

It might have been the arrival of Law that began the process, but Manchester United's rebuilding accelerated after the 1963 FA Cup final. There were two major absentees for the game away against Sheffield Wednesday with which United started the 1963–64 season: Albert Quixall, who was perceived as lacking the stomach for the biggest games and John Giles, who had clashed with Busby on his position, salary and the club's lack of understanding as he recovered from a virus. Slowly,

Busby was reasserting his authority and beginning to shape his third great side. The following month came another step forward, as an injury to the right-winger Ian Moir led Busby to hand a debut to a seventeen-year-old waif: George Best.

From the outset, Best was different. He was frail and beautiful, but agile and tough enough to survive the brutal kickabouts behind the stand. While others used the red carbolic soap hacked into lumps from a larger block provided by the club, he carried his own bag of toiletries with him and washed his hair with Palmolive. Could he cope with the physical demands of the First Division? That first game against West Bromwich Albion offered no definitive answer. Busby left Best out. At Christmas, he sent him home to Belfast, only to recall him after United had been beaten 6–1 at Burnley on Boxing Day.

Two days later, Best was included as United faced Burnley again. By the end Bobby pitied the Burnley full-back John Angus, a friend who had been born in Amble, a few miles up the coast from Ashington, and had played seven times for England. Best destroyed him and United won 5–1. The third member of the Trinity had joined Bobby and Law.

Leeds quickly showed that they could cope in the First Division. They won three of their first four games but, after a 3–3 draw against Sunderland – in which Brian Clough accelerated away from Jack to score his last ever goal but was forced to accept that he would never recover from the knee injury he had suffered on Boxing Day 1962 – Revie was offered the manager's job at Roker Park. A return to the North-East tempted him, particularly as Sunderland would have doubled his salary and given him a Jaguar and a house, but that same week Reynolds was hospitalised with head injuries following a car crash. Revie felt acutely that he had a responsibility to the club, particularly after speaking to apprentices and seeing how upset they were by the prospect of him leaving. He decided to stay, signing a five-year contract, the announcement made the day Leeds faced Blackpool, who had beaten Leeds 4–0 the previous week. This time, despite missing two penalties, Leeds won 3–0, Bobby Collins scoring twice on his hundredth appearance for the club.

The controversial win over Everton lifted Leeds to fourth and by the beginning of December they were third, four behind the leaders Manchester United, who had won thirteen and drawn one of their previous fourteen league games, a run in which Denis Law scored twelve and George Herd ten. On 5 December, Manchester United hosted Leeds, the first meeting of Jack and Bobby as professional footballers.

It was a clash of styles: the individualism and commitment to attack of Busby against the tactical acuity of Revie. On this occasion the new way prevailed. 'Tactically,' wrote Phil Brown in the *Yorkshire Evening Post*, 'Manchester swallowed the Leeds bait and the hook, line and sinker, astonishingly so with the names and experience in their eleven.'[21]

Leeds sat deep, United poured forward and after half an hour without reward were clearly frustrated, at which 'panic was overtaking bafflement. They could not even do the obvious quickly. Of real stratagem there was no sign, nor was there to the end. Approach after approach landed on the penalty area rocks or was driven on to them.'[22]

Collins got the only goal and Leeds were within two points of the top.

The defeat rattled Manchester United, who won only one of the seven league games that followed – in part because Law was suspended after being sent off at Blackpool. Leeds, meanwhile, kept grinding on and, by the time they faced Manchester United in the FA Cup semi-final, they had gone twenty games unbeaten and lay second in the table on goal average, behind

The end of innocence: Bobby at Manchester United's final
game before Munich, the 5–4 win away to Arsenal

The Milburn–Charlton clan. Back row standing: Jim Milburn, Stan Milburn; front row seated: George Milburn, Jock Milburn, Jackie Milburn, Bob Charlton, Cissie Charlton, Jack Charlton and Bobby Charlton

A fifteen-year-old Bobby helps with the laundry at the family home in Ashington

A youthful Jack and Bobby as Leeds faced Manchester United in 1956–57

Bobby practises
heading, flanked
by Dennis Viollet
and John Giles,
1960

Matt Busby and Bobby are interviewed by Jackie Gillot before
their trip to Argentina for the Intercontinental Cup, 1968

Bobby celebrates the 1956–57 league championship with Johnny Berry, Bill Foulkes,
Billy Whelan, Eddie Colman, David Pegg, Tommy Taylor, Matt Busby and Roger Byrne

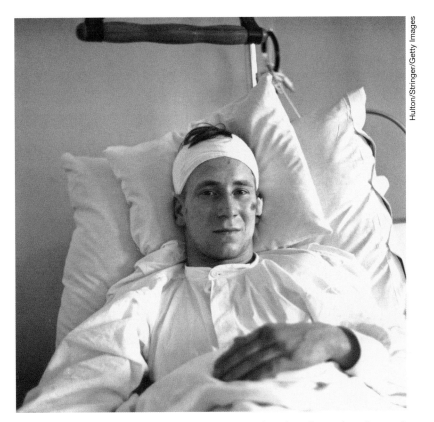

Bobby in the Rechts der Isar hospital in Munich a few days after the crash

Bobby is persuaded to kick a ball around with some kids in the back lane behind his parents' house in Ashington as he recovers, February 1957

An outnumbered Jack still wins the header

Jack and Don Revie in training with Leeds, April 1970

Bobby adds England's second against Portugal in the 1966
World Cup semi-final with a characteristic strike

The proud parents: Bob and Cissie read about their sons'
heroics the day after the 1966 World Cup final

Jack and Bobby with Ray Wilson, Bobby Moore and Jimmy Greaves,
waiting in vain to watch Muhammad Ali spar at a gym in Hampstead
two days before the 1966 World Cup final

Chelsea, who under Tommy Docherty were another modernising force. United, having played a game more, were a point further back.

Their meeting at Hillsborough could have been a showpiece occasion, a glorious contest between the old football and the new, between two sides packed with talent, one of whom focused on structure and the system while the other preferred individual self-expression. Instead, in keeping with the general trend of the season, it was a miserable, scratchy affair, so violent that the *Sun* used the page furniture usually reserved for boxing and headlined its piece on the game 'A Big Fight Report'.[23]

'I cannot remember seeing a match of such importance as an FA Cup semi-final so sordid or such a waste of a big occasion,' wrote Roy Peskett in the *Mail*.[24] 'A disgrace to football,' said Steve Richards in the *Sun*.[25] 'It was too often dirty play, so obviously the fruit of tactics, that prevented goals,' wrote R. H. Williams in the *Telegraph*.[26]

Only Bobby stood out. 'Every idea that Manchester United had,' Williams continued, 'came from Charlton, who settled down to the constructive game he has developed this season.' And yet even Bobby could not help but descend at times to the fray. He was, the *Times* reported, 'usually ... the gentlest of creatures. But now he retaliated immediately in anger, wagged his finger in admonition and from that first act the battle slipped into a black mood that only matched the dark stage itself, a heavy, churned-up pitch made sticky by heavy overnight rain.'[27]

Given the reputations of the sides now, it might be assumed that Leeds were the aggressors. Rather, they were 'massively more sinned against than sinning'[28] as 'Manchester, having heard of the dog's bad name, clearly were determined themselves not to be bitten.'[29] Manchester United committed twenty-three fouls in the game, Leeds just nine. This was a

recurring pattern: Leeds were aggressive, but often their reputation seemed to prompt their opponents to play aggressively.

A scrappy, tetchy game bubbled over just before the hour.
'The expected classic between Leeds and Manchester United,'
wrote Donald Saunders in the *Telegraph*, 'deteriorated into a
brawl that reached its ugly climax with half a dozen players
involved in a midfield fracas.'[30] The trigger, Peskett said, had
been 'Jackie Charlton attacking Denis Law after being body-
checked'. He was then 'butted in the ensuing fight'.[31] 'Some
referees,' wrote Richards, 'would have ordered off Denis
Law ... and ... Jackie Charlton. If they had both received
marching orders no one could have sympathised with them.'[32]

What's curious, at least to modern eyes, is that so little
is made of the battle of the brothers. Perhaps that reflects a
change in the media – then there was a reluctance to person-
alise football stories – but it is also indicative, perhaps, of the
attitude to Jack. Even in 1964–65, he wasn't highly regarded
as a footballer. To focus on him against Bobby would have
seemed absurd: a jobbing centre-half against a world-class
talent. Yes, they were from the same family, but as footballers
they were a different category altogether.

Dick Windle, the referee, was widely blamed for not taking
sterner action – although even the fact he had booked two
players led the FA to wonder whether 'in the circumstances
the committee might decide it would be unfair to ask him to
handle the same players in a second match.'[33] He did, though,
take charge of the replay at the City Ground in Nottingham the
following Wednesday, a game that was anticipated with that
classic journalistic blend of sentimentality and censoriousness.
'I will want to cry if Denis Law and Billy Bremner and Bobby
Collins and Bobby Charlton and the rest of the Leeds and
Manchester United players forget boys like my sons and your
sons who think that soccer is the greatest game in the world,'
wrote Frank Taylor in the *Sun*. 'I did not see the Cup semi-final

at Hillsborough. I have no wish to see the joust at Nottingham. For I love this game too much. I love it too much to see it just a tatty jersey-tearing roustabout of sport.' He concluded with the classic tabloid pay-off: 'If this is soccer in 1965, I wish to have no part of it.'[34]

As it turned out, the replay, uncompromising as it was, was a far less violent game than the first meeting (fouls committed: Manchester United eighteen, Leeds five). Busby's side had the better of it, but Leeds were a constant threat from set plays. Jack headed against the underside of the bar before, three minutes from time, as defenders were drawn to him, Bremner converted a long free-kick from Giles with a deft back-header.

It was a victory for Revie and for planning. 'Magnificent defence was again a prime reason for Leeds's success,' wrote Phil Brown in the *Yorkshire Evening Post*, praising Jack in particular, 'but hard on its heels in value were the sudden, fast and accurate attacking strokes which are just as demoralising as the solidity of their defence. Like the defence, these are planned. Even the astonishing winning goal from Billy Bremner came from planning.'[35] Even now, there is resistance to the idea that coherent attacking is the result of planning, despite the success of the likes of Pep Guardiola, Thomas Tuchel and Jürgen Klopp; at the time the idea was almost too radical to be processed, entirely divorced from Busby's vague sense that over time good players would develop an 'understanding'.[36]

In the dressing room afterwards, Revie had a message for Jack: he had, for the first time, been selected to play for England. Jack, as spontaneous as ever, wanted to share the good news with his brother and so went gleefully into the opposing dressing room where Bobby was slumped on a bench. Wearily, in general silence, Bobby congratulated him, then continued, 'Now fuck off.'[37]

*

Those first three meetings that season seemed to have proved the supremacy of Revie's methods, but it was the fourth – on the third-last weekend of the season – that was critical in deciding the destination of the title.

Four days after the defeat in the replay, United hosted Blackburn. Devastated by a second successive exit in the Cup semi-final, Nobby Stiles 'had no heart for it that day'. He was aware the whole season could slip away from them over the course of a week and yet he was too demoralised to rouse himself. Half the team felt the same, but not Bobby. 'He played them on his own,' said Stiles. 'His spirit lifted us.' [38]

'Manchester United got up off the floor after their Cup knockout to blast Blackburn with a top-notch display,' said the report in the *Manchester Evening News*. 'United, with no evidence of that tough-at-the-top feeling, continued to attack with an almost gay abandon. None more so than Bobby Charlton, who gave a complete inside-forward performance. He worked forcefully and was on hand to score three well-taken goals.'[39] United won 5–0. Nobody doubted Bobby any more; he may not have been a charismatic presence, but his consistent excellence, his drive and his goals meant that by his late twenties he was pivotal to both United and England.

Both Leeds and Manchester United won the following week, meaning Revie's side led by three points going into the league meeting at Elland Road. It was a scrappy game on a hard pitch decided by a scuffed effort from John Connelly after fourteen minutes. In windy conditions, despite a 52,000-strong home crowd, Manchester United 'played with capital poise and thought, with rather more skill and, even when they had moments of failure, they were generally failing doing the right thing. Their better and closer control repeatedly showed in the high cross wind.'[40] Jack had been the key figure in the two Cup games and, thrust up front in the final minutes, probably offered Leeds' greatest threat, but this was Bobby's afternoon. His 'dribbling and passing, against close and hard tackling, were brilliant, and he had nearly as many good moments in defence, his intercepting being superb. Without him Manchester would have lost.'[41]

That pulled Manchester United within a point of Leeds, and Chelsea – who had played a game more. They then beat Birmingham and Liverpool to lie a point behind Leeds with a game in hand the weekend before the Cup final. On the Monday of that final week, Manchester United beat Arsenal 3–1 – Law scoring twice despite six stitches in his knee – while Leeds, apparently beset by nerves, went 3–0 behind against relegated Birmingham in their last league game of the season before fighting back to draw, Jack snatching the equaliser with two minutes remaining. But it was not enough: Leeds's slip-up effectively gave Busby's side the title – their first since Munich – on goal average, something sealed two days later as they lost 2–1 at Aston Villa. 'We were making football,' Bobby said, 'that, apart from winning matches, was also lighting up the sky.'[42]

For Leeds, the disappointments continued. The following Saturday, they lost 2–1 after extra time to Shankly's Liverpool in the Cup final in a meeting of the two sides who most embodied the new vision of football. Many observers, it's fair to say, were not impressed. 'More and more clubs are turning to method and discipline, sick of being sacrifices every season to the teams with talent and the money to buy it ...' wrote a sceptical Ken Jones in the *Mirror*. 'Leeds, short of quality forwards and not yet the team they soon may be, were not capable of injecting excitement into Wembley. Liverpool, too, must share the blame because their quality forwards lacked the purpose to pierce Leeds's line of defenders. In spite of much lateral "method" play it was a tense battle of human qualities ... there was a certain hypnotic element about the whole thing. The fascination lay in trying to assess which side would first break the stalemate.'[43]

To modern eyes, the game, won 2–1 by Liverpool after extra time, is unexceptional, yet it was widely dismissed as one of the dullest finals there had been. Jack bought a film of the match, but never took it from its case. The columnist Peter Wilson, meanwhile, was representative of the general mood as he condemned the game as 'a turbid, excoriating bore'. Looking ahead to the following summer, he was appalled by the direction football had taken. 'I am told that if we are to survive the rigours of the World Cup,' he wrote, 'we must forget individualism, the brilliant flashes of inspiration which transform a treadmill into a flying machine, the genius which transmutes a muddied oaf into a booted genius.'[44] Whoever had told him that was broadly right.

Revie acknowledged in his notorious 1974 Yorkshire TV interview with Brian Clough that 'the first four or five years ... we played for results'.[45] And yet the results didn't quite come (not helped, perhaps, by the fact that, for all the complaints about defensiveness, Leeds conceded thirteen goals more than Manchester United that season). For Leeds, that would become a recurring theme.

9

THEIR FINEST HOUR

The road to World Cup glory began with the appointment of Alf Ramsey as England manager in October 1962 – although, with typically honourable cussedness, he didn't actually take up the role until the following March. He felt it would be unfair to walk out on Ipswich Town who, having won the title in extraordinary fashion the previous season, were struggling at the lower end of the First Division.

The perception of Ramsey now is of a dour, repressed traditionalist, somebody who represented old-fashioned ideals of service with which English football and England is no longer comfortable. Even by the standards of the time, he was reserved. 'What was Ramsey like?' Jack said. 'I don't know. I was only with him six years.'[1]

Ramsey's wife, Victoria, wished 'he would let his hair down occasionally . . . It would do him the power of good, I'm sure.' Whatever problems he was wrestling with, whatever satisfaction he felt, were hidden behind his brusque façade. 'I'm the one in the household who hits the ceiling,' Victoria went on. 'I think it's a good thing to get it out of your system. But not Alf. He's the Rock of Gibraltar. I'm not saying he doesn't feel it, but he doesn't show emotion. He has a will like iron.'[2]

It is true that Ramsey was instinctively xenophobic,

introverted and stubborn. It's also clearly the case that his reputation suffered for England's failure to qualify for the 1974 World Cup – in particular his reluctance to bow to the desires of the media and fans to accommodate at least some of the various maverick attacking talents who dotted English football at the time. England may have been preposterously unlucky to draw against a Jan Tomaszewski-inspired Poland at Wembley in November 1973 when they needed to win to reach the World Cup, but their football had, for a couple of years, lagged behind the Netherlands and West Germany. The game had moved on and Ramsey had not – but he is hardly unique in that regard; most managerial careers end in disappointment.

There is even a surprisingly widespread view that Ramsey somehow stunted English football by winning the World Cup. 'Ultimately,' the historian David Downing wrote, 'the real loser in 1966 was English football. Ramsey's success reinforced English insularity and reduced what willingness there was to learn from abroad, thus condemning the national game to the status of a backwater ... The old values of toughness, speed and never-say-die attitude had been reinforced, but the insistence on fair play which had always accompanied them would weaken as the game became more thoroughly professional.'[3]

Quite apart from the issue of whether a country that has habitually underachieved has any business being disdainful of its only success, the ambiguous attitude towards Ramsey seems to ignore what a revolutionary figure he was. He was not a charismatic showman, expounding his philosophy – and by extension highlighting his own greatness – and he was very evidently uncomfortable with the media age, but in his quietly determined way, he did as much as anybody to drag English football into modernity. Bobby was always going to be central to that; Jack became so.

*

Ramsey played in English football's first two post-war humil-iations: the 1–0 defeat against the USA at the 1950 World Cup in Brazil and the 6–3 home defeat to Hungary in 1953. He knew that English football was being left behind, a mes-sage reinforced by his manager at Tottenham, Arthur Rowe, who developed what became known as the 'push-and-run' style that looked to protect possession by focusing on shorter passes, demanding physical fitness and positional intelligence. Some were enraptured by Spurs' style, others found it a little mechanical, but it was undeniably successful. Rowe's side won the league in 1950–51, confirming in Ramsey's mind the prin-ciple that the team was always more important than any star within it.

Ramsey retired as a player in 1955 aged thirty-five* and became manager of Ipswich Town, then a provincial, Third Division club of no great aspiration. The squad was ageing and there was little money available for investment, but Ramsey slowly imposed a structure and, in his second season, led Ipswich to promotion. They went up again in 1960–61, by which point he had begun to develop a system with withdrawn wingers, who drew full-backs out of position, creating space for a pair of mobile centre-forwards. Remarkably, the follow-ing season – their first ever in the top flight – Ipswich won the league for the first time in their history.

When England appointed Ramsey, they were getting a thor-oughly modern, radical tactician. The switch to the back four and a zonal marking system was the beginning of the end of the individualism that had previously characterised football and that was still espoused by Matt Busby. Ramsey may not have spoken publicly about his approach in the way that Bill Shankly or Don Revie did, but he was no less a force of the new age. As

---

* He lied about his date of birth when he first registered as a player, reason-ing that the war cost him two years of his career, and it was thought he was thirty-three.

much as anything else, England's victory in 1966 was a tactical triumph, one rooted, for all that Ramsey may seem an unlikely trendsetter, in the cultural spirit of the age.

The 1956 Ideal Home Exhibition, held at Olympia, London, featured 'The House of the Future'.[4] The Pathé News film of the design shows something resembling a set for an early sci-fi film, all bare walls and hexagons. A woman, with hair that looks as though a gorgon has been wearing a baseball cap for an extended period, sits and reads a newspaper. A man, dressed in a close-fitting, one-piece suit with an extraordinarily high waist – a sort of jacket and tie, trawlerman's waders, Renaissance stockings combo, like something an Oompa Loompa might wear to a wedding – presses a button and a table rises from the floor, controlled by a large cube that sits on a hospital trolley next to his uncomfortable-looking plastic chair. But what is really striking is the aesthetic: other than their clothing, everything is cold and hard and functional, the design so spare that the only apparent decoration is a line running a few inches in from the edges of the table and floor.

Ludicrous as it may appear to modern eyes, the media reaction was broadly favourable, or at least thoughtful. 'We still have very nearly the same inconvenient, inefficient pattern of living as our parents and even our grandparents,' wrote Patricia Keighran in the *Daily Mail*. 'But consider the progress in other fields.'[5] There was a growing willingness to reject those inefficient patterns and consider what Jonathan Meades called 'the most extreme strain' of late modernism: brutalism.[6]

Football, as surely as any other discipline, follows cultural fashion. In the aftermath of the First World War, it went through its first great tactical disruption of the twentieth century, as the increasing use of the offside trap led to a change in the offside law which, in turn, led to the W-M formation superseding the 2-3-5.[7] In part, that was a result of the social upheavals caused by the war and the rise of an increasing number of managers who cared less about playing the game in the 'right' way – which is to say, the way it had been played in public schools and universities in the previous century – than about winning and claiming their bonuses. But it was also part of the more general project of modernism, the questioning of tradition and the old ways to fulfil Ezra Pound's demand to 'make it new'.

By the late 1950s, nutrition and diet had improved, not least because rationing in Britain had come to an end in 1954 (it's widely believed one of the reasons Liverpool won the league in 1946–47 was that they went on a pre-season tour of the US, where there was no rationing, and so returned in far better physical shape than most of their rivals).[8] There was a greater understanding of sports science, while developments in the design of boots and kits meant players could run faster and for longer. At the same time, there was a growing recognition that the strict man-to-man marking of the W-M – in which symmetry meant it was a simple matter of the right-back picking up the opposing left-winger or the left-half the opposing inside-right – was not the only way to play; players could occupy a position and mark anybody who came into their zone.

That offered far greater flexibility of approach for coaches who were prepared to experiment. Few in Britain were, but that was not only true of football; Britain in the fifties remained an instinctively conservative culture. Le Corbusier and Bauhaus, for instance, were seen as overtly foreign, both continental European and American. 'Brutalism,' the cultural historian Ben Highmore wrote, 'was meant to have a whiff of Gauloises and existentialism, but it was also meant to echo with jive talk and jukeboxes.'[9] (Even the name is French, derived not of brutality but of *béton brut* – raw concrete.)

Whatever was happening elsewhere, 'stone-faced classicism,' as Barnabas Calder put it in *Raw Concrete*, his celebration of brutalism, 'seemed better to represent the timelessness of empire and the solid grandeur of world-power status.'[10] In football, that impulse was represented by the old-fashioned reliance on the classical winger, which reached its apogee in May 1953 as Stanley Matthews inspired Blackpool to victory in the FA Cup final in the Empire Stadium, as Wembley was still known. A month later, just after an imperial expedition had conquered Everest, came the coronation of Elizabeth II. Britain has probably never since felt so self-confident. Yet just six months later, Hungary came to the Empire Stadium with a style of football that proudly declared itself socialist[11] and beat England 6–3, abruptly alerting the English game to the revolution going on elsewhere.[12] Brazil's success playing a 4-2-4 in the World Cup in 1958 effectively signalled the end for a game based around old-fashioned wing-play. The 1953 FA Cup final had been regarded as a celebration of the classic English style; it turned out to be its final hurrah.

As the old certainties fell away, English football entered a period of unprecedented experimentation, which included the employment of Don Revie as a deep-lying centre-forward at Manchester City, directly aping the way Nándor Hidegkuti had played for Hungary. Football inevitably picked up the mood of the time – those inconvenient, inefficient patterns were being stripped away everywhere. After the devastation of the Second World War, architecture found there was no time or money for the luxuries of historical motifs and so, as Calder put it, 'Modernism could present itself as being una-dorned and utilitarian, and so win the stylistic argument by default.'[13] Elaine Harwood wrote of brutalism as prioritising 'pragmatism ... teamwork and [an] emphasis on efficiency.'[14] She was talking about the preferred style of building, but she could easily have been speaking of the football that England ended up playing under Alf Ramsey.

Hindsight always makes the patterns look neater but, still, it's clear that between his first game, against France in February 1963, and the World Cup final against West Germany in July 1966, Ramsey guided England through a process of careful development. That's not to say there was a single vision – he was far from a utopian idealist – rather that he had his principles and a general idea in mind, and then adapted to evidence and changing circumstances. That was simply who he was, a patient English empiricist. 'He weighs everything in the balance,' said his wife Victoria (in an interview perhaps best described as being of its time), 'whether it is a tiddly little problem of my own or one of his own much bigger worries. Then he gives his considered advice. Sometimes when I still go my own way, I think, "If only he would be wrong just once. But he never is, you know."' [15]

Before that game against France, Ramsey gathered a group of senior players and asked if any of them had any suggestions as to how things might be improved. There was some awkward glancing around before, to break the silence as much as because it was a major bugbear, Bobby pointed out that the Hendon Hall hotel in north London, where the squad usually stayed, was around an hour by coach from the Bank of England ground at Roehampton, west London, where they trained. Might it be possible, he wondered, to find a hotel nearer by?

'I've listened to what you have to say,' Ramsey replied, 'and we'll leave it as it is.' [16]

On another occasion, Bobby found himself cajoled by other players into asking whether they really had to wear their heavy suits from Simpsons of Piccadilly for a summer tour of central Europe. Again, he found his concerns abruptly dismissed.

Ramsey, it became apparent, was not somebody to be

challenged in any way. 'He was blunt to the point of being rude,' Bobby said, but that was never something that really bothered him; Bobby preferred a strong leader. 'He knew the game, he knew players and, most of all, he understood what they needed and how they should be led.'[17]

That first match was the second leg of the preliminary round of the 1964 European Championship. The first leg at Wembley had been drawn 1–1 and Ramsey was only notionally in charge, still working at Ipswich while, for the last time, the team was picked by an FA selection committee. His influence, though, was clear, as Johnny Haynes, the gifted but individualistic Fulham inside-forward, was omitted.

Bobby, romantic and in awe of individual talent as he always was, believed Haynes had been left out because he was still recovering after breaking both his legs in a car crash the previous year. Even in his autobiography, he seems to assume a fully fit Haynes would have continued to be selected, but Ramsey wanted team men, players he could trust to follow his instructions.

Ron Springett, the goalkeeper, was kicked in the chest early on and as he struggled England lost 5–2. It was not an auspicious start, but it did mean Ramsey had a little over three years without any competitive fixtures in which to prepare his side for the World Cup which, despite his habitual reserve, he insisted England would win.

Five weeks later, Ramsey was fully in charge for a Home Championship fixture against Scotland. There had been a clamour for Haynes to be restored, but he resisted it. This was a clear implication for Bobby: he was the star of the team. By the time England beat Wales 4–0 that October, with Bobby capping an excellent performance with the final goal, it was clear that Haynes's time with England was over and that Ramsey had won a first victory over those who preferred the flashier ways.

It was the following summer that Ramsey's thinking was clarified with a trip to Brazil for a four-team tournament to celebrate the fiftieth anniversary of the foundation of the Brazilian football federation. Between the end of the domestic season and arrival in Brazil, England had three further fixtures – away matches against Portugal, Ireland and the USA. The night before departure for Lisbon, Bobby, Jimmy Greaves, Bobby Moore, Gordon Banks, Ray Wilson, George Eastham and Johnny Byrne, looking to let off a little steam, headed into the centre of London and wound up in a bar called the Beachcomber off Bayswater Road. There, depending which account you believe, they had a couple of gentle pints or got stuck into a rum-based cocktail called a Zombie. At least five of them (again, accounts vary, but everybody agrees Bobby, Moore and Greaves were involved) missed the 10.30 p.m. curfew.

Bobby snuck back into the hotel and thought he might have got away with it. On his bed he found his passport, lying dark against the white pillow, 'shouting its reproach'.[18] Ramsey said nothing until they got to Portugal, at which he told the guilty players that if he could have found replacements in time he would have sent them home.

That is now widely seen as good management, making his point and asserting his authority without ostracising players who he must have known, even at that stage, would be critical to a World Cup challenge – although, given how things eventually turned out with Greaves, the temptation must be to wonder whether that was the beginning of Ramsey's distrust of the centre-forward.

But what is also revealing is Bobby's reaction. Some may have resented Ramsey's controlling nature, thinking he was making an absurd fuss over a couple of drinks too many at the end of a long season. Others would have taken the point that this was a boss who prioritised discipline and resolved to ensure their socialising remained within bounds. Bobby, though, felt a sense of 'shame'[19] and fear over what his family, his club manager Matt Busby and his club coach Jimmy Murphy would say. He was twenty-seven at the time, yet avoiding the disapproval of his parents and parent substitutes was still his overriding concern. Jack, it's fair to assume, would have reacted differently.

In terms of results, the tournament in Brazil was a disaster for England. They finished bottom of the table, drawing one game and losing the other two. But far more important than that was what Ramsey learned: against high-level sides such as Brazil, Argentina and Portugal, he could not afford to play a 4-2-4. World Cups were not won by putting eight past Switzerland or Northern Ireland, but by a side's capacity to grind out narrow wins against the best; the lesson seems simple, but it has still to be fully absorbed. Even in our far more tactically aware age there are demands from fans and journalists for England not merely to win every game, but to do so with swagger.

That conclusion was not one easily accepted by the press, which demanded constant entertainment. Ramsey began to adapt, withdrawing one of his wingers into an asymmetric 4-3-3. His next question was who to play at centre-back alongside the elegant Bobby Moore. Through most of 1964, the preferred option was Maurice Norman of Tottenham but, as he began increasingly to play at full-back for his club, Ramsey looked for another option. What he needed was somebody tall and combative, somebody who could do the dirty work that did not come naturally to Moore. There was an obvious candidate, but he was almost thirty and had never been capped. Nevertheless, for the Home Championship match against Scotland in April 1965, Ramsey turned to Jack.

Revie had seen Jack's potential and he had blossomed under a manager who eventually agreed with his ideas on zonal marking. 'One minute ...' Bobby said, 'Jack was a happy-go-lucky character ... and the next he was a key player in a very hard, talented and professional team.'[20]

But still, there was plenty of suspicion. Even Jack was slightly baffled by his selection and, characteristically, challenged Ramsey directly. 'I have a pattern of play in mind,' Ramsey replied, 'and I pick the best players to fit the pattern. I don't necessarily always pick the best players.'[21] Jack did not have the elegance or the confidence on the ball of Bobby Moore, but that was precisely the point. 'You're a good tackler and you're good in the air, and I need those things,' Ramsey went on, 'and I know you don't trust Bobby Moore.'

Jack was to be the straight man, the physical enforcer, tough and reliable alongside a more skilful partner; he was, essentially, to do for England exactly what he did alongside Norman Hunter for Leeds United (with the obvious difference that Hunter was a much more physically aggressive player than Moore).

Nobby Stiles also made his debut against Scotland that day, replacing Milne, and adding his tenacity to midfield. He was, Bobby said, 'a real professional, nothing airy-fairy, nothing for show, just a player doing his job at the highest level.' Crucially for Ramsey, he was 'a player you could trust'.[22]

Jack flicked on a corner for Bobby to open the scoring and Jimmy Greaves soon added a second but when England were reduced to nine men by injury Scotland came back to force a 2–2 draw. The performance, though, had generally been good. With a year to go until the World Cup, the foundations of the team that would win were in place: Gordon Banks behind a back four of George Cohen, Bobby Moore, Jack and Ray Wilson, with Stiles and Bobby reprising their Manchester United combination in the centre of midfield.

But national confidence was fragile. That autumn there was a 0–0 draw away to Wales and then, with the same XI, a 4-2-4 with Chelsea's Barry Bridges partnering Jimmy Greaves as the central attacking pair, Terry Paine and John Connelly on the wings and Bobby as one of the two central midfielders, an unfortunate 3–2 defeat to Austria. It was, it's true, only the third time England had lost at Wembley against foreign opposition and true also that Austria had lost 4–1 to West Germany ten days earlier but, still, the reaction from fans and media looks bizarrely overblown from a modern perspective. 'A Night of Shame,' roared the *Sun*.[23] There were boos and jeers from the stands long before the final whistle, which was greeted with a slow handclap. 'England's World Cup plans, thought to be progressing steadily only a few months ago, stuttered to an untimely halt,' wrote Donald Saunders in the *Telegraph*.'[24]

'We will not win the World Cup,' said Jimmy Hill, at the time the manager of Coventry but just as reliably opinionated and wrong as he would later be as a full-time pundit, 'but don't blame Alf Ramsey. No one could with this lot.'[25]

In the *Guardian*, Albert Barham spoke of 'a sorry lack of spirit';[26] even more than now, the tendency was to attribute poor results to the absence of passion. Yet Ramsey professed to be unconcerned, 'disappointed' but not 'very disappointed'. 'We played some brilliant football in midfield,' he said, 'the work rate was high, but we failed where it mattered most, in the two penalty areas.'[27]

So, what, according to the journalists, was the problem? Much of the analysis identified the right problem but drew the wrong conclusion. Barham had regularly expressed his doubts about Bobby's suitability for the central role, but seemed never to consider that the issue might be the 4-2-4 system that meant whoever played in central midfield risked being outnumbered. 'The wingers, especially Connelly,' noted Brian James in the *Mail*, 'got the ball across often enough but with no great accuracy.'[28] So perhaps the solution was not to be obsessed with attacking down the flanks?

And then there were the central strikers. 'So few goals have been scored by this side in the past year that the attack seems to suffer an anxiety neurosis when an opportunity presents itself,' wrote Saunders.[29] He highlighted a specific problem with Greaves, back in the team after illness, but nowhere near his best: 'No manager could afford to banish so gifted a player from his World Cup plans but Greaves at present is not doing the job for which he is chosen.' James referred to Greaves as 'a pale spasmodic shadow'[30] while Barham asked, 'How long can England wait for Greaves to recover his old scoring power?'[31] Yet none seemed to ask the question that, in hindsight, seems obvious: was Greaves, even at his best, the right fit for the England Ramsey was creating?

Greaves did not play in England's following game, a less than convincing 2–1 win over Northern Ireland at Wembley. Nor was he selected for the final game of the year, away to Spain, the reigning European champions, as Ramsey again picked what at the time was generally referred to as a 4-3-3. But with Joe Baker and Roger Hunt through the middle and Alan Ball shuttling back on the right it was really, as Stiles said, something closer to a 4-1-3-2. The journalist Peter Lorenzo used the term 'wingless wonders' in the *Sun*,[32] but it's not clear how many realised just how radical Ramsey was.

England began well, taking an eighth-minute lead through Baker, but he suffered a thigh injury ten minutes before half-time. He was replaced by Norman Hunter, who dropped into the back four alongside Jack in the second half, with Moore pushing into midfield alongside Bobby and George Eastham. With Ball in his hybrid, shuttling role, England suddenly had three runners from deep and Spain couldn't cope. 'Their full-backs,' Ray Wilson said, 'didn't know who to mark. They were standing there, ball-watching, and we ripped them to bits.'[33] It was the same problem Ramsey's Ipswich had posed for opponents, but on both flanks. England, acknowledged the Spain manager José Villalonga, had been 'phenomenal'.[34] They won 2–0, but it could easily have been five. Ramsey barely spoke to the players in the dressing room afterwards, worried, Bobby thought, that his delight might lead to a sense of overconfidence.[35]

'Tonight,' wrote Brian James, 'I saw the shape of England's soccer to come.'[36] But few others had the chance to; Ramsey hid the system away. England played eight further matches before the World Cup but he brought out the wingless system only in the last of them, in Chorzów, Poland, far away from prying eyes.

Ramsey wasn't usually a man given much to the dramatic, but as he read out the team for the friendly away to Poland to the press, he allowed himself a little flourish. The first ten names were familiar enough: Banks in goal; the usual back four of Cohen, Moore, Jack and Wilson; Stiles, Charlton and Ball in midfield; with Greaves and Hunt up front. 'And number 11,' he said and then, after a discernible pause, 'Martin Peters.' There was a moment while the journalists processed the information, and then uproar. But Ramsey by then was on his way out of the room. He had chosen a side with no winger.

Peters was twenty-two and versatile, used to hitting crosses for Hurst at West Ham and a goal threat with his ability to arrive late in the box and attack the back post. For Ramsey, he was almost the final piece, more attack-minded and better on the ball than Hunter, but more comfortable tucking in when Wilson went outside him than Eastham. The move to winglessness was complete: playing a 4-1-3-2, England won, Bobby laying in Hunt for the only goal, while they controlled the game just as Ramsey had envisaged. Greaves played rather

than Geoff Hurst, but otherwise that was the side that would
win the World Cup.

Peters, Geoffrey Green wrote in *The Times*, 'was an out-
standing success. So often when a player was in trouble tonight
he looked for help: Peters was never very far away; he came
close to adding to the goal he had scored against Finland ten
days earlier.'[37] But what was more significant was less his individual display than what Peters meant for the whole. 'A fluid,
tactical plan,' Green wrote, 'had England flowing back and
forth like a red tide in their unfamiliar red shirts.'

Quite how revolutionary that plan was is perhaps hard
for minds conditioned by modern football to grasp, but it's
notable that most papers at the time maintained the illusion
that England were playing a 4-3-3, with the shuttler Ball as
a winger, while Bobby, slightly old-fashioned, referred in
his autobiography to Jack, Moore, Stiles and Peters as 'half-
backs'; that might have been a reasonable designation fifteen
years earlier, but by 1966 they had very different and clearly
defined roles.[38]

Ramsey knew the challenge posed by Uruguay; the fans and
media either did not, or were not prepared to be as pragmatic
as Ramsey. After all the build-up, the opening game of the
World Cup was a massive anti-climax. But then tournament
football, watched by an audience that comprises more casual
viewers than league games and far more closely scrutinised,
often begins against a background grumble of discontent.

Greaves was paired with Hunt, and Connelly started on the
left wing. What is not clear is whether Ramsey – who, characteristically, never explained his thinking – was simply hiding
his tactical innovation or whether he saw the use of a bona
fide winger as an asset against a team who sat deep. England
dominated the ball, had sixteen corners and fifteen shots

and drew 0–0. Ramsey was not surprised, or even especially disappointed: it merely confirmed to him that dribbling was essentially useless against South American teams. In the *Mail*, Brian James spoke of Uruguay as 'unambitious and uncompromising' but true as that may have been, it was the headline of his report that was more representative of the national mood: 'Angry, Baffled, Goalless England'.[39]

Ramsey didn't care. He knew Uruguay would drop deep and defend and that England had to be careful not to overcommit and risk conceding on the break. He also knew that Uruguay were England's main rivals in the group and had been clear that the spectacle was of no concern to him. The group was for getting through before the real test of the last eight and beyond, when control was the most important thing. What mattered against Uruguay was simply to avoid defeat. 'In 1966, the supporters had been weaned on the football just after the war, where everything was open . . .' said Ray Wilson. 'Crowds didn't understand when teams came to defend.'[40]

And it wasn't just crowds. For many, the issue was less that Ramsey was using the wrong tactics, than that he was using tactics at all. The *Mail*'s perpetually disgruntled columnist J. L. Manning, a man who looked at least a decade older than his forty-two years and had the outlook of somebody at least a decade older than that, was adamant that thinking about football at all was a waste of time, some ghastly import from abroad. 'Even the commentators are going all foreign,' he said. 'They talk down to us as if football was a new television panel game which the natives are seeing for the first time. You know the clever-clever fellows I refer to. There are those who say, arrogantly of course, some people thought it was dull, but we in the game were fascinated by the tactics. It's a great pity football crowds are not better educated. They would enjoy it so much more. Educated? About football? To understand football requires the intellectuality of the gnat.'[41]

Absurd though Manning appears now, the view was prevalent at the time – in fact, was the man-in-the-pub, blunt, common-sense variant of a view of the old-fashioned game espoused by Busby and, by extension, Bobby – that it was not for overcomplicating and was, on the whole, better when played with the aim of scoring goals. 'I am willing to bet that a team which plays this rubbish will not survive the quarter-finals,' Manning concluded.

England toiled against Mexico but then, seven minutes before the break, Hunt nudged the ball to Bobby in the centre-circle and sprinted on ahead of him. Bobby recalled what Jimmy Murphy had always told him: if there was space in front of you, accelerate into it, because that would discourage opposing forwards from giving chase and because it would destabilise a defence unsure whether to fall back into shape or to try to regain possession early. As he advanced, nobody stopped him. Mexico, distracted by Hunt and presumably concerned by the possibility of offering an easy through-ball, kept dropping off. Bobby didn't look up. He was just waiting for the ball to sit right in his stride and, when it did, at just about the same spot from which Jackie Milburn had scored his second in the FA Cup final fifteen years earlier, he crashed it goalwards. It flew, on a slight angle from right to left, into the top corner. He may have been twenty-five yards out, but Ignacio Calderón was helpless.

It was a stunning goal, one that, in its fluid power, seemed to release all the anxiety and frustration of the previous 128 minutes England had played in the tournament. It brought, Bobby said, 'maybe the loveliest, most exhilarating feeling I ever had as a footballer'.[42] He was on such a high that at half-time he sprinted from the pitch, just for the joy of running.

England were never in trouble in the game but it wasn't

until the seventy-fifth minute that the decisive second arrived, Bobby's finely calibrated pass laying in Greaves on the left side of the box. His shot was saved, but Hunt knocked in the rebound. With only two out and out forwards, England needed goalscoring runners from deep. Bobby may have been uneasy with talk of tactics but he was essential to Ramsey's system.

That left England top of the group and, after Uruguay drew with Mexico in their final game, they needed only a draw against France to guarantee qualification and a quarter-final at Wembley against the runners-up from the group featuring West Germany, Argentina and Spain. With France needing to win to qualify, they were always going to be more open than Uruguay or Mexico had been. England took full advantage. Hunt poked in after a header from Jack had struck the post and then, after Bobby had had a goal wrongly ruled out for offside, Callaghan – in for Paine, who like Connelly whom he had replaced, never played for his country again – crossed for Hunt to add a second.

There were only two shadows. Firstly, the behaviour of Stiles, who in the space of twenty second-half minutes, punched Robert Herbin, thrust an arm at Bernard Bosquier and broke Jacky Simon's leg with a wild, late foul, but collected only a solitary caution. Standards were different then and players got away with more but Stiles could easily have been sent off and the foul on Simon, in particular, prompted a minor furore. When the FA suggested to Ramsey it might make diplomatic sense to leave Stiles out, he threatened to resign and the issue was widely forgotten – in England, at least.

Far more domestic attention was focused on a gash in Greaves's shin that required three stitches and ruled him out of the quarter-final. Hurst replaced him, and never lost his place. The injury, for all the support Greaves had among fans and the media, for all the sympathy there would later be for him, probably did Ramsey a favour.

The Greaves question was a cipher for a much wider debate.

He was, unquestionably, a brilliant forward, an elegant and graceful goal-scorer and a lot more besides – even if those from outside the capital did wonder whether he was quite as good as London-based journalists insisted. His strike-rate was incredible, whatever the sceptics said: forty-three goals in fifty-one internationals before the World Cup. Yet there had been hints long before the tournament that he would prove to be a fault line. No sooner had England won in Spain without him than the battlelines were drawn. Peter Lorenzo may have described that win as 'a thrilling victory, supreme in its tactical brilliance and mastery',[43] but the very next day he was arguing that 'England must recall luxury goal ace' – just as soon as Greaves was fit again.[44] Others were less convinced. After the win in Poland, Green had observed, 'Greaves continues to follow his own infuriating path,' apparently struggling to reconcile what he had seen in Chorzów with the demands of English received wisdom.[45]

Even Bobby, instinctively given to celebrating the individual and uncomfortable with team structures that risked repressing romantic improvisation, had his doubts. 'If Greaves wasn't scoring,' he said, 'his contribution ... tended to be not much more than the ornamental.'[46] For Dave Bowler, Ramsey's biographer, the question for the England manager from the underwhelming win over Denmark had been not, as was widely believed, whether Greaves should be partnered by Hunt or Hurst, but whether Hunt should be partnered by Hurst or Greaves.[47] Yet after the stalemate against Uruguay, the *Mail* had remained sufficiently distracted by the Greaves legend to ask whether it might be worth bringing in Hurst to replace Hunt – even though the Liverpool striker at that point had scored twelve times in his fourteen internationals.

Antonio Rattín, Argentina's captain, loomed over the German referee Rudi Kreitlein, his expression one of incomprehension.

How could he have been sent off? What had he done wrong? He demanded an interpreter. Kreitlein waved him dismissively away. Rattín lingered. As the game was held up for several minutes England supporters began to chant, 'Why are we waiting?' Eventually, Rattín left, trudging off the pitch to sit briefly on the red carpet beneath the royal box before being persuaded that he should return to the dressing room. He went slowly, with a curious dignity.

The corner flags were small Union flags and, as Rattín walked by, he paused briefly and took the cloth between thumb and forefinger, rubbing it as though to test its quality. Four decades later, Rattín could not recall clearly what the gesture had been supposed to signify.[48] But there is a sense of poignancy and disgust, sadness even, that perhaps makes sense, given the popular stereotype of the British in Argentina – piratical colonialists, yes, but also dignified upholders of fair play. How, Rattín seems to have been asking, could *you* have cheated me? Did the Union flag mean nothing any more? (Rattín, in his defence, had been told by delegates from the shambolic Argentinian football association, quite wrongly, that captains could ask for a translator to help them talk to referees.)

From England's point of the view, the outrage was directed only one way. Argentina, Bobby said, had 'thoroughly debased the meaning of football'.[49] He and Jack both ended up booked, although such was the chaos it would be more than thirty years before either realised. The cautions seem to have been awarded during an incident in the second half during which Jack, challenging for a header, was pushed into the Argentina keeper Antonio Roma and fell to the ground, where he was kicked by an Argentinian who Bobby dragged away as a general fracas broke out.

It was a game characterised by melees and ill-temper. England committed more fouls; Argentina committed the worse ones and, according to various England players, indulged in frequent jostling, shirt-pulling, pinching, spitting and foot-stamping off the ball. Rattín, having already been cautioned, could have been sent off for an ugly lunge on Bobby before finally being dismissed by Kreitlein ten minutes before half-time, essentially it seemed because the West German got sick of him.

A Hurst header eventually gave England a 1–0 win, but that wasn't the end of it. After the final whistle, Harry Cavan, the Northern Irish FIFA delegate, was spat upon, while there are various reports afterwards of Argentina's players trying to break into the England dressing room, with Jack and Ray Wilson happy enough to take them on as others urged discretion. J. L. Manning, of course, was disgusted. 'This is an age,' he lamented, 'of poor taste, nasty smells and ugly sights.'[50]

In the end, there were two significant consequences. Most immediate was the fact that England were through. The longer lasting was Ramsey's ill-judged post-match interview in which he referred to Argentina has having played like 'animals' which, combined with the photograph of him preventing George Cohen from swapping shirts with Oscar Más, became long-lasting ammunition in England's culture war with South America. For his part, Bobby swapped shirts with the left-back Silvio Marzolini, who wore it for years as a pyjama top before sending it back to be exhibited by the National Football Museum.[51]

Ramsey was criticised for not having sent his team on the attack immediately after Rattín had been sent off, but he reasoned that a plan not to overcommit against deep-lying opponents was even more likely to work against ten men than eleven. Including extra time, he had eighty-five minutes to make the man advantage tell – as, eventually, it had. It may only have been 1–0, but in knockout football, as Ramsey had always made clear, progress mattered far more than the margin of victory. And at last that was a message that was beginning to get through to the media, even if they remained unsure about it. 'There is now only one team which can prevent England holding the World Cup for the next four years,' wrote Brian James in the *Mail*. 'That team is England. Since the 1966 tournament began the conviction has hardened. That this World Cup will not be won. It will be lost, lost by teams tempted into carelessness and punished for their blunders.'[52]

There was no space for frippery, only reliability and solidity: this was Ramsey's brutalist manifesto.

Bobby had suffered from fibrositis in his left shoulder for years, so it wasn't a great surprise when he woke the morning after the Argentina game with a stiff neck. FIFA had decided England should play their semi-final, against Portugal, at Wembley and he had three days to recover. (There are various wild conspiracy theories about this, but it was always clear in the tournament schedule that the semi-final likely to draw the bigger crowd would take place at Wembley on the Wednesday with the other being played at Goodison Park on the Tuesday).

Did Bobby watch the news that day or listen on the radio? By the time the papers were delivered the following day, he must have been aware of another sportsman killed in a plane crash: that Sunday the 1964 Open golf champion Tony Lema died as the Beechcraft Bonanza in which he was travelling ran out of fuel and crashed into a pond by the seventh green on the nine-hole course at the Lansing Sportsman's Club in Illinois. Did he make the link to another success in a major quarter-final eight years earlier? Perhaps not; he bore the memories every day and didn't need specific triggers to be thrust back into the tragedy, but it was probably as well the only travel England had to do was taking the bus around the North Circular.

Bobby's neck was still stiff on the Monday. He began to fret about whether he would have to withdraw. It was still tight when he woke up on the Tuesday. It may be that the issue was psychosomatic; at the very least, it gave his anxiety a focus. On the Wednesday, he could still feel it but as the afternoon wore on it loosened to the point that he was confident he could play.

Ramsey, it seems, had never had any doubts. The big question for him, at least as far as the media was concerned, was whether he should recall Greaves. Brian James was sure: 'Ramsey Must Gamble on Greaves', read the headline of his *Mail* piece arguing that, as Portugal were a decent football-ing side who would not sit deep and seek merely to frustrate England, there would be space for a slighter, more skilful for-ward to exploit.[53]

But Ramsey was unmoved. He fielded the same team that had beaten Argentina and was rewarded with a 2–1 win. A long ball from Wilson to Hunt had set up the first in the half-hour, the ball cannoning back off the Portugal keeper José Pereira to Bobby, twenty-two yards out. Confident in the roll of the Wembley turf, he was able to side-foot a finish between the retreating defenders.

It was another long pass from a full-back that brought the second with ten minutes remaining, Hurst latching on to Cohen's ball over the top and cutting it back for Bobby, coming in on the edge of the box to steer his shot, with the aid of a slight deflection, into the top corner. If it were still needed, here was validation of his role as a goal-scorer from deep.

Jack, having just about got the better of his aerial battle with José Torres, then conceded a penalty, flicking a header off the line with his hand – not a dismissal in those days. Eusébio con-verted, but England held on to reach the final. The following day, the *Mail*'s report was headed by a picture of Bobby, mouth just beginning to open in a wild grin, hugging Jack. More than anybody else, the semi-final was their triumph, although their father, characteristically, had refused to change his shift at the pit and missed all but the final minutes. Like Bobby, he always seemed unsettled by the fuss that surrounded his sons and could be snappish with anybody who tried to engage him in conversation about football, a game in which he never developed any real interest. Work and duty always came first; in that, Bobby was very much his son. When the BBC commentator David Coleman found out Bob Charlton had not seen the game, he had a tape sent to Ashington and video equipment installed in an office at the mine so he could watch it.

After all the negativity, there was a sense that, at last, a football match had broken out. 'This has been the rehabilitation of football,' said Jean Eskenazi of *France Soir*. 'It was everything you like in football when you want football played which is not a street battle.'[54]

The morning of the final, Bobby went to Golders Green with Ray Wilson to change a shirt. Wilson bought some shoes for that night's banquet and Bobby picked up a pair of cufflinks he intended to present to the Portugal winger José Augusto – although, as it turned out, they went missing and he was never able to hand them over. What's telling, of course, is not so much the specifics of what Bobby and Wilson bought as the fact they were able to go at all. It's hard to imagine a player of any country being able to wander round a clothes shop on the morning of a World Cup game these days, let alone the final.

For Bobby, the shopping helped prevent him dwelling on the occasion. The night before, the squad had gone to the local cinema to see *The Blue Max*, a film starring George Peppard, James Mason and Ursula Andress about a German fighter pilot. If Tony Lema's death hadn't made Bobby reflect about Munich, this certainly did. Duncan Edwards, he realised, would have been approaching his thirtieth birthday and in his prime.[55] Had he survived, Martin Peters or Nobby Stiles probably wouldn't have been in the side. Or, depending where

Edwards would have ended up as W-M became 4-4-2, perhaps Bobby Moore or Jack would have missed out.

Bobby was also stewing about the conversation he had had with Ramsey the previous day. Ramsey had watched footage of ten previous West Germany games and had realised that the key to stopping them was preventing Franz Beckenbauer, in those days a central midfielder in a 4-2-4, from being able to dictate play. He sat too deep for Stiles to pick him up, meaning Bobby had to do it, reining in his attacking instincts. 'If we win,' Bobby said, 'everything is justified ... But if the mind said "Yes," something in my bones wanted to say "No".'[56] It seems barely credible now that for Bobby this was even a debate, testament to just how strong that original vision of football was, and just how removed Ramsey's conception of the game was from that. Whatever doubts he had, Bobby did his job. Ramsey later criticised Bobby for having snatched at two shots, but at neutering Beckenbauer he couldn't be faulted.

The game itself exists now in the popular memory as a series of fragments. England's third and fourth goals in particular are part of the general consciousness, familiar to many who have little interest in football. But between those brushstrokes of glory, the match was oddly disjointed. There was a feeling that the West Germany keeper, Hans Tilkowski, was vulnerable to crosses and England clearly set out to target him. He had also damaged ribs in training a couple of days before the final; whether England were aware of that before kick-off is unclear, but his discomfort was obvious enough after his first clash with Hurst.

Yet it was West Germany who took a twelfth-minute lead, Helmut Haller capitalising after Wilson had failed to clear a Sigi Held cross. Jack and Banks both hesitated slightly, thinking the other would get there, as Haller's shot bisected them.

Within six minutes, though, England were level, Moore's free kick from the left finding Hurst unmarked to head in.

England had the better of it from then on and seemed to have won the game with twelve minutes remaining when Hurst's shot looped off Horst-Dieter Höttges and was slammed in by Peters who, to everybody's relief, arrived at the dropping ball just ahead of Jack. But in the final minute, Jack was harshly penalised in jumping for a header with Held, giving West Germany a free kick thirty yards out and slightly to the left. Lothar Emmerich took a long run and hammered the ball goalwards. It struck Cohen and fell for Held, who shot from the corner of the six-yard box. Jack lunged for it and missed, but Banks saved, the ball ricocheting back into the middle of the area where it bounced off Karl-Heinz Schnellinger's shoulder and fell for a stretching Wolfgang Weber to force it over the line. Jack was left on his knees, hands on hips: if only he had been able to react a fraction quicker to the deflection off Cohen, perhaps he might have blocked the second shot. It was a luckless goal to concede, one with a dreamlike quality such that no action could ever be taken quickly or decisively enough to avert the result. Twice England almost cleared and it may be that Schnellinger handled, but it didn't matter: West Germany were level and the game was going to extra time.

Jack and Moore fell to the turf in exhaustion, Jack furious about the free kick that had been given. But Ramsey had no time for self-pity. He insisted the players got to their feet: he wasn't going to have any of them looking tired, whereas many of the Germans were down, having their calves massaged. At which he issued perhaps the most famous team talk in the history of English football, a masterpiece of pithiness that belied his reputation for inarticulacy. 'You've won it once,' he said. 'Now go out and win it again.'

And they did. England were clearly much the fitter and created a string of chances. It now seems all but certain that

Hurst's second goal, England's third, did not cross the line after bouncing down off the bar, but those are details that cannot be controlled. From Ramsey's point of view, what was significant was the way the indefatigable Ball had been able to run into space behind Schnellinger, the full-back drawn forward as Stiles played a pass in behind him, before crossing for Hurst.

The fourth was perhaps less to his liking. With less than a minute remaining, Jack was urging Moore just to hack the ball out of play, to kill time, as the captain casually strode into space and measured a pass into the path of Hurst. He ran on and, conscious that if he were going to miss he needed to make sure Tilkowski could not easily retrieve the ball, thrashed a shot into the top corner: 4–2. England were world champions.

Gordon Charlton, the third brother, eight years younger than Jack, missed the final because he was at sea, working in the engine room of a ship. He learned England had won only when his shift ended and he found the captain capering in delight on deck.

Bob and Cissie Charlton were at Wembley. 'My proudest moment,' Cissie said, 'was when they both walked out of the tunnel together at Wembley – then Jack had reached Bobby's peak.'[57] It's an odd formulation, spoken probably six or seven years after the final, that manages to suggest that what made the occasion memorable was less that it was her boys playing in a World Cup final, than that Jack had, at last, got up to Bobby's level. Perhaps there's nothing in that – in the early days of television, baffling circumlocutory constructions were commonplace from non-professionals – but it does hint at how the family dynamic had changed.

Bobby himself became much more comfortable in front of a camera, but in the mid-sixties he was still very anxious. There is an excruciating clip of him getting off the bus at the team hotel that evening and being approached by a journalist who initially misidentifies him as Jack.

'How do you feel about today?' the journalist asks.

'You don't have to ask me, really, do you?' says Bobby, his tone immediately defensive.

'What did you think of the game itself?'

'Very, very hard and tough,' he says, almost over his shoulder, as he walks on by.[58]

'If England, perhaps, did not possess the greatest flair,' Geoffrey Green wrote in the *Times*, 'they were the best prepared in the field, with the best temperament based on a functional plan.'[59] That this was Ramsey's triumph was made clear by the headline of his match report: 'Ramsey Proved Right in World Cup'. In the moment, even his doubters, such as the Swiss journalist Maurice Simon, were forced to acknowledge his triumph. 'The only thing I can do,' Simon wrote in *La Tribune de Lausanne*, 'is to go barefoot wearing a hair shirt, together with some of my colleagues, will have to rub their foreheads in the dust before the new god the English have found for themselves – Ramsey.'[60]

'He has proved us wrong so many times it is an embarrassment to recall them,' wrote Michael Williams in the *Sunday Telegraph*. 'Stiles, we said, would never play ... Jack Charlton, too, we said was never good enough. Good enough? He has been one of the bastions of a great defence ... We said it was suicide not to play wingers ...'[61] What Ramsey had achieved, as Stephen Fay noted in a detailed piece in the *Sunday Times*, written with the help of the former West Ham and Manchester United full-back Noel Cantwell, was nothing less than the reinvention of English football after the 6–3 humiliation against Hungary in 1953.[62]

Central as Ramsey had been, he was also a product of his cultural environment. This was the age of such architecture as the Engineering Building at the University of Leicester (completed 1963), the *Economist* Building in Piccadilly (completed 1965) or the halls of residence at the University of East Anglia (completed 1966), and his England played in a similarly utilitarian style. His triumph was also a victory for the brutalist spirit that underlay much of the more radical aspects of English style of the sixties. 'The World Cup was won by a professional approach, by meticulous preparation and by a superlative team effort,' wrote Tony Pawson in the *Observer*, before noting the centrality of Jack to the success: 'This underrated man was the best centre-half in the competition – a formidable sweeper who could also attack.'[63]

At Wembley, fans delightedly waved Union flags which, symbolically at least, bound the World Cup into a much wider movement.* The previous year, the Who had begun wearing the Union flag and the red, white and blue target symbol of the RAF. The insignia rapidly became an emblem of pop art. There was a sense of irony behind it, an irreverence, but there was also a genuine mood of patriotism. 'Even outside the privileged enclaves of swinging London,' wrote the historian Dominic Sandbrook, 'wages were high, the economy seemed to be booming and every day brought new cultural triumphs.'[64] Mary Quant, for instance, was for a time in the early sixties the most fashionable designer in the world. The Bond film *Thunderball*, released in December 1965, was an astonishing success, easily the biggest grossing film of 1966, selling 60 million tickets in the US alone. Between 1964 and 1966, twenty-eight nominations at the Oscars went to British actors, from Julie Andrews to Richard Burton, Julie Christie to Peter O'Toole. The artist David Hockney and the photographer

---

* Thirty years later, England's progress to the semi-final of Euro 96 felt inextricably linked to another era of British cultural self-confidence, to Blur and Oasis, Danny Boyle and Damien Hirst. By then, though, the Union flag had yielded to the flag of St George.

David Bailey were globally feted, and that's before getting to the Beatles and the Rolling Stones. British culture was not just globally relevant but predominant.

On the weekend of the quarter-final win over Argentina, 'Sunny Afternoon' by the Kinks was displaced from No. 1 in the UK charts after a month but, as Sandbrook observed, it seemed perfectly to capture the mood: 'For many people, England's victory in the World Cup was the perfect ending to a hot, contented summer, stamped with the cultural self-confidence of swinging London.'[65]

The capital erupted in celebration. 'It's like VE Night, election night and New Year's Eve rolled into one,' said an AA spokesman.[66] That night there was a banquet for the players at the Royal Gardens hotel in Kensington, attended by the prime minister, Harold Wilson, but not by the players' wives and girlfriends, who were entertained elsewhere. An estimated six thousand fans gathered outside to welcome the squad.

After 11 p.m., the squad split up and celebrated separately. Bobby and Norma went with Moore, Wilson, Eastham and their wives to the Playboy Club, to which Moore had an invitation, returning to the hotel at around 4 a.m. Jack, desperate to spend the hundred pounds he had been given by Adidas for wearing their boots on getting drunk and alone because Pat was pregnant, left a back entrance to the hotel with the journalist James Mossop and jumped in the first taxi they saw. As it turned out, it was already occupied, by a violinist who had just finished giving a concert and had no idea about football. Once they'd dropped him off, they headed into the West End and started drinking at a club. Mossop described bottles of champagne being sent over and a mood of general celebration but it still all feels remarkably low-key compared to the tightly controlled functions at well-guarded hotels that tend to be how modern teams mark success. Jack and Mossop ended up sitting at a table with somebody called Lenny and his friends. They drank into the early hours before going back to Lenny's house in Leytonstone, where Jack slept on the settee.

The following morning, as he enjoyed a hungover breakfast in the garden, a woman popped her head over the fence to say hello. It was, bizarrely, Mrs Mather, a neighbour of his mother from Ashington, down in London visiting a friend. It was a homely coincidence that created a sense of the whole country coming together, but the significance of the detail perhaps is that such a coincidence was possible. That was a far more democratic age, one before footballers lived in their gilded bubble, in which it was possible for a middle-aged woman from a pit village to glance next door and see a world champion trying to eat his way through a hangover.

A couple of weeks later, just before the start of the new league season, Ashington held a celebration for the brothers, who were to be driven in an open Rolls-Royce from the family home on Beatrice Street to the town hall. Jack arrived early with the whole family, including Pat and their new baby, but as the time for them to set off drew closer there was no sign of Bobby. His mother, Cissie, began to fret that he might have decided to give the event a miss altogether, but he and Norma did turn up at the last, explaining that they'd come earlier but been so unnerved by the mass of people outside the house that they'd gone off and spent some time with one of Bobby's uncles.

Bobby remained uneasy. While Jack sat up on the back seat, grinning and waving, looking for mates in the crowd, Bobby seemed nervous and uncomfortable, as though he were trying to block out the mass of people. At the town hall, he gave a short, gracious but slightly cold speech, while Jack lapped up the attention, reflecting on their childhood and the spirit of the town.

Perhaps it was nothing more than the difference between an

extrovert and an introvert, and it was no secret that Bobby disliked crowds. But there were plenty, particularly in hindsight, willing to see Bobby's discomfort as the first public evidence of a cooling of his relationship with his immediate family and his home.

10

GRAIL

Perhaps it was never going to happen. Since Munich, Matt Busby had been sustained by the dream of winning the European Cup. That was the only way the dead could be honoured. That was the quest, the only way to achieve any sort of closure. But after defeat to Partizan in the European Cup semi-final in 1966, after the dashing of hopes raised – quite reasonably – by an extraordinary victory over Benfica in the quarter-final, everybody began to have doubts. 'I had reached the stage of thinking we were not meant to win this competition,' said Busby.[1]

United lay sixth in the league. Even though they had four games in hand, there was no way they were going to close the sixteen-point gap to the leaders Liverpool. Pat Crerand, who had spent much of the previous hour crying alone in the dressing room after being sent off, tried to console Busby, insisting that United would win the league the following season and the European Cup the year after that, but at that moment a two-year surge to glory seemed a distant prospect.[2] 'We believed,' Foulkes said, 'the team had peaked, and that it might have been our last chance.'[3]

The following Saturday, United lost to Everton in the FA Cup semi-final. Yet everything had seemed to be going so well.

*

Keep it tight early on, Matt Busby had said. Benfica had never
lost a European tie at the Estadio da Luz. The previous time
United had played in Lisbon, they'd lost 5–0 to Sporting,
reminders of which were offered by Benfica fans who hammered on the side of the United bus and raised five fingers as it
made its way to the stadium. They pointed at Best's long hair
and made snipping gestures. A few hours later, a lock of his
hair would have been worth a fortune.

United had won the first leg of the quarter-final 3–2, and
had been troubled not only by the explosive brilliance of
Eusébio but also by the height of the centre-forward Augusto
Torres. The plan was simple. Sit deep, try to restrict crossing
opportunities, let Foulkes handle Torres and Stiles handle
Eusébio and hope the second balls fell their way.

Just before kick-off, Pat Crerand, messing about with a ball,
smashed a mirror in the dressing room. There was a moment
of horrified silence. Everybody knew the superstition. Within
quarter of an hour of the game starting, that had been forgotten. But the workings of fate are rarely straightforward.

The popular version of the story has it that Best simply
ignored the instructions, went his own mesmerising way and
devastated Benfica. Even Busby followed that interpretation in
Soccer at the Top. Best headed in an early free kick, then seized
on David Herd's knockdown of a long kick from Gregg, shim-
mered past an almost laughably clumsy challenge and rolled
in a magnificent second. John Connelly added a third after
fourteen minutes and the game was as good as over. An own
goal from Brennan and late strikes from Crerand and Bobby
completed the 5–1 scoreline. Best was exceptional, but not
because he'd disobeyed instructions. On the contrary, Best and
Connelly had stayed behind the ball for the most part; what
made them lethal was the space they had to run into. Of all the
many accounts of that game, only Bill Foulkes makes the point
that sitting deep not only made United more solid defensively

but also added to their attacking threat.[4] Perhaps that's simply the nature of myth, that the story of Best's rebellious brilliance comes to overwhelm all else, but it does seem to fit with the more general sense that United in the sixties were not especially tactically aware.

Certainly, in the immediate aftermath, tactical considerations were swiftly submerged. United had a little time the next morning before they flew home. Best wandered out of the hotel at Estoril onto the beach. But he couldn't sunbathe as he'd intended. He could barely move for well-wishers, people asking for autographs, women asking for a lot more.

When he disembarked in Manchester, Best donned an oversized sombrero. Gregg tried to persuade him to take it off, but Best understood how a gimmick could enhance an image – and he had a new boutique to promote. The photograph appeared on the front pages, while a Portuguese headline describing him as the fifth Beatle was gleefully reported. Best's father, Dick, had begun his night shift at the Harland & Wolff shipyard in Belfast just as the match was kicking off. By the time he emerged the following morning, his son was a superstar in a way no footballer had ever been before.

This, perhaps, was the curse Pat Crerand had summoned.

United's immediate reaction to the win in Benfica, though, was profound relief and expectation. The defending champions Inter were probably the best side left in the tournament, with their *catenaccio* and the dark rumours about their capacity to manipulate referees; Real Madrid were formidable but not the side they had been a decade earlier; but United got what seemed the most straightforward draw, against the Yugoslav champions Partizan.

Straightforward in a football sense, that is. But, as Bobby said, 'It would have been impossible to come up with a match that carried any heavier load of emotion.'[5] It wasn't just a game in the same city that the Babes had played their final game, but on the same pitch. The day before the game, Vladica Popović, a half-back for Crvena Zvezda in 1958, visited United's hotel to meet the three survivors, Bobby, Bill Foulkes and Harry Gregg. 'I went to say I remembered playing against them and to wish them luck against our arch-rivals,' he said. 'I considered them as friends.'[6]

Busby, as ever, insisted they would play their usual game. 'Manchester United have never played for a draw and we will not start now!'[7] he said before kick-off but, with Best struggling with a knee injury, United never really got going and Partizan, having sized them up in the first half, outplayed them in the second, winning 2–0.

A comeback at Old Trafford still seemed possible, but Partizan defended with a mixture of diligence and violence. Stiles punched Ljubomir Mihajlović, provoking the brawl that led to Crerand and Jovan Miladinović being sent off. United dominated posses-sion, launched ball after ball into the Partizan box, but scored only once, when the Partizan keeper Milutin Šoškić, misreading Fahrudin Jusufi's decision to leave the ball, fumbled a Nobby Stiles effort over his own line. 'It was practically a game of one goal and for ninety minutes Manchester United were attacking it, crossing, crossing, shooting,' said Šoškić, who rated his per-formance at Old Trafford the best of his career.[8]

Bobby spoke of 'a wave of doubt and depression.'[9] Were United simply fated never to win the tournament? But amid all the soul-searching, nobody within the club seems to have made the point that Šoškić did – that United were playing the football of the past. 'My perception,' he said, 'is that Manchester were a hundred per cent the better team, but for such a good team they played quite foolishly. All the time they persisted with high balls. [Velibor] Vasović and [Branko] Rašović and me, we quite easily picked up those balls ... I couldn't understand how a team could keep playing in such a way. They had the players available to play in a different way. They were a very strong team, a very good team and if they'd played another way I think they would have scored five or six goals. Even in Belgrade, United could have won.'[10]

Busby wasn't sure he could commit to the minimum of two more years it would take for continental glory. He wanted, more than anything, to win the European Cup, but the thought of having to lift a fifth league title to get there was almost too much. He seriously contemplated retirement. 'I was fed up,' he said, 'but driving along I stopped at the crossing near the blind school. There I witnessed seven little children with sticks being led across the road. I just sat in the car and thought, Matt, what problems have you got? You've got no problems compared to these poor kids. At that moment I thought one more go. Just one more go!'[11]

Bill Shankly, the Liverpool manager, liked to build confidence in his side before matches by going through the opposition, pointing out the flaws in each player.

'It's a disgrace they're even allowed on the same pitch as us,' he supposedly raged before one game against United at Anfield. 'Pat Dunne is useless in goal. Brennan gets blown over by the wind. Foulkes just kicks it anywhere. Tony Dunne only has one foot. Crerand would lose a race to a tortoise. Herd can belt it but never knows which way he's facing ...'

At which the winger Ian Callaghan interjected, 'What about Charlton, Best and Law?'

'I hope you're not telling me, Callaghan, that we cannot beat three men.'

The journey to that glory began in the summer of 1966. Busby at last accepted – in the wake of the defeat to Partizan and a slightly disappointing domestic campaign – that there was a need to tighten up at the back. Increasingly, Stiles dropped in as a de facto central defender alongside Foulkes and, in September, the goalkeeper Alex Stepney was signed from Chelsea for £55,000. United only suffered three defeats that season after his arrival and, having lost to Sheffield United on Boxing Day, went unbeaten for the remainder of the season. Bobby was third leading scorer with twelve goals but just as significant was that, in total, United conceded forty-five goals, fourteen fewer than the previous season, and fourteen of those had come in the seven games before Stepney arrived.

It was mid-March when United broke from the pack, winning 5–2 at Leicester as Liverpool, who had been level on points, lost at Burnley. Bobby had scored and Law beat Banks with a deft chip, but David Herd, having got the opener, broke his leg. He never played for United again, a reminder of just how precarious the career of a footballer could be. David Sadler, having turned twenty-one the previous month, came on for him and scored the fifth, but given what happened subsequently, there is a sense that Herd was never adequately replaced.

Sadler was a versatile player, but was naturally a centre-back. Nevertheless, the following week he started up front, alongside Law against Liverpool. Stepney made one excellent save from Callaghan, but that aside United, demonstrating their newfound resolve, held Liverpool at arm's length and drew 0–0 – a point 'earned and won by the defence,' as the report in the *People* had it[12] – to maintain their advantage. The title, Bobby's third, was sealed on the penultimate weekend of the season with a 6–1 win at West Ham. Brilliant as United were in that game, scoring four in the opening twenty minutes, the afternoon was soured by the fighting that swirled around the terraces at Upton Park; a return to those prelapsarian days of 1957 this was not.

The following season began at a similar pace. As well as seeing off Hibernians of Malta and FK Sarajevo in the European Cup, United lost just three of their first twenty-seven league fixtures and, at the beginning of February 1968, stood three points clear of Leeds with a game in hand. But as injuries and fatigue began to bite, the season threatened to fall apart. United went out of the Cup to Spurs then lost five games out of eight in the league. They edged by Górnik Zabrze in the European Cup quarter-final but when they beat Real Madrid 1–0 in the home leg of the semi-final, the consensus was it would not be enough.

Defeat at home to Sunderland on the final day allowed Manchester City to pinch the league title. A season that had begun with huge promise was suddenly one game in the Bernabéu from ending with nothing. Nobody said it, but everybody knew: for the European quest, this was it. They didn't have the energy to reset for another two-year campaign.

The second leg began dreadfully. United's advantage was extinguished just after the half-hour by a near-post header from Pirri. Within ten more minutes, Madrid had the lead and, from United's point of view, it was a horrible goal to concede. Shay Brennan, under no pressure, missed a simple ball, allowing Paco Gento to get away down the left. He then drilled in a shot via the shin of a retreating Stepney. Not that the goal that got United back into the game was any better, Ignacio Zoco hopelessly slicing a Dunne cross into his own net. Before half-time, though, an Amancio snap-shot had restored Madrid's aggregate lead.

Busby said he felt 'sick'.[13] 'The old man was speechless,' said Bobby. 'I'd never known him speechless before. Even Jimmy said nothing. We were gutted.'[14] The players 'had their heads between their legs'.[15] It wasn't just that they were behind, in a frenzied stadium against the most successful side in European history. It was that they were, to a large degree, responsible for the scoreline. A near-post free kick, two schoolyard gaffes and a failure to clear a cross: this was self-inflicted damage. In the gloom, Busby found the perfect words, pointing out

United only needed one goal to force a replay.* Others, Bobby among them, felt just as significant had been an incident before Madrid's third. Stiles, having been kicked by Amancio and, struggling as the muscle tightened, took the law into his own hands and delivered a crunching right hook to the winger's jaw. A rattled Amancio was far less influential in the second half.

Various United players suggest Madrid thought the game was done, that there was a 'cockiness'[16] to them in the second half. If there was, they had underestimated United's resilience, the sense they had that if destiny was with them it had to be now. The equaliser came with seventeen minutes remaining as Best flicked on Crerand's free kick for Sadler to bundle in at the back post.

And then, five minutes later, came a scarcely credible winner. That Bill Foulkes was even playing was extraordinary. On New Year's Day, he'd been observing a training session in the gym as he prepared for a move into coaching when some horseplay led to Brian Kidd falling into him. The collision caused cruciate ligament damage and kept Foulkes out for four months, including the home leg of the semi-final. In that crucial game against Sunderland on the final day of the league season, four days before the match in the Bernabéu, he had to be taken off in the second half. He was thirty-six, and nowhere near fully fit. That he was in the box was more remarkable still. There was no reason for a centre-half to go forward like that, nor was it the sort of indulgence Foulkes usually permitted himself. 'Something prompted me to advance,' he said. 'I could offer no rational explanation.'[17]

It was Foulkes who was there at the top of the box to receive the cutback after Best, beating two men, had darted in from the right. In the distant past, when Foulkes had trained part-time

---

* The away goals rule had been introduced for the European Cup for the first time this season, but only for the first round. A provisional date had been set for a play-off in Lisbon the following Friday.

at United while still working shifts at the pit in St Helen's, he had played a few games at centre-forward but that was a long time ago: he had scored only eight goals in his sixteen years as a footballer. Bobby admitted his heart sank when he saw who it was moving on to the pass, expecting him to blaze it over. He didn't. Rather Foulkes stroked his shot almost casually into the far corner, an implausibly deft finish for such a big man. To point out that this too, this moment of ecstasy, was not part of some coordinated tactical plan but the result of inspired improvisation may seem churlish, but it is nonetheless true.

Busby called it United's 'greatest night', while Bobby, weeping, could find no words for his emotion.[18] At the final whistle, he had fallen, exhausted, to the turf. He felt the job was done, that the European Cup would finally be United's. Later, drained and dehydrated, he lay on his bed in the hotel, unable to join the celebrations.

Benfica remained to be beaten. They were, but it was a desperately close-run thing. On a hot, sticky evening at Wembley, neither side played well. Bobby got the opener eight minutes after half-time. He had intended his run across the near post to be a decoy with Best and Kidd behind him, but Sadler's cross dipped perfectly for him, and he scored with a well-placed glancing header. But Jaime Graça levelled with eleven minutes remaining and six minutes later came the decisive moment.

Bobby was lured into trying to dispossess António Simões in midfield and when, stretching, he lost out in the challenge, he turned in horror to see Eusébio clean through, bearing down on goal. 'Not again,' he said to himself,[19] the same words Busby muttered on the bench. For a moment, the game, all United's dreams, came down to that most elemental contest: striker against keeper. All anybody else – Bobby, Busby, the other players, the ninety-two thousand fans at Wembley, the millions listening on the radio or watching on television – could do was wait. Stepney stood tall and Eusébio flinched. The ball was bouncing, but he had time to place his shot. He didn't. He hit it as hard as he could and it flew, with some force, straight into the midriff of the keeper. United survived and in that moment Benfica were broken.

Like the World Cup final on the same ground two years earlier, the game went to extra time. Just as had happened two years earlier, Bobby's manager pointed at their opponents as they lay sprawled on the turf; he insisted the other team were exhausted. 'If you pass the ball to each other,' Busby said, 'you'll beat them.'[20] A simple instruction, simplistic even, but it worked. Just as had happened two years earlier, Bobby's side ended up scoring four.

Two minutes into extra time, Kidd touched on a long clearance by Sadler, Best ran clear, rounded the keeper José Henrique and rolled the ball in, a goal similar in construction to his second away against the same opposition two years earlier.

Two minutes later, Kidd, on his nineteenth birthday, headed a third, looping the rebound over Henrique after the keeper had saved his initial effort from a corner.

And five minutes after that, Bobby released Kidd down the right and continued his run into the box. Kidd beat the left-back Fernando Cruz and pulled the ball back for Bobby to sweep the ball across goal and in at the far post.

At last, it was over.

When the final whistle went, Bobby's immediate reaction was fatigue. Just as had happened two years earlier, he felt neither great euphoria nor any real sense of fulfilment. He just felt tired. It had been a humid night and he had run himself into the ground. Even after the fourth goal, the game had been won,

Benfica had been beaten and the title had been secured, the sense had been not of glory but of having to drag weary limbs over the line. 'There was an understanding,' said Bobby, 'that something was over, something which had dominated our lives for so long.'[21]

That final was the culmination of one of the greatest stories in sporting history and yet it's remarkable how many people involved that night had a sense that something was awry. Bobby's first thought was to congratulate Matt Busby but, by the time he got to his manager, he was already surrounded, by other players, by coaches, by directors, by hangers-on. His instinct was protective – 'He really was, I felt, an old man'[22] – and he began pulling people away, something he later regretted, worrying characteristically about how impolite he must have seemed. Eventually, he got through and hugged his manager, before making his way to the dressing room. He was handed a beer and downed it, then sank another one.

He soon wished he hadn't. He felt terrible and, when he got to his room at the Russell hotel, he fainted. He had felt something similar after the semi-final, but this was worse, a debilitating combination of dehydration and emotional exhaustion. Three times he tried to get up from his bed to go downstairs to join the celebrations and three times he collapsed before reaching the door.

In the end, Norma went to the dinner alone. 'It's all been a bit too much for Bobby,' she told the other guests. 'He is just too tired physically and emotionally to face up to all this. He couldn't take it, with complete strangers coming up and slapping him on the back and telling him what a wonderful night it is ... he's remembering the lads who can't be here tonight.'[23]

In the early hours of the morning, Busby clambered onto a table and to the backing of the Joe Loss Orchestra sang, 'What a Wonderful World'. For him it was a moment of vindication. Nothing could bring back the dead of Munich, of course, but at least he had done due honour to their memory. In his moments of darkest doubt, the thought that *they* would have wanted him to go on had been a powerful motivation and reassurance. *They* would have wanted United to win the European Cup and now *they* had been satisfied.

Bobby wasn't the only one who wasn't there; George Best might have scored a sublime goal, but what he later described as 'the greatest night of my football life' was also 'one of the most unsatisfying'. He had been kicked incessantly by the full-back Fernando Cruz but had kept going back for more, his relentlessness helping create the space for John Aston to have the game of his life on the opposite flank. But that wasn't enough for Best who, by then, felt he needed to be the key presence in any game he played. Amid the laughter and the celebrations, he felt a profound sense that he 'didn't belong'. And so he left.

After the preliminaries, he returned to his room, packed away his medal, got changed and took a taxi to a flat in Chelsea belonging to the scriptwriter Jackie Glass, his girlfriend at the time. And then, for the first time in his life, he got properly drunk, drunk to the point of blacking out, so drunk he had no memory of the game. 'It *should* have been the start of something wonderful and beautiful,' he said. Instead, he later acknowledged, 'It was the beginning of the end.'24

11

SUCCESS AND SUPERSTITION

Second in the league and runners-up in the FA Cup in 1964–65, a first trophy was surely just around the corner for Revie's Leeds. They went out of the FA Cup in the fourth round to Chelsea. But the Fairs Cup, Leeds United's first experience of European competition, still offered a realistic chance of glory.

It had already been a tournament that had taken its toll. In the first round, against Torino, as Leeds wore unfamiliar numbers to confuse their opponents, Collins had his thigh bone broken by a foul from Fabrizio Poletti. Leeds had lost only two of their opening fourteen games at that point and, although the decision to shift Giles into the centre to partner Bremner eventually proved beneficial, the wobble that initially prompted it – three wins from seven league games – was enough to lose significant ground in the title race. Leeds came second, six points behind Shankly's remorseless Liverpool.

Then, having seen off SC Leipzig, Leeds faced Valencia in the third round in February 1966. Violence bubbled below the surface of the first leg at Elland Road and erupted when the Valencia defender Francisco Vidagany kicked Jack on the ankle. Jack retaliated, only to be intercepted by a punch from the goalkeeper Ñito. As Jack turned his attentions to him, Ñito backed off, high-kicking, eventually leaping into West Stand paddock to avoid the confrontation. As a mass brawl broke out, police intervened and the experienced Dutch referee Leo Horn took the players off, eventually dismissing Jack and Vidagany before restarting the game. An FA inquiry ended up fining Jack twenty pounds. The game itself finished 1–1 but a Mike Grady goal at the Mestalla took Leeds through.

Újpest Dózsa were beaten in the quarter-final, setting up the semi-final against Zaragoza. A 1–0 defeat and a 2–1 win, in which Jack got the winner, meant a replay. Jack scored again, but Leeds lost 3–1.

A poor start – just three wins from the first eleven games – effectively ended any hope of a title challenge in 1966–67 and Leeds finished fourth.

The FA Cup, though, generated great excitement. In the fifth round, Jack had equalised away at Sunderland to force a replay for which so many turned out that the gates had to be shut twenty-three minutes before kick-off. Fans lined the roof of the Scratching Shed and when a crush barrier collapsed after ten minutes, eighteen people required hospital attention. That game was also drawn, but Leeds came through a feisty second replay in which Sunderland had two men sent off. Jack scored the winner in a hard-fought quarter-final against Manchester City, but he missed the semi-final through injury. Chelsea won 1–0 as Peter Lorimer had what had appeared to be a free-kick equaliser ruled out because the referee had not signalled for it to be taken.

Again, hopes of a trophy came down to the Fairs Cup. There was a far more comfortable victory over Valencia and a sense that luck was perhaps turning as Bologna were beaten on the toss of a coin in the last eight. Kilmarnock were despatched in the semi-final, but familiar misfortune was waiting before the final, against Dinamo Zagreb. A flight cancellation meant Syd Owen was unable to get to Yugoslavia to scout their opponents, which perhaps contributed to a 2–0 defeat in the first leg. Back at Elland Road, Leeds could only draw 0–0, leading to criticism that they were overly negative. 'I don't think Don ever really believed until the last couple of years what a great team he had,' said Peter Lorimer. 'He could be quite negative, probably because he hated losing so much.'[1]

For Jack, though, there was a personal triumph, as he followed Bobby in being named footballer of the year by the Football Writers' Association (FWA), a decision that seems to have been greeted with bewilderment at Leeds. 'Not only was Jack not the best player in England that season,' said John Giles, 'he was far from being the best player at Leeds, and, in truth, he was one of the worst.'[2] For years afterwards at Leeds, the worst player in training would be given a yellow shirt to wear and named 'footballer of the year'.

The banter, though, should not deflect from what an important player Jack was. 'He was like a policeman on duty,' said Norman Hunter. 'He would be standing there in the middle ... waving his arms about, telling us what to do.'[3]

Jack had been anxious before the FWA dinner about having to give a speech but, once he started, he found it came naturally. He found his audience gripped by his anecdotes and laughing along with him. Public speaking soon became another money-making avenue.

Why did it keep going wrong? How could a side keep on getting that close only to falter at the last? Revie was meticulous. He left as little as possible to chance and yet chance kept going against him. Towards the end of the 1966–67 season, he received a letter telling him that Elland Road was built on the site of a traveller encampment and that, as they'd been forcibly moved on during construction, they had cursed the club. Others might have been sceptical, but Revie had the example of the 1956 FA Cup final, when he'd played superbly after touching the pieces of wood he'd been given by a Roma woman; he was already predisposed to believe in the power of 'gypsy magic'. But he was not somebody to rush precipitously into action and took the letter to the local vicar. Reverend Jackson had vague recollections of having heard something similar: the land – named the Old Peacock Ground after a nearby pub – had been owned by Bentley's brewery and he thought there had been a camp there before Holbeck Rugby Club bought the site and began to develop the area.

Revie turned to Laura Lee, a Roma woman based in Blackpool. When the *Yorkshire Evening Post* tracked her down in 1971 – by which time she was forty and living in a caravan on a farm near Scarborough – she said she'd been doing readings for Revie for two years.[4] Confidentiality prevented her revealing exactly what she had done, but there were evidently areas into which Syd Owen and Maurice Lindsey's dossiers could not reach.

Revie invited Laura Lee to Elland Road that summer. 'There was,' she said, 'the smell of a curse – and curses do have smells – in the dressing rooms at Elland Road, and obviously something was wrong.' She had Revie clear the ground and then lock all the doors and gates so that only the two of them remained, then walked to all four corners and the centre-circle, scattering seeds and 'other things I can't reveal'.

It was simultaneously very strange and yet totally in keeping with Revie, who was always a deeply contradictory figure. On the one hand he was the epitome of northern English solidity, a big man averse to extremes of emotion who projected an air of authority; and yet he was also deeply insecure. Nobody in the English game at the time prepared so thoroughly for games and yet he seems always to have been haunted by the fear it would not be enough.*

Training at Leeds was rigorous, innovative and regularly tweaked to adapt to specific opponents. The night before games players would stay in comfortable hotels, partly to try to ensure they arrived relaxed for matches and partly so Revie could keep an eye on them. There were the infamous dossiers but also meetings after matches in which players were encouraged openly to critique each other's performances. But none of that was enough. He was also, by his own description, 'probably the most superstitious person in the world'.[5]

When he had been very young, Revie remembered, he had been walking to the shops in Middlesbrough with his mother when their way had been blocked by a man up a ladder painting his windows. The young Revie ran ahead only to be called back by his mother and made to step off the pavement and walk around: you didn't, he was told sharply, ever walk under a ladder because that brought bad luck. By the time he was a manager, Revie had accumulated an array of superstitions. Each year he had a blue mohair suit made and wore it for every game, even when it began to wear through. He had a lucky tie. He carried charms in his pockets. He always sat in the same seat on the team bus and in the hotel restaurant. Once he'd set off for the ground, he never turned back, even if that meant sending somebody to collect something essential he'd left behind. After

---

* In that there is a curious echo of Marcelo Bielsa, Leeds manager from 2018 to 2022, who, in January 2019, having provoked a furore by sending a club employee to watch Frank Lampard's Derby train, gave an extraordinary press conference in which he acknowledged that a lot of the work he did analysing opponents was largely useless but helped assuage his sense of guilt. 'All the information I need to clarify [my tactics] I gather without watching the training session of the opponent ...' he explained, 'but we feel guilty if we don't work enough. Watching it [the opponents training] allows us to have less anxiety and, in my case, I am stupid enough to allow this kind of behaviour.'

he'd checked into a hotel, he would always walk to the nearest lamp-post and back. He hated ornamental elephants and was so uncomfortable about images of birds that he had Leeds take the owls off their badge and drop their traditional nickname of the 'Peacocks' (taken from the pubs, the Old Peacock and the New Peacock, that used to stand near Elland Road).

He imposed his superstitions on others. For five years he insisted his wife Elsie should wear the same fur-lined suede coat to games. He made the players put on their left boot first and, as far as possible, replicate any actions or gestures that had preceded a successful performance: if somebody tossed a ball to somebody else just before they left the dressing room and Leeds won that day, he would have them do it again the following week.

The players picked up the mood. Jack obediently always put his left boot on before his right, but with the additional twist that only then would he put on his jockstrap and his shorts. He would then take the programme to the toilet and leave it on the left side of the bowl. Only as the players left for the tunnel would he put his shirt on. He liked to be last out, which was why he shunned the captaincy and came into conflict with Revie's preference for his players to follow in shirt number order after the captain.

And yet the more Revie tried to control every aspect of preparation and the game, natural and supernatural, the more it came to seem that the fates had conspired to thwart him.

Other than seeking to lift the curse, Revie's other significant act in 1967 was to sign the centre-forward Mick Jones from Sheffield United for a hundred thousand pounds, partly because Alan Peacock continued to struggle with injury and partly because the previous season only Giles had managed to get into double figures for goals scored.

After a slow start to the season, in which they won just one of their opening five games, Leeds improved rapidly. By the end of February, they were second in the table, a point behind Manchester United, having played a game more. They were also in the final of the League Cup, the fifth round of the FA Cup and the fourth round of the Fairs Cup.

Yet for all Revie's meticulousness, a crucial element in Leeds's transition to success came about by chance. Messing about after England training at Roehampton one day, Jack, Bobby and Jimmy Greaves took to practising crossing. One of them would go in goal, one would swing in a cross and the other would try to head it in. When it came to Bobby's turn to go in goal, Jack, knowing that Bobby fancied himself as a keeper, decided to annoy him by standing right in front of him as Greaves whipped in inswingers. Again and again, Jack nudged the ball into the net. Bobby became increasingly irritated but found that against somebody of Jack's height, there was nothing he could do if the cross was good enough.

Jack, always alert to new possibilities, went back to Leeds and told Revie. At the next training session, without briefing the goalkeeper Gary Sprake, Revie had Lorimer and Gray bend in crosses to Jack at the near post. Sometimes he scored, sometimes he flicked it on; either way, Sprake was helpless and became so frustrated that he threw a punch at Jack. Revie knew he was on to something.

Near-post corners became a Leeds trait. Opponents struggled to cope. If they put two or even three men on Jack, they just got in the goalkeeper's way, but leaving him untended, and relying on the goalkeeper to get to the ball in front of him, was a risk. The Everton keeper Gordon West decided to start at his back post and take Jack out if the ball was delivered towards him. There was a sense that somehow what Leeds were doing wasn't quite on, that this was another aspect of their wider nefariousness, although quite what was wrong with it nobody was able to articulate.

As it turned out, the innovation was critical to ending the

curse, as Leeds faced Arsenal in the 1968 League Cup final. Eighteen minutes in, Eddie Gray swung a right-wing corner in towards Jack at the near post. As Paul Madeley, replacing the cup-tied Mick Jones at centre-forward, also challenged, the Arsenal keeper Jim Furnell missed the cross, forcing George Graham to clear off the line. On each of the three previous nights, the full-back Terry Cooper had dreamed of scoring the winner; when the ball fell to him, eight yards out, he smashed a volley cleanly through a gaggle of players.

Arsenal protested that Furnell had been fouled, and Pathé* showed an angle from behind the goal, pausing the action with Madeley's left arm in contact with the keeper's face. But still images can be deceptive. Madeley's arm is low, certainly not thrust into the keeper, and Furnell is already on his way down, having been brushed off by Jack. That said, Madeley has jumped towards the keeper and his knee clatters into his hip. Today, given the protection keepers are afforded, the goal almost certainly would be ruled out; back then, the case was far less clear-cut.

Arsenal's frustration that the goal stood contributed to the niggles into which the game soon descended, with Leeds content to sit on their lead. It had been, the Pathé voiceover observed, 'One of the most unglamorous soccer matches ever witnessed on the perfect turf of the famous stadium.'[6] A challenge by Frank McLintock on Sprake sparked a multi-player fracas just before half-time and the threat of violence simmered throughout. But Leeds didn't care, as they held on to win the first trophy in their history.

'From that day on teams started to fear us,' said Eddie Gray. 'Once you have lifted a major trophy the way others look at you

---

* Alan Hardaker, the secretary of the Football League, opposed television broadcasts, believing they would result in lower match attendances, from which the bulk of revenues were in those days derived; early League Cup finals were not shown live.

changes. We felt more confident to kick on, too. The success
that followed all came from that League Cup win. The club
had been so close in the past but, finally, we had a trophy. Any
burden felt by the club had been lifted.'[7]

Traces of the curse, though, lingered. Leeds went top of the
table and beat Bristol City and Sheffield United to reach the
FA Cup quarter-final. Rangers were seen off in the quarter-
final of the Fairs Cup. The possibility was there for a season of
extraordinary success. But that was their undoing. The fixtures
piled up. Exhaustion set in. Leeds lost to Everton in the Cup
semi-final, the winner the result of a Gary Sprake error. They
lost their last four games of the league season to slip from first
to fourth. They beat Dundee in the Fairs Cup semi-final, but
with Jack and Norman Hunter called up to play for England
in the European Championship quarter-final, the final ended
up being pushed back to August. The sense in mid-May, even
after a first trophy, was of weariness and anti-climax.

As it turned out the Fairs Cup was the beginning of perhaps
Leeds's greatest season. By the time they beat Ferencváros in
the 1967–68 Fairs Cup final to lift their first European trophy,
Leeds had played seven league games of 1968–69 and dropped
just one point. Jack and Billy Bremner settled into a routine,
going to their local every Thursday and having a couple of pints
while they played dominoes. Television meant that footballers
had begun to be recognised when out and about, but most were
still a long way from being celebrities in the modern sense.

Although they lost twice in October, they then embarked
on a twenty-six-game unbeaten run to the end of the season,
winning the league with a record points total. Just nine goals
were conceded at Elland Road. It helped perhaps that, for once,
Leeds had gone out of the League Cup and the FA Cup early.

*

Defeat finally came to Everton on the final Saturday of August 1969, ending a record run of thirty-four games unbeaten. Revie had spoken at the beginning of the season of targeting the 'triple' and they came extraordinarily close. Chelsea beat them in an FA Cup final replay. Leeds had led the league at the beginning of March, only to fall away as fatigue took its toll, winning just one of their final six games to finish nine points behind Everton. In total Leeds played sixty-two games that season, with eight players making fifty or more appearances.

On Easter Monday, two days before the first leg of the European Cup semi-final against Celtic, Leeds went to Derby and rested a number of players, losing 4–1. It didn't help; Leeds lost the first leg 1–0, beaten by a deflected George Connelly shot that dribbled over the line in the opening minute. They were subsequently fined five thousand pounds by the league for not fielding their strongest side.

The Cup final, against Chelsea, was a notoriously brutal game, played on a dreadful pitch that had been churned up by the Horse of the Year show held at Wembley a week earlier. Jack put Leeds ahead with a trademark header from a near-post corner, but another Sprake error gave Chelsea an equaliser. Mick Jones looked to have won it with six minutes remaining, but Ian Hutchison equalised two minutes later and the game went to a replay at Old Trafford.

Four days later, Leeds went to Glasgow for the second leg of the European Cup semi-final, a game that drew a British record crowd of 136,000. Despite taking the lead with a brilliant goal from Bremner, Leeds lost 2–1.

Still, there remained the Cup final replay. After the drama of the first game, the second drew what was at the time the sixth-highest television audience in British history. If it was the prospect of violence that had drawn them, they were not disappointed: in 1997 the referee David Elleray said he would have shown six red cards in the game; in 2020 the referee Michael

Oliver suggested eleven. The referee on the night, Eric Jennings, restricted himself to a single yellow. Jack, remarkably, stayed on the pitch after flooring Peter Osgood in retaliation for a late challenge. Crucially, Chelsea switched Ron Harris and Dave Webb, so the notorious hard man could take care of Eddie Gray, who had tormented Webb at Wembley. Harris scythed him down early and Gray was nowhere near his best. Again, Leeds took the lead and again they were pegged back, before Webb's extra-time header gave Chelsea victory.

It was another season of agonisingly near misses.

Jack liked money. He had never hidden the fact. He wasn't flash with it, far from it, but even as a child he had his schemes. He set up a souvenir shop at Elland Road, Pat running it until the club decided it was lucrative enough to buy. But that was just the first of many ideas. Bizarrely, given how unkempt his general appearance was, he would buy cloth from a mill in Bradford and sell it at away matches to opposing players for bespoke suits. His connections led to him working for Maple Clothes in Leeds, becoming a director in 1973.

Leeds began 1970–71 superbly but Arsenal had closed within two points when West Brom went to Elland Road in the middle of April, having won none of their previous sixteen away games. West Brom led at half-time before Hunter's misplaced pass hit Tony Brown and ricocheted forwards towards Colin Suggett. The linesman, Bill Troupe, flagged and everybody stopped. But then, as Suggett stepped out of the way and referee Ray Tinkler allowed play to continue, Brown ran on, surged forward and squared for Jeff Astle to roll in. 'Leeds will go mad,' said the commentator Barry Davies, 'and they have every right to go mad.' Players protested, a missile struck the other linesman, Colin Cartlich, and fans invaded the pitch, only being dispersed by police. The goal stood. 'He was in an offside position and the linesman flagged,' Tinkler explained, 'but he was not interfering with play. So no offence was committed and I could let play go on.'[8] Allan Clarke pulled one back, but the game, and top spot, was lost.

Some hope was restored on the penultimate weekend of the league season as Jack headed the winner against Arsenal, the goal standing despite the fact he was offside. Leeds beat Nottingham Forest and Arsenal beat Stoke on the final weekend, but Arsenal still had one game to play, away at Tottenham. A draw would have handed Leeds the title, but Ray Kennedy's goal gave Arsenal a 1–0 win and the championship. A second Fairs Cup, claimed with an away goals victory over Juventus in the final, was meagre consolation.

On the way to the 1972 FA Cup final, the Leeds team coach passed a bride going to a wedding. Having been the bridesmaid so often, Revie took it as a good omen – and it was, at least in terms of that game. In the league, though, it was a familiar story.

As punishment for the Tinkler incident, Elland Road was closed for four games and Leeds were fined five hundred pounds while being ordered to pay the away sides compensation for the loss of revenue.* Leeds nevertheless started the season superbly. They lost just one of their first seven matches and, after returning to Elland Road, dropped only three points there all season. There was a conscious effort to improve their PR and a link with Paul Trevillion, a thirty-eight-year-old illustrator known for *Roy of the Rovers*. He designed numbered sock tags for the players which were then thrown into the

---

* At this time, 25 per cent of gate receipts went to the away side.

crowd along with souvenir footballs before kick-off, while the players warmed up in personalised tracksuit tops. It may not have been the most glitzy or insidious form of marketing, but it was a very long way from the ramshackle club Jack had joined.

That season, Leeds played some stunning football. They beat Manchester United 5–1, Nottingham Forest 6–1 and Southampton 7–0 – the game that featured the famous thirty-pass move described as 'almost cruel' by Barry Davies in commentary. Jack was the only Leeds player not to touch the ball and afterwards he was furious.

'Why didn't you pass to me?' he demanded.

'Because,' Giles replied, 'we wanted to keep it.'[9]

But brilliant as the football was, it prompted one obvious question: what if Revie had released the handbrake earlier? Had they shown that attacking intent in the previous half a dozen seasons, might more chances have been taken, might their story have been one of perpetual success rather than regular frustration?

When Leeds beat Birmingham 3–0 in the FA Cup semi-final, they were again on course for the double, fourth in the league table but just three points behind leaders Derby with two games in hand. But fatigue, again, was lurking. The following Wednesday, Leeds lost at Newcastle but beat West Brom and Chelsea, leaving them with one game left to play after the Cup final, against Wolves. They trailed Derby, who had finished their season, by a point and although Liverpool, who faced Arsenal, were a point further back, their goal average was such that a draw would guarantee the title.

Eight minutes after half-time in the centenary Cup final, Jack intercepted an Alan Ball pass and found Paul Madeley. He fed Peter Lorimer, who spread the ball right to Mick Jones and his cross was met by a plunging header from Allan Clarke. One goal was enough and, for the first time, Leeds were Cup winners.

But the attempt to complete the double, on Jack's thirty-seventh birthday, ended in frustration. Leeds had three strong penalty appeals turned down. Still weary from the Cup final, they fell behind just before half-time and conceded a second midway through the second half, losing 2–1. Liverpool were held 0–0 by Arsenal, meaning Brian Clough's Derby, gathered around a phone in a hotel lobby in Mallorca, were champions. For the fifth time in eight seasons, Leeds finished as runners-up in the league. A reception had been arranged at the Queen's hotel for the squad on their return from Wolverhampton to celebrate the season, but the feeling was one of desolation. Only Giles and Lorimer went in for a drink.

There would be one more league title under Revie, in 1974, but by then Jack was gone. His final season as a player followed a very familiar pattern: third in the table, with defeats in the FA Cup final to Second Division Sunderland and, amid more refereeing controversy, in the Cup Winners' Cup final to AC Milan. Jack, suffering a hamstring injury, played in neither match.

Perhaps Leeds would have won more had Revie not been so focused on the fear of defeat but, ultimately, the reason they slipped up so often late in the season was probably that they were too good for their era. They were a side whose consistency, whose ability regularly to go deep in every competition, demanded a much larger squad and the sort of rotation that wouldn't be common practice for another three decades. Revie had been able to modernise a lot but that, perhaps, was an innovation too far.

12

A FAREWELL TO ARMS

This time, Bobby Charlton had not been assigned to neuter Franz Beckenbauer. But Beckenbauer had been assigned to neuter him and the effect was much the same. With their best player and main creator having little impact, West Germany struggled to get a grip in midfield. At Wembley, in the 1966 World Cup final, they had at least been able to take the game into extra time. In Léon in the 1970 World Cup quarter-final, they found themselves 2–0 down four minutes after half-time. England were in control.

But midway through the half, Bobby saw Colin Bell warming up and realised he was about to be taken off, as he had been in the last two group games. Bobby was thirty-two and although he was still in good physical shape, there was some sense in trying to preserve him for the challenge of a semi-final against Italy at even greater altitude in Mexico City. But momentarily, Bobby lost concentration, allowing Beckenbauer to get away from him.[1] It still shouldn't have mattered. Beckenbauer's shot lacked venom, but it squirmed under Peter Bonetti and West Germany, from nowhere, were back in the game.

England's form after winning the World Cup had been mixed. Bobby and Jack both played in the notorious 3–2 defeat to a Jim Baxter-inspired Scotland in April 1967, Jack not merely carrying on but scoring after breaking two bones in his foot but four wins and a draw from their other five games in the 1966–67 and 1967–68 Home Championship were enough to secure qualification for the quarter-final of the European Championship. Spain were beaten home and away, Bobby getting the only goal in the home leg, before a hard-fought semi-final against a very good Yugoslavia brought the sending-off of Alan Mullery – the first England had ever suffered – and a 1–0 defeat.

Jack didn't play in that game; at thirty-three, he had begun to be phased out for Brian Labone of Everton. After playing in the home leg of the win over Spain, he only ever played in two more competitive internationals. He accepted his reduced role and Alf Ramsey's slow evolution of the side seemed to be working. Between the defeat to Yugoslavia and the start of the World Cup two years later, England lost only one of twenty games, and that away to Brazil. In that run they conceded just eleven goals.

The Brazil game was part of a tour undertaken in 1969 that had begun in Mexico City. Ramsey had been concerned by a band that played through the night outside the hotel, apparently with the intention of keeping England awake, by the non-appearance of the motorcycle escort that was supposed to take them to the stadium and by the hostile reception England received from fans. Ill-advisedly, he complained about those issues publicly, which only made the antipathy the Mexican public felt towards England worse. Quite why they were so hostile remains unclear; most players of the time seem to have blamed Ramsey's comments in 1966 about the Argentinians playing like 'animals', although that seems a curiously minor issue to inspire uncharacteristic Latin American solidarity.

Ramsey learned from the experience. When England returned a year later, they brought with them a luxury, air-conditioned coach and their own food. The team doctor,

Neil Phillips, had been sent on courses to learn about dealing with heat and altitude and the players took pills every day to ward off the threat of dehydration and infection. But Ramsey remained Ramsey, high-handed and suspicious of foreigners. A better diplomat, perhaps, would have ensured that the food he was importing had the right licences; as it was, heaps of meat were burned on the dockside.

After initial acclimatisation – during which sunbathing was limited to half an hour a day with a whistle being blown after fifteen minutes to tell the players to turn over – England headed for friendlies against Colombia in Bogotá and Ecuador in Quito, to try to prepare them for playing at altitude in Guadalajara.

It was around 4 p.m. when the squad arrived at the Tequendama hotel in Bogotá. There was a delay in allocating rooms, so the players sat around in the lobby chatting and playing cards. After a while, Bobby wandered over to a jewellery store called Fuego Verde, looking for a gift for Norma. Bobby Moore joined him and Peter Thompson popped in. Bobby asked about the price of a ring, but decided it was too expensive and, after a looking at a couple of other items, they returned to the sofas. The shop's owner, Daniel Rojas, then said he was missing a gold bracelet encrusted with diamonds and emeralds worth six hundred pounds. His assistant, Clara Padilla, pointed at Moore and said she had seen him take it.

At first it seemed a fuss over nothing, especially when police measured Moore's hand against the opening in the display case and decided he couldn't have reached in to take the bracelet. England beat Colombia 4–0 and then went on to Ecuador where they won 2–0. They were stopped off in Bogotá briefly on their way back to Mexico. Unknown to the rest of the squad – indeed, from his autobiography it seems Bobby never knew – after a street hawker called Alvaro Suárez had said he had seen Moore secrete the bracelet in his jacket, Colombian police were waiting for the England captain at the airport, although a deal was done to spare him the indignity of a public arrest.[2] As the players went to the cinema at the Tequendama and watched the James Stewart western *Shenandoah*, Moore slipped out to speak to detectives. He was taken to see a judge, who decided he had to be detained pending further investigation, but allowed him to stay under house arrest at the home of Alfonso Senior, a director at the Colombian football federation.

The rest of the players returned to the airport and boarded their plane without their captain. Bobby was mortified and volunteered to stay behind to give his side of the story. Ramsey forcefully told him he would do no such thing. The widespread opinion is that it was just as well it was Moore who was accused: he dealt with the situation with characteristic sang-froid; the naturally fretful Bobby would have been shattered by the experience.

The judge staged a reconstruction at which Padilla said, 'Bobby Moore and two of his teammates came to my counter and started talking to me. Then I saw Mr Moore open a glass case, take out the bracelet and put it in his pocket.'[3] Moore asked which pocket and when she indicated the left, he showed her and the assembled officials that the jacket did not have a left pocket at which Padilla tearfully acknowledged she hadn't actually seen Moore with the bracelet at all. The judge allowed a provisional release and Moore arrived in Mexico four days before England's first game in which he was, despite it all, immaculate.

A document was subsequently found showing that Rojas paid Suárez 5000 pesos (around a hundred pounds), although whether that was to lie or, as Rojas claimed, to compensate him for the strain of the case, has never been adequately resolved. Nor, in truth, has the case. On 17 December, Moore and Bobby gave statements at Bow Street magistrates and, eventually, the charges against Moore were dropped. In a 1976 authorised biography of Moore by Jeff Powell, the author states clearly, 'There was no bracelet,' but when the book was reissued after Moore's death, that line is absent and Powell suggests Moore told him late in life that he had been covering for a prank by a younger member of the squad. In the book, Powell said he had no idea who that was but, in 2002, he told a BBC documentary that he did know but had vowed never to reveal the culprit's identity.

Padilla's testimony referred to a third squad member in the shop and it has been widely assumed that this was Thompson, but he was twenty-seven by then, only eighteen months younger than Moore. It's hard to imagine Moore would describe him as a younger player. That revelation prompted a lot of speculation as to who the younger member of the squad could be, but players of the time deny it and the assumption in Colombia seems to have been that the whole affair was a scam aimed at getting a wealthy foreign visitor to pay to make a problem disappear. Intercontinental Hotels, who owned the Tequendama, did not renew Fuego Verde's lease, citing the bad publicity the incident had brought. Padilla, meanwhile, emigrated to Los Angeles a few months later and vanished, leaving behind a mystery that has never truly been solved.

That was a very good England squad; better, many believe, than the side that had won the World Cup four years earlier. Alongside Jack's replacement, Labone, was Mullery for Nobby Stiles, Keith Newton and Terry Cooper had come in at full-back and Roger Hunt had given way to Franny Lee as Geoff Hurst's striker partner. The shape of the team remained familiar; they knew one another's games and they were playing with confidence. The problem, as Bobby observed, was that 'In

Mexico, Alf Ramsey wasn't the master of his environment – he was at war with it.'[4]

England began in characteristically unspectacular fashion with a 1–0 win over Romania. Jack was left out but Bobby played the full ninety minutes. Then came the famous 1–0 defeat to Brazil: Banks's save, Jairzinho's goal, Moore's tackle and the misses from Lee and Jeff Astle. Beyond the fragments that, even half a century later, continue to form part of the collective memory of the national side, it was a match that perhaps showed just how gifted that England side was. Forced by circumstances to play in a way that was alien to them, slowing the pace and holding possession, England pushed Brazil – and that 1970 side remains probably the most feted of all international teams – as close as any side in that tournament. Aside from a fifteen-minute period just after half-time, England were their equals.

Ramsey risked a number of changes against Czechoslovakia in the final group fixture, selecting Jack over Labone. A draw would have been enough, but England won through an Allan Clarke penalty.

And so to Léon and the defeat to West Germany. Two years earlier, in a friendly, England had lost to a German side for the first time, a result that wasn't taken overly seriously, but stands in hindsight as the second of five key games in six years that transformed the footballing relationship between England and Germany. A process that had begun with the 1966 World Cup final would end with the two legs of the European Championship quarter-final in 1972 – West Germany outplaying England at Wembley before England's grim and ineffectual response in Berlin. Mexico 1970 was the critical third act.

Ramsey would have returned to what was clearly his first choice XI, with Labone replacing Jack, but the day before the game Banks went down with food poisoning. The efforts of Ramsey and Dr Phillips to protect the squad had failed only once – but it was a crucial player at the most crucial time. It's too simplistic to say that Banks would have saved Beckenbauer's shot – all goalkeepers make mistakes – but that it should have been Bonetti who erred added to the sense that everything had conspired against England. Sometimes planning isn't enough.

As Bobby was replaced by Bell, an anxious Jack left the stadium. Unable to watch the final twenty minutes, he found a nearby café and sat down with a coffee, hoping the flow of spectators away from the ground would signal an England win. When it didn't come, he knew that West Germany must have equalised and the game gone into extra time. He returned, despondent, just in time to see Gerd Müller score the winner.

Neither Bobby nor Jack ever played for England again.

13

DECLINE AND FALL

The sense that a chapter had closed for United with the European Cup success was never dispelled. They began 1968–69 poorly and were sixteenth in the table when, on 14 January 1969, Busby announced he would retire in the summer. A burst of good form in the spring meant United finished the season eleventh and reached the sixth round of the Cup, while their European defence got as far as a controversial defeat to AC Milan in the semi-final, but Busby was exhausted. Besides, there were no more mountains left to climb.

'You could almost hear the energy and ambition sighing out of the club,' said Best. 'Everybody was talking as if the good old days were over.'[1]

But they *were* over. 'We didn't admit it to ourselves,' said Crerand, 'but a few of us were badly past our sell-by dates.'[2]

It wasn't just personnel. The style of play, Busby's whole approach, was outdated. Half a century of hindsight makes that win look miraculous, not just in terms of the emotional strain but in what it represented as a final flowering of an individualistic notion of football in a world that was rapidly turning to systematisation. Quite apart from the personalities, the friction and the mismanagement, that was what caused the decline. What was extraordinary was less United's slump than that they had remained at such heights operating in such an outmoded way. 'We were the last man to win Wimbledon with a wooden racquet,' as John Aston Jr put it.[3]

Bobby drove Busby to Turnberry for a golf tournament in the summer of 1968 and on the way the subject of Busby's successor cropped up. Characteristically, Bobby had been wary of offering too forceful an opinion, but the only name that seemed under consideration was Dave Sexton, an alumnus of the West Ham academy who had had an impressive first season in charge of Chelsea. According to the goalkeeper Alex Stepney, there had been a plan to appoint another of those who had used to meet at Cassatarri's, the former United captain Noel Cantwell, but that was abandoned when three senior members of the coaching staff – Wilf McGuinness, Jack Crompton and John Aston Sr – threatened to resign if he got the job.[4]

When it came down to it, though, Busby preferred to promote from within, elevating somebody steeped in his ways: McGuinness. He was named head coach while Busby remained a general manager, remaining in the same office he had occupied at Old Trafford since the club had been able to return there after the war. After suffering his broken leg aged twenty-two, McGuinness had become part of the coaching staff at United and was seconded to work with England during the World Cup. There was a certain logic to the appointment: running a football club, particularly one as popular as Manchester United, was an enormous job. For Busby to oversee the business side of operations while training up a younger man who could run training and select the team wasn't an unreasonable plan, but the dividing lines were never clear enough.

McGuinness was only thirty-one and still, in many ways, one of the players. He continued to play cards with them, which on one occasion provoked a public row with the winger Willie Morgan, who had signed from Burnley in the summer of 1968. McGuinness, said Morgan, was 'a complete arsehole.

He was trying to establish himself but he did it completely the wrong way. He had the mind of a three-year-old'.[5]

And perhaps there was some truth to that. But McGuiness was also in an invidious position. Any time he tried to impose some sort of discipline, it riled players who regarded him as a peer and struggled to accept his authority. Towards the end of the 1969–70 season, for instance, Stepney sought permission to go to London a day early before an away game against Arsenal to drop his pregnant wife and four-year-old son with her parents, where they would spend the summer while he was away with England at the World Cup in Mexico. McGuinness, apparently thinking Stepney wanted to attend the FWA annual dinner and, perhaps, looking to flex his muscles, refused him permission; the goalkeeper went to Busby, who overruled his coach.[6]

The most notorious example was the curious incident of Bobby and the press-ups, a story of which there are as many variants as there were witnesses. Nobody can agree on anything, other than that Bobby had to leave training early and had already changed into his suit when McGuinness called the players together. After that, nothing tallies; nobody even seems certain when whatever happened, happened.

Perhaps it was raining or perhaps it wasn't. Perhaps the pitch was muddy or perhaps it was dry. Perhaps the meeting was out in the open or perhaps it was under cover. Bobby put his hands in his pockets, an offence during training for which the punishment was ten press-ups. McGuinness issued the standard sentence and Bobby got down and performed them. Perhaps it was all light-hearted and nobody was bothered, or perhaps Bobby was furious with his old friend. Everybody has a different version. Stepney's is the most inflammatory; Bobby's the least – but then it would be typical of Bobby to play the incident down.

Whatever actually happened, the story encapsulates a broader truth: McGuinness was never able to command the respect of the squad, many of whom saw him as petty. Nor was anybody quite certain who was responsible for what. McGuinness wanted to sign Colin Todd from Sunderland, Mick Mills from Ipswich and Malcolm Macdonald from Luton, but was presented with Ian Ure from Arsenal, despite chronic knee problems. 'I certainly wouldn't have signed myself,' said Ure, describing his medical as 'a farce'[7] – once again, the suggestion was that United lagged behind in basic facilities for players.

United got off to a dismal start under McGuinness. There was a draw at Palace and then home defeats to Everton and Southampton. For the fourth game of the season, the return fixture at Everton, came a startling decision: no Law and no Bobby. Again, explanations vary. McGuiness trying to lay down a marker, said his critics, while he himself insisted Law was injured and that he had left out Bobby because of the way the first game between the sides had gone. 'The centre of the pitch had been a pretty frantic place,' McGuinness explained, 'very crowded and with everything moving at a hundred miles an hour and I felt Bobby had been bypassed.'[8]

Bobby himself seemingly disagreed with McGuinness's reading of that first game, suggesting it was 'one of those rites of passage' the new head coach had to go through, to demonstrate there would be no favouritism shown to his friends.[9] Busby, meanwhile, insisting he had never interfered with team selection, also subsequently made clear that he 'did not agree' with dropping both on the same day.[10] But that, in a sense, was the problem. Whether Busby directly interfered or not, he was there – an alternative source of authority, a higher court – and not only that, but one who regularly socialised and played golf with certain players.

All of which made McGuinness's attempts to modernise United's approach harder. Players resisted the new ways because they weren't convinced the old ways were over. McGuinness, said Law, 'was a blackboard manager who liked to spend ages explaining moves and tactics ... we were usually quite baffled by the time he had finished each session. We used to nod our heads at the right times, but these robotic plans meant very little to us.'[11]

And that in turn further complicated the increasingly difficult situation with George Best, offering him an excuse as his extra-curricular activities began to take over. 'Football started to become a chore at some stage during this period,' said Best. 'Kickers and systems. I was coming off the pitch with mixed emotions when Wilf took over. I knew I was playing well but we were losing.' More even than Law, Best resented the attempt to impose a structure. 'The fun went out of it,' he went on. 'People started bickering, slagging each other off, then there were fights, fists-up jobs.'[12] With Best, though, there was always the doubt: did United's poor form contribute to his dissatisfaction or did his dissatisfaction contribute to United's poor form? And, more generally, which was cause and which effect, the bad results or the backbiting? In that regard, the sixties ended for United as they had begun.

A statue of Bobby, Best and Law, arms hooked over each other's shoulders in celebration, may stand outside Old Trafford, but the Trinity never really got on. Law was both opinionated and deeply private; he could be acerbic in the dressing room and on the pitch and he rarely socialised with his teammates. Almost as soon as he arrived at United in 1962, he took to referring sarcastically to Bobby as 'Sir Robert'. Bobby, meanwhile, came to see Law as another disruptive influence. 'You got the feeling sometimes he wanted to create havoc, that he liked to cause a commotion,' he said in 1973.[13]

There was friction between Bobby and Crerand. As a Scot of Irish descent who was vehemently pro-Republican, there was an instinctive Anglophobia about Crerand, and it's perhaps true that he was unlikely ever to be sympathetic to

Bobby, an England World Cup winner whose reserved nature seemed representative of a particular kind of Englishness. But equally, Bobby *was* increasingly dour. He'd get up and go in the bathroom to smile, Crerand said, just to get it out of the way for the day.

United got to two semi-finals under McGuinness but by the time he was sacked on Boxing Day 1970, his demise had long felt inevitable. 'It was the wrong time for him,' said Bobby, with characteristic diplomacy.[14]

As the players left the field at the end of the first leg of the 1969 League Cup semi-final, a Manchester derby, George Best approached the referee, Jack Taylor. He was raging. City had had the better of the first half, but Bobby had cancelled out Colin Bell's opener and United had been much improved in the second. The game, though, had been settled by an eighty-ninth-minute Francis Lee penalty. Had Lee dived? He had a reputation for doing so, and the reaction of the United players suggested they thought he had. The video, though, in as far as it's possible to tell through the murk, shows Ian Ure lunging hopelessly at Lee as he darts by him and a photograph from behind the goal appears to show Ure's studs clattering into Lee's left ankle. Perhaps Lee anticipated, even induced, the foul and perhaps he did relax his back leg so that when contact was made he was certain to go down, but to modern eyes the offence seems clear enough.

Best was then bundled over, having burst beyond City's defensive line and United had a penalty appeal turned down when Joe Corrigan, the City keeper, having saved Best's free kick, dived at the feet of Ure as he charged onto the rebound. But the issue really is not whether Best's remonstrations had any validity. It was the form they took and the way his actions seemed to encapsulate a growing petulance on his part and an indiscipline in United more generally. He flipped the ball out of Taylor's hands, an obvious and unacceptable show of dissent, that was only ever going to bring heavy punishment. He was banned for twenty-eight days.

For the public, that was the beginning of his decline.

When did the decline actually begin? Perhaps it was always implicit in Best. Perhaps with his personality, in that environment, at that time, it was inevitable. He got bored easily. Even in 1966, he spoke of how Wednesday, Thursday and Friday nights, having to stay in and be tucked up in bed at his landlady Mrs Fullaway's by 11 p.m., were 'murder'.[15] He was desperate for the game on the Saturday and the nights out that could follow.

In those days he didn't drink especially heavily. Within a couple of years, though, as his celebrity grew, booze became a refuge. In 1968, both Mike Summerbee and David Sadler married and Best lost his two principle chaperones. Sadler had been another lodger at Mrs Fullaway's, pretty much the only person in whom Best could confide. Summerbee, a winger at City, had gone halves with him on a house in Cumpsall that they used as a hideaway to disguise their night-time excesses from their landladies and clubs. Suddenly, Best was alone.

Nights would follow a regular pattern: a drink, a casino, a club, ending up at the Clifton Grange hotel in Moss Side, a drinking house run by Philomena Lynott, the mother of the Thin Lizzy vocalist Phil Lynott. It had heavy curtains that were always drawn and no clocks, while a vat of Irish stew bubbled permanently on the stove. It was a place where time stopped, where it felt, at least for a while, that consequences could be endlessly deferred.

Another favourite haunt was the Brown Bull on Chapel Street, an old-school boozer with swing doors and a sticky carpet run by a former GI. The stories are legion. Best with Michael Parkinson or Germaine Greer, Best with people from the nearby Granada Studios for whom the Brown Bull became a local. Best playing drinking games, including one called 'jacks', in which players turned over a card from a deck: the first to find a jack got a drink from the bar, the second tasted it, the third downed it, the fourth paid for it. Best disappearing to a room upstairs for a quick shag. Best, after another heavy night, dozing under a coat, waking to see people staring in at him from the upper deck of a passing bus. And, repeatedly, Best standing at the end of the bar, in company but alone, drinking mechanically, joylessly, grafting his way to blessed oblivion.

Thirteen days before the 1968 European Cup final, Best had been named footballer of the year by the FWA. He collected the statuette at the ceremony and hit the vodka hard. He went to a club and was drunk enough and happy enough to overcome his usual reserve and dance on the stage with a chorus line, still clutching his trophy. He picked up a woman and went back to her place. Still holding the award, he tried to remove his trousers. Finding it difficult, he attempted to sit on the bed and missed by four feet. But still he didn't let go of his trophy.

The following morning, sheltering from the rain as he waited for a taxi, Best huddled in a doorway. He fell asleep and was woken by a policeman, who only believed he was who he said he was when he unwrapped the brown paper parcel he still held and showed him his footballer of the year award.

Bobby Charlton and George Best didn't speak much on the train back from Cardiff. It was 28 July 1969 and they'd just played for the Rest of the UK against Wales in a friendly to mark the investiture of Charles as Prince of Wales. But as they pulled into Crewe and Bobby prepared to get off, he asked Best if he wanted to join him for dinner; Norma and the children were away, and there was some scampi in the freezer.

To his surprise, Best said yes. While Bobby cooked the dinner, Best flicked through magazines, played with Bobby's dog, a chow chow, and watched television. As they ate, Best suddenly became talkative, bombarding Bobby with domestic questions. Who walked the dog? Did he have a cleaner? How much did a gardener cost? A little taken aback, Bobby answered, and only later realised Best was contemplating marriage.

The following weekend, United played a friendly in Copenhagen. There, Best was smitten by a blue-eyed, blonde woman, Eva Haraldsted, who had asked for an autograph. He asked a Danish newspaper to help track her down and, within eight days, they were engaged. The story is usually told as a what-might-have-been: what if Bobby had pushed the case harder and convinced Best to settle down? But the truth is that Bobby was so persuasive in describing the charms of married life that Best proposed to pretty much the next woman he met.

Marriage had clearly been on Best's mind. He'd discussed the idea with his girlfriend Jackie Glass and she had agreed to his implied proposal, giving him a gold chain from which hung a disc bearing the world, 'Yes.' She later stepped back, suggesting that Best wouldn't dare arrange a wedding in case he fell in love with one of the bridesmaids. Best rather proved her point by having matching chains made up for his friends Malcolm Wagner and Danny Bursk, although what they were indicating acquiescence to was a far more temporary union.

To nobody's great surprise, Best's engagement didn't last and instead became one of the more preposterous sagas of his life. He broke things off after three months, leading Haraldsted to sue for breach of promise. Best then became involved in a fracas in a nightclub with Haraldsted's new boyfriend and his brother, at which Pat Crerand weighed in and found himself charged with assault. Crerand was represented in court by George

Carman, later a high-profile QC who successfully defended the Liberal leader Jeremy Thorpe against charges of conspiracy to murder. One night, as Carman fell into a drunken sleep downstairs, Best seduced his wife. Two years later, as Carman represented Best in another case, they resumed the affair. Carman found out and asked a local gangster to break Best's legs in retribution. Fortunately for Best, the gangster was a United fan and not only refused but threatened to take violent revenge should anything untoward befall the player.

With Best banned, United's form improved over Christmas 1969. Although they had drawn against City in the second leg of the League Cup semi, they beat them in the fourth round of the FA Cup. Might it be, some asked, that they were better off without their great star?

He returned for the FA Cup fifth-round tie, away to fourth-division Northampton Town, and scored six times in an 8–2 victory. His last, sitting Northampton keeper Kim Book down with the subtlest sway of his hips before smashing the ball into an empty net, was a distillation of his graceful brilliance. Best spoke of how he loved the FA Cup, of finals watched on television back in Belfast and of his childhood dreams of dominating a game at Wembley.

Six weeks later, United faced Leeds in an FA Cup semi-final replay at Villa Park. In the hotel before the game, a bored Best wandered about. He spotted a woman, 'chic, self-possessed ... exquisite legs'[16] reading the John Le Carré novel *A Small Town in Germany*. They made eye contact. When they later passed on the stairs, she asked him to come and autograph a photograph she had in her room. She was married, her husband attending a conference in the hotel, but that had never bothered Best before. He agreed to meet her after the team lunch.

Trying to avoid detection, Best ate deliberately slowly, but

McGuinness – then still the manager – was well aware of his tactics. A few minutes after Best had left the dining room, McGuinness found the hotel porter and borrowed a master key from him. He opened the woman's bedroom door, sent Best back to his room then, furious, went to the bar. Best heard him order a whiskey, and returned to the woman's room. He stayed with her until a few minutes before the bus left for Villa Park.

Everybody knew what had gone on. The Leeds players, outraged at what they saw as an insult to professionalism, gave Best an especially hard time. 'That wasn't the way to behave before an important game,' said John Giles, 'and I gave George a bit of a kicking for it. He complained afterwards that I'd called him unprofessional about ten times during the match and kicked him each time, which was true.'[17]

Had Best played well, had he contributed anything at all, it might have been the basis for a classic anecdote about his maverick genius. But Best rarely played well against Leeds, struggling to elude the man-marking of Paul Reaney. 'That was mainly because of the information in the dossiers,' said Jack.[18] By Best's own assessment, that night he 'played like a wanker'.[19] The game was drawn 0–0 and Leeds won a second replay.

The Northampton match is often hailed as one of the great Best highlights, but United won only four more games that season, and one of them was the irrelevant FA Cup third-place play-off that was mystifyingly introduced that season and soon abandoned.

That year, 1970, Best moved into his new house in Bramhall. It was a disaster, a white-tiled symbol of good intentions gone awry through a lack of practicality and of the impossibility of living with the sort of celebrity that ate away at him. The house, named 'Che Sera' following a competition in the News of the World, was designed by the modernist architect Frazer Crane and featured a baffling array of mod-cons – a sunken bath, remote-control curtains, a television that unfurled at the touch of a button.

It was striking and ambitious and wholly unsuitable – and not just because the electronics frequently failed, particularly when planes passed low overhead, leaving Best at times unable to close the curtains or unable to sleep because the television in his bedroom was constantly opening out and retracting. Best's sole input in the design had been his request for a snooker room but, as it turned out it was too small to cue properly at the baulk end. Nothing worked.

But the biggest oversight was the absence of a hedge or a fence. Day-trippers would turn up, at times in their hundreds. 'The visitors peeped through the windows,' reported the *Mirror*, 'gazed into the fishpond, tramped around the garden and climbed the outside verandah stairs to get a close look.'[20]

Fish were stolen from the pond. One man installed an armchair on the lawn and never removed it. Others picnicked in Best's garden. Best would be mobbed if he tried to go out and at times found himself having to ask tourists to move their cars so he could get back in. Trapped, he would sit in his living room, pulling faces and making V-signs at people pressed up against the one-way glass. The situation was vaguely comic and had the feel of a morality tale on the lines of the emperor's new clothes, but it was also hugely detrimental to Best's already declining well-being.

Two weeks before McGuinness was sacked, United had lost the derby 4–1 to City and Best had been booked for a foul that broke Glyn Pardoe's leg. It was his fourth caution of the year, which may not sound much now, but back then meant another FA disciplinary hearing, held in early January, by which Busby had taken over from McGuinness on a caretaker basis. That week, a brick was put through the window of one of Best's boutiques, presumably in retribution.

The night before the hearing, Best got drunk. He missed the

train from Manchester, but Busby was able to get the hearing postponed from noon until 4.30 p.m. When Best finally turned up, he vomited in the lift. The FA gave him a £250 fine and a six-week suspended ban. Busby had once been renowned for his ruthlessness with those he saw as undermining him but he never was able to control Best, nor was he willing to lose a player of his extraordinary gifts. Bobby felt Busby was more forgiving than he had ever been, more forgiving than he should have been. Best, he said, was never 'exposed to the discipline I experienced during my early days'.[21]

Best himself thought how he lived was none of Bobby's 'fucking business'[22] and admitted that, when getting a dressing down from Busby, he would stare at the wall behind him, ignore what was being said and count the animals on the wallpaper.[23]

Later that week, Best missed training and so Busby, determined to try to restore discipline, dropped him for the weekend league game away at Chelsea – although he could only get the message to him by calling Best's friend, the hairdresser Malcolm Wagner. Best, though, was still expected to travel with the squad as a show of solidarity. But on the Saturday, he missed the train again. He rushed to the airport and caught a flight to London and from Heathrow he went not to Stamford Bridge but to a flat in Islington belonging to the actress Sinéad Cusack, whom he'd met a few weeks earlier. There he saw on *Grandstand* that United had won 2–1, ending a run of ten games without a victory. Before long, the flat was besieged by fans and the media. Trapped inside, Best and Cusack kept up to date with what was going on in the street outside by watching the news. When he was eventually smuggled out of the flat and returned to Manchester, Best was banned for fourteen days.

Busby arranged for Best to see a psychiatrist. He attended one session, resentfully.

*

Under Busby's management, United's form improved, Best
started playing well again and United finished eighth. 'From
the moment he took over,' said Law, 'the boss had told us that
we were to forget all the blackboard stuff and concentrate
on playing football the way we always had when he was in
charge.'[24] It's telling not only that 'the boss' was always Busby,
but also that the squad was so scathing of attempts to drag it
into modernity. They needed to be more organised and coherent, but McGuinness was resented for trying to bring about
that organisation and coherence.

Busby stood down as manager for a second time in the
summer of 1972, and the sorry dance began again as United
gave the job to Frank O'Farrell, another graduate of West Ham
and Cassatarri's. He was somebody with very different ideas
from Busby, and they soon clashed. Busby's continued presence
had hampered McGuinness, but it was to an extent logical – at
least, in theory, a phased withdrawal while the new man got
used to the job. O'Farrell couldn't tolerate Busby remaining
in the same office he had occupied for years, or the way his
friendships with players so often seemed to cut across what
O'Farrell was trying to do. Worse, the squad he inherited was
a mixture of ageing greats and signings who struggled to meet
expectations. And the one bona fide star he had, Best, was in
the grip of alcoholism and what looks – from the perspective
of half a century later – a lot like depression.

Best and United began the season well and they lost only
twice in the league before Christmas. In January, though,
everything began to go wrong. Best skipped training, just lying
in bed at Che Sera. He was dropped. When he returned to the
club, he was asked how the squad had reacted. 'They've been
great,' Best replied. 'All except one. I'm not saying who he is
but his name is Bobby Charlton.'[25]

That their relationship had been worsening had been clear
for a while, but this was the first time the hostility had been

publicly acknowledged. That summer, Best had asked Busby to make him captain instead of Charlton. When Busby refused, it confirmed to Best what he'd long suspected: he would never be fully accepted by the United hierarchy. That his behaviour suggested he was entirely unsuited to the pressures of captaincy seems never to have occurred to him.

Best briefly returned to live with Mrs Fullaway, but he slept wherever the night found him. He drank more and more. He suffered worse and worse blackouts. His form disintegrated and so too did United's. They lost seven in a row in the league. Best announced he was sick of United. 'It's just not good enough,'[26] he said, frustrated at how everything seemed to depend on him. He fled to Spain and on his birthday announced his retirement. He was twenty-six.

After six weeks he returned and was suspended for a fortnight. There were the familiar promises – that, having rediscovered his love of the game, he would recommit, return to fitness and form. But a death spiral, once embarked upon, is not so easily exited.

The rest of the squad was already losing faith. That summer, on his way to Bermuda for a holiday, Bobby was stopped at Heathrow by a journalist who asked him about Best's future. 'If it wasn't for him we wouldn't be going on holiday to Bermuda,' he replied. 'It's impossible to go anywhere in Europe because you get pounded by British tourists asking what's happened to George Best.'[27]

George Best's celebrity and his inability to handle it, his addictions to booze, gambling and women, destroyed him.

They also destroyed his mother, Ann. She had never touched alcohol until she was in her forties but she began drinking as her son became more famous and more remote. When Best first went to stay in Manchester she would ring him once a week.

Increasingly, it was Mrs Fullaway who answered the phone and kept her updated. When Best went home to Belfast, it became a circus and so he stayed away. By the end, what Ann Best knew of her son was what she saw on television on read in the paper. The end came horribly early, in October 1978. She was fifty-four and had drunk herself to death.

And they destroyed Busby's vision of Manchester United. This was the problem with a team built without a systemic underpinning. Busby could talk airily of 'pattern' and dismiss notions that there needed to be an underlying structure, but football had moved on. His side of the mid-to-late-sixties was great because it had three exceptional talents, three winners of the Ballon d'Or. But when he retired in 1969, all were in decline. Bobby Charlton was thirty-one and age was closing in. Denis Law was twenty-nine but had never fully recovered from his knee injury. George Best was twenty-two but had already won his last trophy.

'I represented the future of Manchester United – or should have done,' Best acknowledged. 'Charlton represented the past.'[28] That was not simply about age; it was also about attitude. Best once said that he was 'grateful' to have been born in 1946 and not 1926. 'We don't have to stick rigidly to the short back and sides and wear-your-club-blazer-at-all-times routine of the past,' he said.[29]

But those *were* the values of Bobby, who had been born in 1937. 'It's a great pity,' he said in 1967, taking a despairing look at the youth revolution, 'that young people today seem to shy away from close relationships with their elders because it's part of a "square" conception of life. So many young people on the "scene" have the attitude that nearly everything and ordinary people are "sick". They behave as if the peak of senility is reached at the age of twenty-five and they must wring every drop out of life by then whether they offend other people or not.'[30]

Given Bobby wasn't yet thirty, it's a remarkable piece of fogeyism, even down to his clear discomfort with the modish slang. He goes on to attack those who insist on being 'cool', 'gas' and 'with it'. And yet there he was, playing alongside one of the great icons of that rising youth movement. Inevitably, there was friction. 'I just don't understand him,' Bobby said in April 1973. 'What do you come into football for? It's your duty to give your best to the people who come to support you, but he didn't seem to see this.'[31]

Best, meanwhile, accused Bobby of having 'a holier than thou attitude', commenting, 'I wish I could hear him say "fuck", just once.'[32]

Bobby, as club captain, felt trapped in the middle. Players looked to him for leadership, and he looked to O'Farrell, who looked back to him. Bobby would complain that Best had not turned up, had disrupted training or had become an embarrassment, and O'Farrell would suggest that Bobby, as a senior figure with more than a hundred England caps, might like to take action himself. But Bobby, for all his moaning on the pitch, hated conflict off it, and so the issue festered.

Their sniping, though, was asymmetric. Bobby was bound by convention, by a sense of decency, by a hope that Best would, at some point, see sense. Best cared for none of those things and made no attempt to disguise his disdain. Asked in a television interview who the biggest influence over his career had been, he replied, 'Cissie Charlton.'[33]

Bobby's testimonial, a goalless draw against Celtic, was held on 18 September 1972. Best refused to play, claiming an injury to his right ankle, although he later said to have played would have been 'hypocritical'.[34] He did turn up to watch but lasted just five minutes before leaving for the Brown Bull. There he sat gloomily at one of the heavy oak tables, drinking and throwing darts and two dozen eggs at a portrait of Bobby that hung on the wall.

O'Farrell, a quiet, decent, thoughtful man, found himself in an impossible position. Best was a problem perhaps beyond any solution, but he was far from the only issue. Law was struggling with injury and becoming increasingly truculent. And then there were the internal politics of the club. The power structures that had sustained Busby and provided him with his authority inevitably resisted any successor. O'Farrell thought Crerand was past it, but Crerand was close to Busby. He didn't rate Morgan or Stepney, but they played golf with Busby at Davyhulme. An attempt to sign Peter Shilton was rebuffed, ostensibly for reasons of cost, although O'Farrell believed it was because it would have meant Stepney being sidelined.

In his autobiography, O'Farrell's successor, Tommy Docherty, who also had an attempt to sign Shilton rejected, reproduced a letter he received from O'Farrell on 12 May 1977. 'You will have found out by now, as I did to my cost, that the Knight is not covered in shining armour as he makes out to many who do not know him so well.'[35] He also predicted that Busby would be desperately manoeuvring to be rid of Docherty. Nine days later, United won the FA Cup and yet, by the start of the following season, Docherty was gone, sacked for a relationship with the wife of the club physio long after the initial furore seemed to have blown over. The significance of a pair of private detectives Docherty discovered were following him has never really been explained.

Best felt Busby and the club had been over-loyal to players who had lingered too long. That included Bobby who, as he saw it, had become 'part of the problem'.[36] O'Farrell did end up dropping Bobby. 'It was the Wilf thing all over again,' Bobby said. 'They all seemed to think that if they dropped me it would prove something.'[37] He took to training alone, running endless laps of the pitch. But even if he resented the decision to leave him out as some sort of power play, Bobby knew deep down that his powers were waning.

'He first of all started trying to put the blame on himself,' said Best. 'It was all his fault, which tended to make him a little worse.'[38]

Bobby became increasingly morose. There were days when he would walk into the dressing room at the training ground and go straight to his peg and change, staring at the wall and ignoring everybody. 'The big three ... were at loggerheads,' said Stepney. 'There were long days when they would simply not speak to each other ... I am sure it was George's complete lack of concern for the club that threw Charlton into the desperately black mood which seemed to envelop him every time he was at the club.'[39] And for Bobby, the club was far more than a club. He, perhaps more than anybody else, idealised Manchester United. It remained for him a land of potential wonder, the place that had produced Duncan and Eddie and David and its fall from that state disgusted him.

Even three decades later, Best was unable to acknowledge that. He produced five autobiographies, pumping them out every time money ran short. They are frequently contradictory, so what he actually thought about anything is very difficult to assess. His 2001 book, *Blessed*, is remarkable, even by the standards of the genre, for its self-pitying tone. Everything can be blamed on other people, on his fame or his disease; nothing is ever his fault. 'Others didn't understand the pressure I was under ...' he said. 'I was finding it increasingly difficult to get motivated because the team was so poor.'[40]

But as Bobby saw it, it was Best's job to make sure it wasn't so poor, and his frequent absences and inconsistency weren't exactly helping. And Bobby, of course, existed as perpetual rebuke to Best: look what he had gone through and look how he had coped. In the end it got so bad that Bobby and Best stopped passing to each other. Bobby could be just as stubborn as his brother or his father, but in this case it was perhaps understandable: if he didn't maintain the old values, the standards that had made United great, who would?

Yet while attitudes had changed, there was still resistance to modernising how United went about the game. And still there was resistance to change. O'Farrell said he kept hearing the phrase 'Let's play the football'[41] – let's play the old way, Matt's way, with lots of self-expression and little discipline or organisation. And Busby was always there for dissatisfied players to complain to.

Crerand was adamant that Busby didn't interfere with O'Farrell and that what undermined him was Bobby 'running to [the chairman] Louis Edwards all the time.'[42] Perhaps Bobby did complain and perhaps that was unsettling, but Busby clearly asserted his influence. At the end of October 1972, United lost 4–1 at home to Tottenham. That night, at the club's annual dinner dance, Busby commented to O'Farrell's wife, Anne, that her husband was 'an independent sod'[43] and that he should come in for a chat. O'Farrell confronted him the following Monday, leading to a heated conversation in which Busby suggested Martin Buchan was playing poorly and questioned the decision to leave Bobby out. O'Farrell was startled: Buchan, as far as he was concerned, was one of the few players behaving with professionalism. When he pressed Busby for details, it became apparent that the former manager had confused two players. It was then that O'Farrell realised just how insidious the Davyhulme cabal had become. It was those players who played golf with Busby who resented Buchan, precisely for his overt conscientiousness.

Eventually, Busby invited Bobby to come and see him at his

King's Road home, the first time he had ever visited. Bobby complained about Best, but received a homily about forgiveness. And perhaps it's even true that, by then, Best, problematic as he undoubtedly was, had become a convenient excuse for other failings.

Although he would later revert to Busby loyalism, Bobby around then seems to have lost at least some faith in the Old Man, to have realised that the pre-Munich world was not so perfect as he had thought. The hardness that perhaps was natural for somebody who lived through two world wars and the general strike could translate into something uncomfortably cold. Ruthlessness in dealing with players who are perceived to have stepped out of line – Johnny Morris after a training-ground row, Charlie Mitten for accepting an offer from the rebel league in Colombia, Dennis Viollet for his womanising – is part of management, but did Nobby Stiles not deserve a testimonial when he was sold to Middlesbrough in 1971 after eleven years at the club?

Even worse was Busby's treatment of Jimmy Murphy. As the sixties went on, Busby and Murphy had drifted further apart. Murphy remained forever below stairs, probably by choice; he only went to the Cromford Club once, for Roger Byrne's wedding. When McGuinness was promoted, he got Murphy's office and Murphy was moved to share with Joe Armstrong while his travel allowance was cut, forcing him to pay for his own taxis as he didn't drive. By the end, they were strangers. A few years before Murphy died in 1989, he fell seriously ill. Bobby went to visit. Busby, who lived just five miles away, did not.

Busby's actions tested Bobby's relationship with him. The first evidence of strain had come when it became apparent that Busby had gone back on a promise made to Bobby in 1966 that he could always be the top earner at the club. The money bothered Bobby less than the sense of betrayal: if even the Old Man's word wasn't sacrosanct, what was? But what happened to Murphy was a far worse betrayal, one that highlighted the cruelty of football, the way people were discarded once their purpose was served. Duncan and Eddie and Billy never had to face that, but in Murphy's treatment Bobby perhaps sensed his own sporting mortality. At a tribute dinner to Murphy, Bobby gave a typically nervous speech. 'Whatever I have accomplished in football,' he said, 'I owe to one man only: Jimmy Murphy.'[44] Nobody in the room doubted the implied snub to Busby was deliberate.

Jack had been joking, probably. In 1970, shortly after the World Cup, he'd given an extended interview to Tyne Tees Television in which he'd been, in his usual way, funny, provocative and blunt. 'I have a little book with players' names in it,' he'd said. 'If I get the chance to do them, I will. I will make them suffer before I pack it in. If I can kick them four yards over the touchline I will.'

Why had he said it? Nobody believed he actually had a little book. But might he have a metaphorical book? That possibility is impossible entirely to discount, but it didn't seem to fit either with his history or his personality. He was somebody who would kick an opponent and be kicked in return for ninety minutes and then happily have a pint with them afterwards. It might be difficult to change his mind once it was made up, but he was not somebody to bear a grudge. In a Leeds side noted for its cynicism, Jack was physical but notably not vicious. Then, perhaps encouraged by the laughter of the audience, he compounded the fault. 'If I was chasing a player in an international match,' he said, 'and I could not catch him, I would flatten him.'

As the tabloids whipped themselves into a moral hysteria – the *Express* called for him to be sacked – the FA issued Jack with a temporary ban from playing for England, a token gesture given he had already retired from international football. A subsequent tribunal established by the FA and League accepted that, in context, what Jack had said did not look as bad as it appeared when reported by the tabloids and effectively exonerated him of bringing the game into disrepute, imposing neither a fine nor a ban, merely asking for an apology.

In his autobiography, Jack explained that while he didn't have a literal 'black book', he did have 'perhaps five or six players in mind who had committed nasty tackles on me' and that he'd always vowed 'I'd get them back if I could'.[45] Contrary to widespread belief, that list did not include either Peter Osgood or Denis Law, but John Morrissey of Everton, George Kirby of Southampton and a Chelsea player who 'did' Jack in 1970 whom he wouldn't name because he hoped he still had a chance for retribution.

But perhaps the most significant aspect of the whole affair was that Bobby then broke his long-standing habit of avoiding controversy. 'The remarks on the record would not have come well from a lad of twenty or twenty-one who had been in the game five minutes,' he told the *Express*, 'but the effect is that much worse when they come from someone of Jack's experience and prestige. Jack must know what effect this business is having, that it is not doing the game any good. But he appears to be sticking to his guns. That is Jack, all right. He is as stubborn as they come.'

Cissie, who had been in the audience for the interview, responded in the *Mail*, insisting Jack's words had been taken out of context. 'I am amazed at our Bobby. He's in the same position as all of Jack's other critics. He hasn't seen the television programme.'

For the first time, the tensions within the family were exposed publicly.

Bobby may have been his mother's favourite growing up, but their relationship cooled after his marriage to Norma. The issue initially seems to have been one largely of class. Jack felt Norma looked down on the rest of the family, while the United keeper Harry Gregg said he thought Bobby was embarrassed by his mother's visits to Old Trafford. Norma, meanwhile, found Jack boorish – and given his bluntness and untidiness, nobody could pretend he was an easy house guest – and insisted Cissie, whom she found 'domineering', never gave her a chance. Cissie never sent Bobby's two daughters a Christmas or birthday card.

Jack bought his parents a semi on a new-build estate the year after the World Cup win, and later, with his father suffering from pneumoconiosis, moved them into a farm in the Yorkshire Dales; Bobby visited less and less often.

In his autobiography, Jack tells the story of his father and his uncle Tommy Skinner visiting Manchester and Bobby, making the excuse he had decorators in, putting them up in a hotel. Jack seems to have regarded this as an unforgiveable slight and another example of Norma's coldness. His father also seems to have been offended. 'Cissie,' he supposedly said shortly before his death from cancer in April 1982, 'if your Bobby sends any flowers for the funeral, hoy the buggers aback the fire.'[46] But perhaps Bobby had had the decorators in. And anyway, even if he didn't, protecting personal space is hardly a crime, particularly for somebody as private as Bobby.

With her husband gone, Cissie returned to Ashington, living first in a council flat and then in a nursing home at Newbiggin. There were times when Bobby would do an event in Ashington and not even pop in. 'As my married life progressed ...' Bobby said, 'the links with Ashington became frayed and strained ... It quickly became apparent that my mother ... would never freely embrace the girl with whom I intended to spend the rest of my life ... It seems unbelievable to me that it can happen that a son does not get on with his mother.'[47] But that was how it was.

*

George Best returned to training. He lost weight. But his pace had deserted him. 'All the skills were there,' he said. 'There was simply no way I could get my old speed back. No amount of training made any difference.'[48] Nothing made any difference.

He dismissed United's new signings: Wyn Davies was 'too old'; Ted MacDougall was 'a bad buy'; Ian Storey-Moore was 'injury-prone'.[49] He left his long-time agent, Ken Stanley. He would drink more and more then, realising when he woke that he stank of booze, skip training to avoid a bollocking. Then he would skip training the following day to avoid a bollocking for skipping training.

At the end of November 1972, having again been dropped for missing training, Best ended up sitting at the bar in a club called Reuben's. He had been drinking all evening. A woman came up to him and asked him to dance. Best offered his set line that men from Belfast didn't do that sort of thing. The woman, drunk on Babycham and brandy, reacted badly, called Best 'a big-headed bastard'[50] and took a swing at him. Best slapped her, leaving her with a hairline fracture of the nose and bleeding from a cut inside her mouth.

Five weeks later, Best was given a twelve-month suspended prison sentence. By then, Madame Tussauds in Blackpool had melted down his waxwork and refashioned it into Rodney Marsh. O'Farrell effectively gave up on him. Best had already rejected O'Farrell and 'all that bollocks about zonal defence and 4-4-2 and all that crap'.[51]

Everything fell away. Best went on a two-day bender in London and was given another two-week suspension by United. His Rolls-Royce was vandalised, the company that had taken on his boutiques removed his name and he lost his boot deal with Stylo to Kevin Keegan. But unknown to O'Farrell, the United board decided to allow Best to train with the squad again. The following day, United, then second bottom of the First Division, lost 5–0 at Crystal Palace, who were bottom.

On the Monday there was a testimonial dinner for Bobby. O'Farrell suspected something was up when he looked at the seating plan and saw he wasn't on the top table. The following morning, he was sacked, and so too was Best.

As Busby left Old Trafford after the dismissals he was photographed passing in front of a group of fans who had gathered to find out what was going on. At first glance it appears he is walking over churned snow. Closer inspection shows that the ground is covered by a damp carpet of ripped-up photographs, most of them of Best. 'Every manager,' Busby later said, 'goes through life, looking for one great player, praying he'll find one. Just one. I was more lucky than most. I found two – Big Duncan and George. I suppose in their own way, they both died, didn't they?'[52]

Tommy Docherty took over three days after O'Farrell had been dismissed. United did, eventually, improve sufficiently to avoid relegation, but for Bobby a 3–1 defeat at Birmingham City in March 1973 came as confirmation he was coming to an end. 'I couldn't remember ever running so hard and so long,' Bobby said. 'I chased and chased, but there was nothing there for me.'[53] He went to see Docherty and told him he would retire at the end of the season.

Denis Law also left the club that summer. George Best was reprieved and given yet another final chance but managed only twelve games in 1973–74 before finally leaving United for good. With the Holy Trinity scattered, Law symbolically scored the winner for Manchester City in United's final home game of the season as relegation was confirmed.

14

NEXT STEPS

Neil Philips, the England team doctor, was also a director at Second Division Middlesbrough. He got on well with Jack and admired the way he thought about football. Stan Anderson had quit as Boro manager in 1972–73, with Harold Shepherdson – the trainer who had been the recipient of Alf Ramsey's 'Sit down, Harold,' comment as he celebrated England's fourth goal in the 1966 World Cup final – taking over as caretaker. Philips thought Jack would be an ideal candidate for the job.

Jack liked the sound of a return to the North-East and suggested he should meet Boro's directors at a hotel he knew halfway between Leeds and Middlesbrough. When they got there, it turned out the hotel had been demolished some months earlier. That was not an auspicious start and seemed to confirm what many feared: that Jack was too disorganised ever to make it as a manager. Even Pat, his wife, worried about whether he would prove too tactless for the job. Bill Shankly, though, felt Jack's directness was evidence of a clarity of thought. And what nobody doubted was that Jack thought a lot about the game: the likes of Shankly, Busby and Brian Clough may have been scathing about Lilleshall and dismissive of coaching courses, but Jack relished his annual trips there and the discussions about how football should be played.

After that shambolic first attempt at a meeting, Middlesbrough's directors invited Jack to Ayresome Park. But when they began questioning him about his plans, he stopped them. As far as he was aware, he said, it wasn't an interview. He took a piece of paper from his pocket on which he had written a list Revie had given him of what he should demand from the board, insisting on complete control of team affairs. He left it with them and went outside to wait in the corridor while the board decided whether to accept his terms. When there'd been no response after quarter of an hour, he popped his head back through the door. He'd give them ten more minutes, he said, and if they still hadn't decided, he was off.

They gave him the job.

Jack refused a contract, saying he wanted to be able to walk away should he feel the need and that the directors should have the right to get rid of him as soon as they felt it wasn't working out. He warned them he would leave after four years; Revie may have still been going strong twelve years into the Leeds job but Jack felt that there was a limit after which familiarity would breed staleness.

Middlesbrough had finished fourth in 1972–73, fourteen points off second and a promotion spot. That suggested there wasn't too much wrong with the playing squad and, anyway, it wasn't in Jack's nature to make major changes quickly. On the Thursday before the 1973 FA Cup final, he had sat next to the Celtic manager Jock Stein at the FWA dinner and tapped him for advice. Stein told him to take the squad on a tour as soon as possible; that, he felt, was the quickest way to get an insight into their personalities. Jack took Middlesbrough to Scotland for three pre-season games and soon identified a couple of moaners he wanted to get rid of.

Stein also warned that there was a danger of players

becoming too comfortable and losing their edge, advising Jack that every now and again he should make a big deal out of a minor incident just to keep everybody on their toes. The first opportunity came in the second weekend of the season as Boro, having played well in pre-season and beaten Portsmouth away in their opening game, lost at home to Fulham. 'Jack lost his temper and it was the first time that we'd really seen him get angry,' goalkeeper Jim Platt recalled. 'I remember him talking with some of the older players – I was quite young at the time – and they were arguing with him or not so much arguing but disputing things. He turned around and said, "You'll do it my effing way ... or you won't do it at all."

'He said one thing afterwards which I thought was right. It was only two points for a win then and we conceded two late goals because we were pushing on with about forty minutes to go, trying to win it. He said, "At the end of the day, you have to realise you can't win every match and those matches you can't win you want to make sure you don't lose."

'He said that the points would add up and that point could have been the difference between getting promoted or not. So he was blunt, but he was fair. After he'd lost his temper, he came in on the Monday and apologised. He said he shouldn't have done it after the match, he should have let things settle down first. But then we had a meeting later in the day, he lost his temper again and skulked off. But that was Jack.'[1]

Jack wasn't the only manager to worry that familiarity could breed staleness; the great Hungarian Béla Guttmann, who won two European Cups with Benfica, was even more stringent, maintaining that 'the third year is fatal'.[2] So concerned was Jack by the possibility of staleness that he only turned up for training on a Thursday and a Friday. The first team coach would lead fitness work early in the week, the players would have Wednesday off if there wasn't a midweek game, and then Jack would come in for tactical sessions.

'His idea,' Platt said, 'was that if we listened to him five days a week we would get bored with him.'[3]

Conveniently, that also left Jack with plenty of time to go fishing.

That summer Jack had rung Stein and asked him if there were any players in Scotland he thought worth a look. Stein promptly offered him Bobby Murdoch on a free transfer. Murdoch had been part of the Celtic side that had won the European Cup in 1967 and had played in both legs of the European Cup semi-final against Leeds in 1970 but, by 1973, although he only turned twenty-nine that August, he was struggling with injury and fitness. Jack was happy to pay the signing-on fee: he knew how good a passer Murdoch was and reasoned that, as he had never been quick, a slight loss of pace was less of an issue for him than it might have been for other players.

Murdoch was the only signing Jack made that summer, but there were plenty of other changes. Following Revie's theory that white was the easiest colour for players to pick out on the field, he added a horizontal white band to Boro's red shirts.* Feeling the rusted gates at Ayresome Park reflected badly on the club, he went to ICI – based just up the Tees in Billingham – and asked for some free paint to do them up. Blocks of seats were painted in different colours so that fans could easily see which section of the ground they were buying tickets for. Jack also had a gantry installed under the roof, improving camera angles so Boro's games looked better on television. For somebody who could at times seem very self-absorbed, he had a very clear idea of ways the supporter experience could be improved.

Similarly, he welcomed journalists and television cameras,

---

* It may be more accurate to say he restored it: Middlesbrough's kit had white shoulders between 1912 and 1936 and again between 1964 and 1966; 1973 was the first time the white detail manifested as a hoop across the chest.

seeing promotion as part of his job. 'It's no good making enemies of the press by being awkward ...' he said. 'They know
they'll be looked after and welcomed at Middlesbrough ... and
in getting them to talk about us, it gets through eventually to
the public.'[4]

Jack also had clear ideas of how he wanted Boro to play. By
the early seventies, the majority of teams had grasped the rudi-
ments of pressing and were pushing high up the pitch to try to
catch the opposition offside. What that meant was that there
was often space behind defences that could be exploited by a
runner from deep. In Alan Foggon, who had been a 220-yard
champion at school, Boro had the perfect man to do just that.
Or, at least, they did once Jack had got him in shape, which
he did by sending Foggon to stay with his parents in their
farmhouse in the Dales where he was placed on a strict diet:
lunch was three ounces of roast beef, four ounces of potato and
vegetables; dinner was cottage cheese; there was no tea, sugar,
biscuits, cake or sweets and he was allowed to drink only
Bovril or black coffee, plus half a pint of milk a day.[5]

The two physically powerful centre-forwards, David Mills
and John Hickton, would push out with the defence, while the
midfield included not only Murdoch but also David Armstrong,
who would go on to win England caps, and a young Graeme
Souness, whom Jack moved from the left into the middle. They
were good enough to weight balls into the space advancing
opponents left behind them for Foggon – starting from an
advanced midfield position – to chase. And, Jack knew, there
was nothing central defenders hated more than having to play
on the turn.

'He was clever,' said David Mills, 'because he found a system
to suit the players rather than trying to get the players to fit a
system. He didn't ask players to do things that he didn't think

they were capable of doing. If you did what he asked you to do and it didn't work, he'd take responsibility. If you went off-piste a little bit, didn't do what he asked and it went wrong, then you were in for the high jump. Jack was uncompromising. It was relentless: practice, practice, practice, tactics, tactics, set plays. Every day was relentless. It was like a machine.'[6]

Critics dismissed the approach as kick and rush – Tommy Docherty quipped that Jack had taken over a sleeping giant and put the fans to sleep – but it was undeniably effective. After losing their second game of the season away to Fulham, Boro didn't lose again until the beginning of February. When they beat Luton at the beginning of November, it meant they were top, despite having scored fourteen goals in fourteen games.

The external grumbling had clearly begun to rankle. 'The club pay me wages to win matches ...' Jack explained in his newspaper column. 'If anybody can come up with a brilliant attacking idea to make the back four obsolete, I'd like to hear it first ... It's a professional game now. The coaches are eliminating mistakes – and it's easier to achieve with defenders. Show me a team just playing on its natural ability and I'll show you errors that can be exploited.'[7]

Jack, of course, had spent his career playing football that had been questioned, both for club and country. 'Leeds,' he said, 'are responsible for some of my success with Middlesbrough. But Alf Ramsey is also responsible for some of it ... We will play effective football ... We will continue to play to our strengths and there will be no fancy football.'[8] In that declaration, made just before the start of the new season, the influence of Ramsey is clear. When they won away at Tottenham early in September, Geoffrey Green described Boro as 'well-drilled, streamlined, durable'[9] – those were Ramsey's brutalist virtues.

Not only did Jack not care what fans thought; he argued after Liverpool had been beaten in the European Cup by a canny Crvena Zvezda – who sat deep and played on the counter[10] – that English fans, with their demand for all-action, helter-skelter football, were actively holding English football back. 'I know it is our job to knock out the Red Stars of football,' he wrote. 'But will you let us? Or will you play hell the more passes we string together?'[11]

Jack didn't change, and nor did Middlesbrough's form. Promotion was secured with a 1–0 win over Oxford with seven games of the season remaining, and the title wrapped up with a 1–0 win over Luton the following week. Jack was named manager of the year, the first lower league manager to be so honoured.

Having played his final game for Manchester United, Bobby had gone away with his family for a fortnight, returning with little clear idea of what he was going to do. He experienced a 'terrible uncertainty'[12] as he waited for the phone to ring and, when it finally did, after three weeks, he was ready to say, 'Yes,' to anything. Bobby later acknowledged he had accepted the offer of a job too quickly.

Preston North End had its appeal. It was a proud old club, the first league champions, and the team of Tom Finney. But it was also a club that was losing money with a squad that needed a significant rebuild. 'There were a lot of older players that were coming to the end of their careers,' said Mike Elwiss, whom Bobby signed from Doncaster in February 1974, 'and, putting it bluntly, they weren't up to it, some of them didn't have the desire to do it.'[13]

There were plenty who wondered whether Bobby might be 'too soft' to make it in management. Jack was not among them, insisting Bobby was 'as ruthless and single-minded a character as anyone I know in football'. That he was capable of playing his cards close to his chest had been made clear to Jack when Bobby had taken the Preston job. The night before his appointment was made public, Jack had seen Bobby at the FWA dinner, when his brother had not so much as hinted at it. Within a few days, he'd persuaded Nobby Stiles to leave Boro and join him at Deepdale (although, in truth, the desire of Stiles's wife to return to the North-West probably had more to do with it than Bobby). 'When people suspect his toughness,' Jack concluded, 'they ought to wonder how he feels every time he boards an aeroplane.'[14]

His support suggests that, while relations between the brothers may have been strained, they were far from hostile. But they would deteriorate.

Things began well at Preston. He was, after all, Bobby Charlton. 'It caused great excitement in the town and among the players in the dressing room,' said the centre-back John Bird. 'There was a definite aura about him and it was plain to see in training sessions: he still had the skill and he still had the flair.'[15]

Bobby surrounded himself with familiar faces. As well as bringing Nobby Stiles back to the North-West, David Sadler and Francis Burns were picked up from United. But perhaps most telling was the appointment as coach of the former United goalkeeper Jack Crompton, somebody whose methods Noel Cantwell had dismissed as hopelessly outmoded a decade earlier. There was very little sophistication in Bobby's methods. 'It was enjoyable,' said Elwiss. 'It wasn't a chore, he just let you express yourself. There were no real restrictions put on you.'[16]

A feeling grew that Bobby struggled to develop players who didn't have anything like the talent he did and that, in a sense, management for him became a way of extending his playing career. 'In training,' said Bird, 'we went through various things, as you always do, but we always finished off with a game and that was his joy ... He generally thought every player had the same enthusiasm as he did and he expected players to have that will to win and enjoy playing – but he was a natural which sometimes was a little bit difficult because not all players are naturals.'[17]

But that wasn't the only problem. Although Bobby later became a fairly regular public speaker, he never relished it and at this stage in particular there were occasions when he found addressing his players an ordeal. 'When he used to read the team sheet out for the opposition just before the game,' said Elwiss, 'you could see he was nervous and his hand was shaking.' For him, Bobby lacked the 'ruthless streak' that was a prerequisite for a manager,[18] despite what Jack had said. The contrast with his brother was clear. Jack 'never showed any signs he found the job difficult,' said Souness. 'He didn't put a lot of hours into the job, but it worked.'[19]

The brothers first met as managers in early December and appeared together on Tyne Tees, Jack jovially shouting at his players as they sprinted up a hill, while Bobby stood in an empty stadium, wearily noting that the job 'takes a lot of your time up'. The pitch at Ayresome Park was covered in snow. While Bobby fretted about the spectacle and player safety, Jack got on with encouraging the staff working with shovels. The clip ended with Jack going to the boot of his car, taking out a pheasant and a hare and giving Bobby instructions in how to hang them.

They were very different people. They'd been different as boys, they'd been different as players and they were different as managers. They were different, too, as men, in politics as well as personality. As Jack became a columnist and found his opinion sought on a range of issues, he began to offer vaguely socialist sentiments. He would quote Arthur Scargill, later a neighbour, approvingly. There was never much sense of a coherent philosophy from him but he generally sided with the working man. Bobby, characteristically, never spoke publicly about politics, although few seem to doubt he was a patriotic, *Daily Mail*-reading Conservative.

What was the state then, as they began their managerial journeys, of their relationship? 'There's no war between me and our kid,' said Jack at a pre-match press conference. But his look was of sadness. 'There's no war.'[20] Middlesbrough beat Preston 3–0. Jack's journey would last another twenty-two years; Bobby's would be over within twenty months.

Nobody seems to have disliked Bobby or been offended or hurt by him but, equally, a number of players from that squad have spoken of his tendency to moan in training when things were going badly. For Mark Lawrenson, who was just emerging from Preston's youth ranks in Bobby's spell as manager, his approach was inspirational to the better players, but intimidating to those who struggled to match his level.[21]

Once the initial fillip that Bobby was their manager had worn off, there was very little to sustain Preston's form. His Busby-derived vision of football was attacking, dependent on brilliant individuals and ill-equipped to deal with the realities of Second Division football in an era becoming rapidly more tactically sophisticated. Having taken one point from their first three games of the season, Preston went eight games unbeaten. A 1–0 win over Sunderland on 13 October took them third, three points behind Jack's Middlesbrough.

But they only won four more games all season and finished second bottom, a miserable campaign compounded by the deduction of a point for fielding an unregistered player. The only solace was that, by the time they lost 4–2 to Jack's Boro on the final day of the season, they were already relegated; Jack did not send his younger brother down. Nonetheless, it was, Bobby acknowledged, 'an embarrassing comparison'.[22] A third of Preston's 4,500 season-ticket holders refused to renew and at a board meeting that April, three of the nine directors openly contemplated sacking Bobby.

His status had given the team its initial boost and now it protected him. Nobody wanted to be the club who sacked Bobby Charlton.

The final day of the 1974–75 season: Middlesbrough against Derby. Middlesbrough led 1–0 through a David Mills goal and were on course to qualify for Europe in their first season back in the top flight. In the last minute, they won a corner. Jack shouted at Bobby Murdoch to take it short. He did not, arcing a cross into the middle where it was turned behind for another corner. Jack screamed at him again to hold possession, to keep the ball in the corner. Again he sent a cross into the box. This time it was cleared, Derby broke and Kevin Hector equalised.

Except that isn't what happened. That's how Jack tells the story in his autobiography.[23] But Middlesbrough's game against Derby was their fifth-last game of the season. And, even if they had won that match – although they would have climbed above Stoke and Sheffield United on goal average – they would still have missed out on Europe by a point. What really cost them was the back-to-back defeats to Leicester and Wolves that followed. But it is telling that it is that incident that should have stuck in Jack's mind, his indignation at a goal and a point squandered, standing out two decades later after other details had fallen away.

Seventh place, though, still represented success, particularly given he essentially used the squad he had inherited. Jack felt that the players who had got Middlesbrough promoted deserved their chance and his only major signing that summer was his former Leeds teammate, full-back Terry Cooper. His unwillingness to spend was to become a major theme of his management. 'I treated club funds like my own,' Jack said[24] – and everybody knew how tight he was with his own cash.

*

Bobby, fundamentally, just wanted to play football and, in summer 1974, after a year out of the game, he decided he had retired too early. George Best may have thought he had held on too long, but Bobby reasoned that the problem was that he had continued to train at full tilt. If he had managed his training better, done just a few sprints, he thought, he could still have operated at the highest level. And so for 1974–75, with Preston in the Third Division, he registered himself as a player again.

Was he a success? On the face of it, yes. He started thirty-eight of forty-six league games that season and scored eight goals, including his two-hundredth in league football. Plenty of journalists and fans have spoken of how Bobby would control games while barely moving from the centre-circle, spraying passes all round the park. But those who played with him are less convinced. 'It was his sheer enthusiasm and love of the game that made him come back – and also to help the team out,' said Bird. 'But doing it on the training field is not the same as playing in a match and in my opinion he shouldn't have come back.'[25] Elwiss spoke of the 'pleasure and honour' of 'being in the same team photograph as him and playing on the same pitch as him' but, in the end, concluded, 'His best days were behind him.'[26]

Again, Preston began the season well. This time they sustained their form until the end of February, but a run of two wins in their final fourteen games of the season saw them finish ninth, well out of the promotion picture.

Middlesbrough had never played at Wembley, but victory over Burnley in the League Cup quarter-final put them in a two-legged semi-final against Manchester City from a first-ever appearance in a major cup final. They won the first leg, Hickton heading in a Cooper flick for a 1–0 win. The only concern was that they had been dominant enough to have won far more easily, that this had been perhaps an opportunity missed. 'Souness sparked off wave after wave of red-shirted Middlesbrough attacks,' wrote Gerry Harrison in *The Times*, but Middlesbrough were hampered by 'their nagging ailment, the inability to score from good chances'.[27]

City's Dennis Tueart was suspended while Dave Watson and Colin Bell were injured, but Boro failed to take advantage of the absence of three internationals in the second leg. Their bus turned up late, a not uncommon occurrence under Jack, and they then got stuck in traffic. 'We had about twenty minutes to get ready and out on the pitch for the start of the game,' said David Mills, 'and, basically, I don't think we'd calmed down, organised ourselves and decided how to go about it.'[28]

Five minutes in, the full-back John Craggs left Asa Hartford's crossfield pass, thinking it was going out of play, only for Peter Barnes to steal in and cross for Ged Keegan to score. Alan Oakes added a second five minutes later and Boro suddenly were chasing the game, which didn't suit their style of play. Two further 'uncharacteristic defensive lapses'[29] led to a 4–0 defeat.

In their centenary year, Boro did win the Anglo-Scottish Cup, but it was a disappointing season. They lost eight of their remaining fourteen games that season and finished thirteenth. 'I think he was devastated first time round with the Man City tie,' said Mills, 'because Middlesbrough hadn't really had any success for a significant number of years and it was a real opportunity to take the team to the final. Deep down, I think Jack was hurt by it all. He'd had so much success as a player and he wanted that same success as a manager, but it just didn't happen for him.'[30]

Bobby believed that in lower league football the two most important positions were centre-back and centre-forward, and he was fortunate at Preston to have an excellent centre-back in John Bird, who had turned twenty-five the summer he had taken the job. 'He believed in me,' said Bird, 'and trusted me and he also said to me that, after Bill Foulkes, I was one of the best centre-halves he had played with.'[31]

But that naturally meant that Bird attracted attention from other clubs, particularly after Preston had been relegated to the Third Division. Gordon Lee had wanted to sign him when he was Blackburn manager and renewed his interest after taking the Newcastle job in 1975. With annual losses approaching eighty-thousand pounds, the Preston board were keen to sell and negotiated a fee of £100,000 plus Alec Bruce,* a diminutive Scottish forward who hadn't settled after joining Newcastle from Preston for £140,000 the previous summer.

By the time Bobby found out, the deal was almost done. The Tuesday after beating Colchester 2–1 in the opening game of the season, Preston faced Blackburn Rovers of the Second Division in the League Cup. That afternoon, one of Bird's neighbours came round to ask him about a headline in the local paper that said he was about to sign for Newcastle. 'I didn't know a thing,' Bird said. Bemused, he went in to see Bobby before that evening's game. 'I know nothing about this,' Bobby replied, 'but you are not leaving.'[32]

Bird had mixed feelings. 'The board couldn't push you to go,' he explained. 'It was a difficult situation for me. It was an opportunity which really you shouldn't miss, going into the First Division with a team like Newcastle United and I didn't tell anybody that I didn't want to go. But I absolutely loved playing for Bobby and being captain of Preston North End. In a sense, I hoped the deal fell through.'

After a 2–0 win over Blackburn, probably his best result as

---

* There is no consistency in the reporting of the fee. A hundred thousand pounds was what was reported in the *Daily Mirror* at the time, but others suggest a substantially lower figure.

a manager, Bobby gave the board an ultimatum – if Bird went, he quit – it looked like the deal had fallen through, but when it turned out directors were still negotiating, Bobby submitted his resignation. 'I didn't want to stay where my opinion as manager didn't carry weight when the club were about to take what I considered a backward step,' he explained.[33]

What is striking is how supportive the players were, despite poor results. The midfielder Alex Spark submitted a transfer request, while the defender John McMahon, who had seen the board cancel a trial at Manchester United after Bobby's resignation, effectively threatened to go on strike. 'I don't want to kick another ball for this club,' he said.[34]

After a crisis meeting, the players issued a statement: 'We will play against Port Vale on Saturday and give our best for the club – if only for the sake of Bobby. But we feel a manager must be allowed to manage and that the directors should concentrate on money-raising and leave football to the professionals.'[35]

Preston drew at Port Vale in the league and had completed their League Cup victory over Blackburn with a 0–0 draw at Ewood Park when the news broke. 'It came out of the blue ...' said Bird. 'We beat Blackburn Rovers, which was a hell of a result and, coming out of the dressing room, to get on the coach to come back to Preston, a representative of Newcastle United, I can't remember who, and the chairman, were at the back of the coach and they said, the deal is back on, because Bobby had gone.'[36]

Bird is reluctant to make accusations, and acknowledges he has no proof, but he was not the only one to wonder if that had been the plan all along. Nobody, after all, wanted to be the director who knifed Bobby Charlton. 'Bobby had made me captain,' he said, 'and I am sure in the boardroom they would have said, "He won't like this if we let him go." I don't think it is too much to say they used the situation. Around the time, locally, that is what a lot of people thought. I think it was pretty obvious ...'

That impression was only strengthened after Bird became manager of Hartlepool and returned to Preston for a Division Four game at Christmas 1986. 'There was one director still left there,' he recalls, 'and, from what was said in there, I think there was more than meets the eye in terms of them using the situation.'[37]

At the very least, Preston's directors don't seem to have tried very hard to persuade Bobby to stay. The chairman Alan Jones, though, was adamant, 'We did nothing at all to force it.'[38]

What was clear was that Bobby bore Bird no ill will, sending him a telegram before his first game for Newcastle, against Manchester City, saying, 'You can do this standing on your head, have a great debut.' As it turned out, he couldn't, or at least not straight away. Bird had found it difficult to adjust to the step up in level and couldn't get into the game as City won 4–0: 'We got absolutely murdered and I didn't get very good press.'

The following week, Newcastle beat Aston Villa at home. Bobby came into the dressing room after the game. 'The players nearly dropped dead when they saw him walk in,' said Bird, 'and he put his arms around me and shouted out loud, "This is one of the best centre-halves I ever played with." Their jaws dropped, and I think he had known I had had a bit of a rough start and had gone there on purpose to make a point. In that dressing room my esteem just jumped up a bit.'[39]

Other players remember him just as fondly. 'Great times, great man,' said Mike Elwiss. 'I loved playing under him and it was just an honour. The older I get, the more I look back and think how lucky I was that our paths crossed. There are not many players who will have been signed by him.'[40]

And yet it is also clear that players did see the flaws in Bobby's management – as, indeed, did Bobby. Before the season began, he had given a remarkable interview to the *People* in which familiar managerial expressions of confidence were repeatedly undercut by his admissions of doubt. 'If I don't get success this season, I shall have to consider the possibility that I might never make it in this business,' he said, insisting he was 'convinced' Preston would finish in the top three while admitting he couldn't feel confident in his future if he didn't.

Much of the interview was spent acknowledging that he'd had no real concept of what management entailed. 'When I first came to Preston I was very raw,' Bobby said. 'I'd been in the game a long time, but there is a vast difference between playing and managing. Players spend all their lives being looked after. They are important commodities. They have to be protected. Now I'm the guy doing that protecting, the one who has to organise their lives ... the amount of effort has come as a shock ... As a manager I was warned I would come up against hard, cynical men who would not make life easy. I've always been prepared to trust anyone until they let me down. I've still been doing that and I've been let down. But I am learning.'

He had decided that the return to playing had been a bad idea that left him unable to 'fulfil my other duties properly'. He remained registered as a player but said he would 'have to have half the staff down with flu' before he pulled his boots on again.[41]

The sense is of somebody extremely naive in a difficult world; naive not just in his dealings with directors but also – even after everything that had happened in the later years at Manchester United – about players. 'He just loved football,' said Bird. 'He couldn't understand how anyone could be any different to him in a sense – just the joy of playing, he just thought it was a privilege to be on a football field and that came across. Probably he couldn't understand why players couldn't do certain things and the reason is because he was a natural. He came across as a very caring and kind sort of person.'[42]

Perhaps that was largely a matter of personality; Bobby had never had Jack's canniness. But there was also something wilful about his attitude. Only seven pages of Bobby's autobiography – out of 685 across two volumes – are given up to his two years at Deepdale and it's evident from the tone that he didn't much care for the sort of detailed preparation coaching in the seventies had come to entail. There is almost something peevish about his comment, 'A network of coaches was creating a new culture, one which could leave you on the outside, however much fame you had won on the field.'[43]

But why would fame on the pitch guarantee success as a manager? He admitted that he considered going on a coaching course as Jack had but that his 'first reaction' was, 'Oh, God, this will take ages.'[44] Bobby may have been the more academically gifted brother as a child, but by the end of their playing careers, it was Jack who had taken the time to gain an education. Bobby still dreamed of those prelapsarian days of instinctive, unregulated attacking football with Duncan and Tommy and Eddie.

And it didn't help, of course, that his model as a manager remained Matt Busby, whose scepticism about coaching had made him seem deeply old-fashioned by the time he retired in 1969. 'I had always thought that if you were a strong enough character,' Bobby said, 'and if you had been around the right people all your career and tried all you could to learn from them, you probably knew more than could ever be imparted in a lecture room or out on a training field under the supervision of someone wearing a bib and holding a sheaf of notes.'[45]

The realisation that wasn't true was not merely a shock, but one that Bobby hadn't wanted to believe true. What he loved was playing and so, other than a brief caretaker stint at Wigan in 1983, his departure from Preston marked the end of his managerial career.

*

On 9 October 1976, Middlesbrough beat Norwich 1–0 to go top of the First Division. The following week they went to Birmingham, who sat off. Foggon suddenly had no space to run into, and Boro lost 3–1. Jack realised his team had been found out and knew that word would soon get around. A run to the quarter-final of the Cup, in which they lost to Liverpool, stretched an already thin squad. Jack had been unable to replace Murdoch, with Phil Boersma never really settling after his move from Liverpool. He'd tried to get a centre-forward to come in for John Hickton, but had refused to pay Coventry eighty-thousand pounds for David Cross – who ended up moving to West Brom for £150,000 a few weeks later. As Boro's form disintegrated, Jack blamed his own financial caution. He believed Boro had been two players short of a title-winning squad.

And perhaps he was right. They had, after all, finished only five points behind the champions Derby in 1974–75. Hickton had turned thirty in September that season. What if Jack had managed to sign a high-class replacement? 'John had a great career at Middlesbrough,' said Jim Platt, 'but time was running out for him. Jack admitted later that he should have brought in a centre-forward and, if he'd done that, I think we'd have been very close to winning the league. But Jack was miserable at the time; he'd never spend money. He never spent money! He smoked and he was always cadging cigarettes off the fans at the training ground. He'd get a cigarette and then he'd say, "Have you got a light as well?"[46]

David Mills remembers picking up the paper one morning and seeing he'd been linked with a £200,000 move to Liverpool. He popped into Jack's office at Ayresome Park and asked what was going on. 'He said, "Yeah, it's true. I've told them I don't want to sell you and it's not enough,"' said Mills. 'So I'm thinking away as he's talking and I go, "Right, well, if you value me at more than £200,000 then will you pay me the salary that a £200,000-plus player is worth?"

'He said two words to me. The first word began with "f" and the second word began with "o". Then he stood up, walked past me, went down the stairs and went off to get changed so he could take training.'[47]

Middlesbrough ended the season twelfth. By then, Jack had long since told the Boro board he intended to honour his decision to leave after four years. To take Boro up and make them a mid-table club with very little expenditure was, by any reasonable measure, a fine achievement – but Jack wanted more.

15

THE LONG
GOOD WEDNESDAY

Don Revie's decision to abandon the England job for the UAE in July 1977 didn't just create a public furore; it also seems to have left a number of managers with a permanent sense of grievance against the Football Association. Jack wrote to the FA applying for the job. He never received a reply and resolved never to apply for another job in his life.[1] When Ron Greenwood was appointed on an interim basis until the end of World Cup qualifying, Jack asked, not unreasonably, what the logic was. How could it possibly make sense to appoint a new manager in December, in the middle of the season? And what was he supposed to do? Hang around without a job until then, on the off chance?[2]

Jack felt he had been messed around. A decade or so later, the chairman of the FA, Bert Millichip, who had been a member of the FA executive in 1977, had met his Irish counterpart Des Casey and told him he'd made a mistake appointing Jack as national manager. When Jack's Ireland then beat England at Euro 88, Casey, of course, was then able to respond that it had been a pretty good mistake.[3]

Yet beyond the FA's basic lack of courtesy in not replying to his letter, it's hard to understand why Jack was so aggrieved to be overlooked. Brian Clough, who was shortlisted but rather undermined his application by criticising England's new Admiral kit to a board member shortly before his interview, also believed he should have been appointed, but after winning a remarkable league title with Derby, he had publicly fallen out with their chairman Sam Longson before a disappointing spell at Brighton and his volcanic forty-four days at Leeds; at that stage of his career, having just led Nottingham Forest to promotion, there was nothing to suggest he would soon win another league title and two European Cups.

Jack's record was nothing compared to Clough's and neither man – plain speakers who knew their own mind and had little truck with social decorum – was ever likely to appeal to FA mandarins who, not entirely unreasonably, worried about the ambassadorial nature of the role. Ramsey had caused them enough problems and, after the chaos of what was seen as Revie's betrayal, it was understandable that they should favour a more diplomatic, safe pair of hands. Ron Greenwood, who was eventually appointed on a permanent basis in December 1977 after beating Italy in a World Cup qualifier during his time as caretaker, fit that description – but he had also been a successful club manager, winning the FA Cup and Cup Winners' Cup with West Ham.

Jack, as became clear from a column in the *News of the World* that summer, had become worried he was being written off because of his style of play. 'I'm fed up of hearing that I'm suspicious of skilful players and no matter where I went next I'd produce a dull side,' he said, before suggesting his approach at Middlesbrough had been forced on him by circumstance. 'With the squad I had at Middlesbrough we had a remarkably efficient and effective side ...' he said. 'I had four or five lads at Ayresome Park who had no right to be in the First Division.'

And then, typically – almost in passing – he made a revealing tactical point about the importance of skill: 'Any manager who knows anything about the game can balance a team so that it won't leak goals every week,' he said, as though he saw organisation as a basic part of the job. Far more difficult was sourcing and accommodating the players good enough to create and take chances: 'Seeing goals missed every week is so damn frustrating.'[4]

For the first time since 1950, Jack didn't have to worry about football. For him, the summer of 1977 was a time of great freedom. He took his family for a holiday in the Caribbean, he did a lot of fishing and ensured he still had money coming in by stepping up his television work.

His documentaries for Tyne Tees had shown how comfortable he was in front of the camera and he became a regular television presence, introducing shows on a range of topics, from the predictable – hunting and fishing – to the unexpected. In 1980, for instance, he looked wholly out of place visiting the new romantic Blitz Club in Covent Garden – whose cloakroom attendant George O'Dowd later found fame as Boy George – with a TV crew and yet seemed at the same time entirely at ease. He told a clubber in heavy makeup and his mother's braided coat that 'your get-up is magnificent' and reflected, 'When I was a young lad there was none of this.' What shines through is a basic humanity and sense of fascination about a culture very different from his own, particularly given his comments on the role of women when he'd returned to Ashington for *Big Jack's Other World*. It's unfair, of course, to generalise based on isolated instances, but the contrast to Bobby's horror at the revolution represented by Best is striking.

Football, though, continued to provide the majority of Jack's media work. He wasn't just a fine analyst of the game but was very good at conveying that knowledge to the audience. There was a period in the late seventies and early eighties when he was unsurpassed as a co-commentor. His tactical acuity was there also in the columns he wrote for the *Daily Mail*. In 1973, for instance, when England beat Austria 7–0 in a friendly in preparation for their crucial World Cup qualifier against Poland, he insisted the ease of the win against a team of 'no tacklers', far from suggesting England were in good shape, actually made their task psychologically harder. It also alerted Poland to the fact they could safely force England to attack down the left where they had 'no finesse'.[5] Sure enough, needing to win to reach the World Cup finals, England were held to a draw.

Jack's co-commentary on the 1980 European Cup final, in which Nottingham Forest beat Hamburg 1–0, is remarkable in its prescience. About five minutes before John Robertson jinked past the right-back Manny Kaltz to score what turned out to be the only goal of the game, Jack had suggested that Robertson had the beating of the West Germany international and that that was the likeliest source of a goal. In the second half, as the commentator Brian Moore grew increasingly anxious about the extent to which Hamburg were dominating possession, Jack remained calm, pointing out that they'd been limited almost entirely to long-range efforts and saying – rightly, as it turned out – that he couldn't see that changing.

However good his punditry, Jack's heart lay in management. In October 1977, he took a call from the Sheffield Wednesday director Roy Whitehead, saying that Len Ashurst would soon be leaving and had recommended Jack as his successor. Jack told him to get back in touch when there was actually a vacancy. A few days later, Ashurst resigned, and Whitehead rang back.

Jack and Pat went to watch Wednesday play Chesterfield.[6] They won 1–0, but they were still bottom of the table and, in Jack's assessment, had been 'bloody awful'.[7] He met the chairman, Bert McGee, and, despite reservations about the quality of the squad, accepted the job. As at Middlesbrough he preferred to work without a contract but, this time, he did bring in an assistant. He recognised he had no experience at that level and wanted somebody who did: in Maurice Setters (Bobby's best man), he found the perfect candidate. Setters had managed Doncaster Rovers between May 1971 and September 1974 but after being dismissed had taken them to a tribunal for wrongful dismissal. Although he won, taking legal action was against football's unwritten code and effectively rendered him unemployable.

Accepting the job was far from an obvious step. Wednesday were sinking, had made a loss of £43,966 the previous season and crowds were down to fifteen thousand.[8] Jack had turned down several more lucrative offers from clubs in better shape. But he knew what Wednesday had been and what they could be. And he liked the idea of a project, something he could run on his own terms. There would be no referring back to past glories, nobody telling him how previous managers had gone about their business. Not that there was much sense of excitement on his part at his first meeting with the players. He told them to gather in the boardroom. When he walked in, they fell silent, waiting for a rousing speech from their new boss.[9] 'I don't know why I've taken this job,' he said. 'I don't need to work; I'm a millionaire.'[10]

It was not some vague boast and it certainly wasn't Jack setting himself above his players. The point was significant because it meant he had freedom to do things his way. 'When people don't have to work,' the forward Rodger Wylde said, 'then they do a job exactly how they would like to do it, rather than how they are perceived to have to want to do it.'[11]

'Facing the ball,' Jack realised, 'the majority of the players were quite good – it was when they tried to turn and play they got themselves into trouble.'[12] So he decided his approach had to be rudimentary: get the ball into the box and play from there.

His first months in the job were about laying down ground rules and that meant for the board as much as the players. When McGee went to speak to the players after the reserves had lost to Everton, Jack erupted. Directors were banned from the dressing room and were also discouraged from talking negatively about the club when out in public.

For a couple of months, results remained poor. Wednesday went out of the FA Cup to Wigan Athletic, then of the Northern Premier League; when their team bus got stuck in the mud trying to leave, it seemed an apt metaphor for the plight of the club. Jack, though, was unconcerned. 'We're expecting a rocket when we go into the dressing room,' said the goalkeeper Chris Turner. 'Jack just said: "I knew you'd get beat today, lads. I looked at the pitch, I looked at the conditions, it's not what you're used to so, hey, listen, I expected it. Anyway, the bad news, lads, is that the coach is stuck in mud, we can't get it out and there's two foot of the stuff. We're having to wait for another coach to come from Sheffield to pick us up so, hey, go and have a few beers in the bar and let's move on."[13]

The goalkeeper Bob Bolder was eighteen when he joined Sheffield Wednesday in March 1977. He found the move from Dover to Sheffield difficult and was aware that the reserve team manager Ken Knighton didn't rate him, preferring Peter Fox as backup to Chris Turner. When Len Ashurst resigned and Knighton became caretaker manager, he knew his prospects weren't bright. Sure enough, before the game against Chesterfield, Knighton told him he was being loaned to Crewe and that he should collect his belongings the following Monday.

'I'm Mr Doom-and-Gloom when I turn up at the ground and go into the boot room,' Bolder recalled. 'Ken Knighton is there, "Blah, blah, blah." I can't remember what he said. I'm getting my gear together, so I take my boots off the peg. Next thing, Big Jack walks in. He came in, he looked at me straight away and he said, "Who are you, big lad?"

'"Bob Bolder."

'He went, "What position do you play?"

'"Goalkeeper."

'He goes, "Well, what are you doing?"

'I say, "I'm just getting my boots and getting ready to go to Crewe."

'He said something like, "No one's going anywhere, not until I find out what I've got here. I like big goalies."'[14]

Nine days after the defeat to Wigan, on Boxing Day 1977, Wednesday lost 3–1 at home to Tranmere, a defeat that left them bottom of the table, five points from safety.

But slowly, Jack could see improvement coming. The players may not have been of the standard he was used to, but he worked on improving them, on making the system work for them. They spent a lot of time practising free kicks, an area in which significant gains could be achieved even by limited players. The contrast to Bobby, whose solution to a failing team had been to bring himself out of retirement, was obvious.

Chris Turner broke a finger against Tranmere and so Bolder was brought in the following day to make his debut against Rotherham. Wednesday won 1–0. On New Year's Eve they beat Hereford by the same scoreline. The corner had been turned.

At the end of February, Wednesday went to Shrewsbury and in his pre-match team-talk, Jack turned to the midfielder Jeff Johnson and told him to watch out for Brian Hornsby: 'He's a very skilful player ... I'm buying him to replace you.'[15] As it turned out, there was room in the Wednesday midfield for both of them, Hornsby offering a valuable goal threat. Although Wednesday won only one game in that first season under Jack by more than a single goal, they lost only one of their final twelve and stayed up comfortably, finishing fourteenth, ten points above Port Vale in fourth bottom.

In two months, Bolder had gone from discard to first-team regular. 'It was sheer luck really,' he said. 'If I'd not come in on the Monday, I might not have seen him.'[16] Turner, as he would go on to prove at Sunderland and then Manchester United, was an excellent, agile goalkeeper, but he was smaller than Bolder and so didn't fit Jack's system. 'He wanted a big, strong spine to the team,' said Bolder. 'He wanted his centre-halves to be big and he wanted his goalkeeper to be big. We were always quick on the break so the instructions he used to give me were, "As soon as you get the ball in your hands, you need to release it early." I had a big kick then and could get the ball three-quarters of the way down the field, so I used to hump it downfield with plenty of height. He thought if we went with a big kick from the goalie we'd see bonuses from that: corners, throw-ins and keeping the ball in their danger area all of the time. He didn't like too much fannying around, especially when he saw that the ball was on. If you had that opportunity to get the ball forwards, he wanted people to make the right decision and, if you didn't, you'd get an absolute bollocking.'[17]

Jack's other innovation was the use of the central defender Jimmy Mullen as a deep-lying midfielder. 'In those days you might have had sweepers playing behind two centre-backs,' said Chris Turner, 'but there was never a front sweeper. Jimmy played in front of the two centre-backs, which wasn't really heard of – or certainly not in the Third Division. It was a massive success.'[18]

'We're playing a game in the midweek, a night game, 7.30 kick-off in those days,' said Rodger Wylde. 'The backroom staff at that time was Jack, Maurice Setters, Ian St John and Tony Toms, who was on fitness and physio. He had no qualifications or anything as far as I'm aware, but he was a great bloke, a great bloke.

So, we're there at the normal time, an hour before kick-off, pre-paring for the game. Everybody's in the dressing room except Jack. Nobody's really that worried, though you could see at that time there was a bit of a conversation going on between the coaches, Maurice, Ian and Tony. When it got to about quarter past seven and there was still no Jack, everybody was panicking.

'We get to kick-off time, because in those days you just sort of went out for a few minutes [to warm up] before the game began, went in and came back out again. It wasn't a long warm-up, like it is these days. It's five minutes before the game starts, we go out without Jack, come back in at half-time and there's Jack. You could tell from what they'd been saying that he wasn't at the ground. So what we find out later – because there were no mobile phones in those days – is that Jack had been shooting up in the North-East and was travelling back down when he tuned into Radio Sheffield as he picked up the signal and they're talking about the game. That was Jack, he used to forget everything. He'd get everyone's names wrong, he was terrible like that. I got a phone call a week later from a journalist saying, "Look, we've heard what's happened. We just want somebody to back up the story, we think we can get Jack the sack." I said, "What?!?" I knew that the story was right but there was no way I was going to say anything.'[19]

One afternoon, St John was watching racing on television at Jack's house when Jack's eldest, Peter – born two days after the 1966 World Cup final – came in, swishing a cane from the garden. Jack told him to put it down, but Peter kept whipping it about and eventually knocked an ornament to the ground, smashing it. A furious Jack chased after him. Peter ran from the living room, slamming the door as he went, inadvertently trapping his father's finger. As Jack howled in pain, Pat ran in from the kitchen and wrapped his hand in a cloth. St John drove them to hospital where an A&E nurse asked for Jack's autograph before realising how serious the injury was. Jack lost the tip of his finger.

Jack worked as co-commentator on the 1979 FA Cup final and, while on the gantry at Wembley, completed the seventy-thousand-pound signing of the bustling centre-forward Andy McCulloch from Brentford. Wednesday had finished four-teenth again that season and Jack had accepted the need to make signings. McCulloch's arrival effectively meant the end for Wylde, a tall centre-forward, but one who preferred the ball to feet. 'Jack wanted a big, cumbersome, tough, hammer-throwing striker,' Wylde said.[20]

The left-winger Ian Mellor was signed from Chester that summer and he and McCulloch stayed at Jack's house. They both paid him fifty pounds a week for board and lodging and only found out later that he was charging the club the same. 'That's the type of bloke he was,' Wylde said. 'He was quite stingy, especially with contracts and stuff.'[21]

'I was always a good earner,' Jack would say.[22] Perhaps it was simply in his blood; he was, after all, Tanner Milburn's grandson.

Jack's other signing that year was a remarkable coup. Terry Curran had been a regular in the Nottingham Forest side that had been promoted to the First Division under Brian Clough in 1976–77 but the emergence of John Robertson as a playmaker operating from the left while Curran was out injured cost him his place in the team and he was loaned out to Bury before joining Southampton. He played regularly there, but Jack persuaded him to drop two divisions to return to his native Yorkshire, paying £100,000.

There are those who would dismiss Jack as a long-ball merchant, as though there were nothing more to his football than a desire to get the ball forward as quickly as possible, but the case of Curran shows his acuity. He played him through the middle, off Andy McCulloch and, because Curran was a natural winger, he played in a way defenders found difficult to counter. 'He'd come back and get the ball off me, get the ball off the full-backs, he'd be running with it, he'd be dribbling with it,' said the defender Mark Smith. 'He was coming in from different areas, different angles and, back in the day, he'd be asking questions of centre-backs who'd be thinking, Do I go in there and mark him or do I stay here? By that time it was too late – Terry had got the ball, picked it up, gathered speed, gone past people – great dribbler – got fouled and got penalties galore.

'Some of Jack's team talks sometimes would be, "Right, listen, just give it to Terry." He wasn't playing as an orthodox centre-forward, he wasn't playing on the last defender, so Jack would say: "If he comes off, just give it him." He realised – and I think this was the simplicity about Jack – that if you've got good players and you starve them of the ball, you're not going to be successful.'[23]

Everything was simple, straightforward, succinct. 'I remember him coming up to me on the coach coming back from Swansea once when I was about eighteen or nineteen,' said Smith. 'We'd lost and I'd made a mistake for a goal. It was the time when you could roll it back to goalkeepers and they could pick it up, but I'd be stepping over it, pulling it back and stuff like that. He came up to me – I'll always remember it – on a long journey back from Swansea, and I was sat on my own. He leant across to me and went, "It's not a crime to put the ball in the stand, you know?" That was it! We moved on.'[24]

*

Bobby and Jack celebrate together after the final
whistle blows on the World Cup final

An awkward homecoming: Jack revels in the adulation at Ashington's
World Cup victory parade, but Bobby is uncomfortable

Jack, Cissie and Bobby celebrate the World Cup semi-final win over Portugal in 1966

Bobby, Jack and Brian Labone play cards in Guadalajara during the 1970 World Cup. Alf Ramsey's preparations extended to taking British china to Mexico

The elder statesman: Bobby in action for United against Fulham, August 1971

Bobby, Norma and their two daughters at Buckingham Palace as Bobby receives his OBE

Jack and Pat at Ayresome Park, Middlesbrough, 1973

Jack and Bobby at the start of their managerial careers, August 1973

Bobby in pre-season training with his Preston North End squad, 1973

Jack with the Wycombe manager, Brian Lee, during Middlesbrough's 0–0
draw at Loakes Park in the FA Cup third round in 1975

Jack issues instructions to Dennis Lemmon before extra time in Sheffield Wednesday's FA Cup third-round second replay against Arsenal in January 1979

Jack, as Newcastle manager, poses with an inflatable bottle of Newcastle Brown Ale as Peter Beardsley and Chris Waddle look on

Jack fishing in Kelso

Jack talks to his players before the penalty shoot-out against Romania at Italia 90

Jack presents Bobby
with a Lifetime
Achievement Award
at BBC Sports
Personality of the
Year in 2008

The start of the adventure: Jack on the touchline in Brussels for his first competitive game as Ireland manager, September 1986

'I remember,' said Chris Turner, 'seeing Jack on the training ground when we were practising free kicks one day. It was absolutely launching it down with rain and Jack turned up with an umbrella and a long coat, with a pair of wellies on. Jeff [Johnson] was trying to hit the ball, bend it over the top, whatever. Jack's just strode on and said, "Look, Jeff, this is what we need, something like this." He walked up, and toe-ended it with his wellies right into the top corner. It was outrageous. He could never have done it in a month of Sundays if he'd tried it again but this time, *bosh*. He walked up, said, "This is where we want the ball," and, bang, right in the top corner. We just stood there, we couldn't believe it.'[25]

Like Bobby, Jack still loved playing; unlike Bobby he was able to combine that with management.

'He was a lad,' said Bob Bolder. 'He used to join in with the games every now and again. He thought he was the world's best at penalty-taking, with his welly boots on and stuff like that. That's the way he was, he was like a big kid all the time really. You could see that he still wanted to be out there playing himself, but his enthusiasm for being out there on the training field was huge.'[26]

Paul Bradshaw was a gifted winger whose career was undermined by injuries, which forced him to retire in 1978 when he was just twenty-four. As he tried to recover, he went in to see Jack to ask if he had a future at the club. 'Jack was drawing all these crosses on the board,' said Rodger Wylde, 'saying stuff like, "I want you to play in there with so-and-so playing there, so-and-so up front and at the back."

'Braddy was quite a clever lad – when he finished he became a school teacher – and he was quite astute. He went, "Oh, right, OK, so, I am in your plans then, Jack?"

'He said, "Yeah, yeah, of course you are."

'Braddy went, "Can I just point out to you that you've got eleven outfield players there? Are you not going to play with a goalkeeper?"

'Jack went, "Oh, right, yeah. Perhaps you might not be in my plans, after all."[27]

It was towards the end of 1979 that Wylde realised there was no longer any place for him at Wednesday. Having beaten Lincoln in the first round of the FA Cup, they faced Carlisle in the second. 'Training that week was me up front, four in midfield and five at the back,' Wylde recalled. 'We had Terry [Curran] on one side and Ian "Spider" Mellor on the other side, out wide. The instructions to Bob Bolder in goal were, "Bob, I want you to boot the ball as high and far as you can to Rodger."

'That was what we did all that week in terms of tactics. We went up to Carlisle and it was pissing down with rain. It was a bog. All I remember from that game was the ball being booted to me, their centre-half coming towards me from the back, Terry and Spider running towards me from the front and it was just ridiculous. We ended up getting beat 3–0. On the way back, Jack pulled me and he said, "Rodger, I'm never going to play you away from home again." He blamed me for the defeat!'[28]

Wilde was the club's second-leading scorer that season, despite having missed a month with a metatarsal injury. Jack, though, did leave him out for the next game, away at Reading. Wednesday won 2–0. And the game after that was the Boxing Day derby against Sheffield United.

It was the first time the Sheffield rivals had met in the league since 1971 so it was always going to be a game of great significance. And it meant a lot in the promotion race with United top of the table and Wednesday four points back, in fifth.

Security concerns meant the game kicked off at 11 a.m. and was all-ticket, with a fifth of South Yorkshire police's entire manpower on duty. A record crowd of 49,309 still turned out at Hillsborough for what turned out to be one of the greatest games in Wednesday's history, a game that is remembered as the Boxing Day Massacre.

Ian Mellor, selected ahead of Wylde – 'That sort of finished it for me, because it was a big game,' Wylde admitted[29] and he left for Oldham six weeks later – opened the scoring with a long-range effort seven minutes from half-time. At that point it was a relatively even game and only a remarkable double save from Bob Bolder, tipping a Jeff Bourne shot on to the bar and then blocking the follow-up from John MacPhail, kept Wednesday ahead.

Nine minutes into the second half, McCulloch hit the post and Jeff King fired the rebound against the bar. But the goals came: a McCulloch cross for Curran to head in after sixty-three minutes, a Curran cross for King a minute later and then a Mark Smith penalty after Curran had been brought down. 'It could have been six, or seven, or eight, when you think of the chances we missed,' said Curran.[30]

Although Wednesday lost their next game, at home to Plymouth, they then went on a sixteen-game unbeaten run that carried them to promotion.

Terry Curran challenged for a ball with Oldham's Simon Stainrod and, he believes, was punched as he did so. He went to retaliate with a knee to the groin but, he says, at the last second stopped himself.[31] Stainrod went down anyway. Curran was sent off and, as Stainrod got up, he appeared to be grinning. Wednesday fans rioted, invading the pitch. Jack begged them to return to the terrace, tears of frustration pouring down his face. For half an hour the game was held up; when the players returned, Oldham won 2–0. Sheffield Wednesday fans were banned from their next four away games and the terraces at Hillsborough closed for their next four home games.

Jack called the rioters 'the scum of society' and described hooligans as 'the dregs who just turn up anywhere there might be trouble'.[32] As hooliganism became a major problem, Jack – writing in his autobiography – claims he tried to quell it by encouraging police at away games not to report arrest figures, thinking publicity fuelled the problem. But this was not just a football issue: before the start of the following season, there had been major riots in Brixton, Toxteth, Moss Side, Handsworth and Chapeltown and elsewhere. Thatcher's Britain was become an increasing disaffected and violent place.

Football, and the world, was changing in ways Jack hated.

John Pearson was a local lad who had come through Wednesday's youth system and made his debut because of Curran's suspension. Jack saw his talent early and 'nurtured' him, to use his word – although that often meant taking him and Gavin Oliver, a young central defender from Felling near Gateshead, to act as beaters. 'When he was hunting, say on a Wednesday, he'd go, "Right, you two. You're coming with me tomorrow."

'We'd say, "What do you mean, boss?"

'"You're coming with me; don't worry. We're going up to me mother's."

'He and Tony Toms would drive me and Gavin up to his mum's. He wouldn't take us out for a drink or anything, we were only seventeen or whatever. They'd go out and we used to stay at his mum's. She used to make this massive pie, game pie or whatever it was, really nice. Then we'd be up at six o'clock in the morning, we'd be at one end of a field and we'd be beating for him. They'd all be stood at the other end, him and about twenty others, shooting the grouse. I found it horrific. I didn't want to do it. They'd be falling dead at my feet and I'd be going, "I'm not picking that up, no chance!"

'But that was Jack's thing, he loved all that. So sometimes he'd take us off to do that, or sometimes he'd get all the apprentices together, get the minibus and we'd have to go and do his garden. He'd take us up near Barnsley where he was living and he'd have us pulling up weeds.'[33]

Ante Miročević was an elegant midfielder for the Montenegrin side Budućnost Podgorica and part of the Yugoslavia squad that reached the semi-final of the 1980 Olympics. Shortly before the Olympics, he was approached by an agent who told him that Jack Charlton was looking for a creative player and that a scout had recommended him. That August, Miročević turned twenty-eight, allowing him to leave the Yugoslav league. England, he knew, meant much higher wages than he was on, and he flew to Sheffield for ten days of tests and agreed a deal before flying to Moscow with his national side.

The move was, at best, a qualified success. Miročević was Wednesday's first foreign player but, although he totalled seventy appearances for the club over three seasons, he never really produced anything like his best form – in part because Jack's tactical setup meant he had to shift from his usual number 10 role behind a forward to the left flank. 'It was a standard game of long balls, 4-4-2, but Jack wanted to get some more technique in the side and that's what I was for,' Miročević said. 'He had Terry Curran and Andy McCulloch, who were very strong players, but they needed some kind of player to make the passes and crosses for them. I can't say I was the same level, but I was a player like Bobby Charlton. So we had like a mix of an English style and something different. Everybody played with a high offside line so it was a very compact game with no time on the ball.'[34]

Miročević never really got to grips with the intensity of the England game. 'In England at this time there were fewer training sessions than in Yugoslavia, but far more games, so in some ways the English players were more professional,' he said. 'And Christmas we played, what, three games in four days? In English football there was fair play, no intent to cause injuries. It was just very hard, very fast.'

He didn't like the cold and Jack's training methods at times appalled him. In the summer of 1980, Tony Toms had the players – wearing full military kit – attempt a commando assault course at a training base at Lympstone, Devon. Miročević tried to avoid much of it by pretending he didn't understand English (as Jack pointed out, 'he never had any problems when the talk got round to money').[35] Eventually, faced with crawling through a tube submerged in a stream, Miročević decided enough was enough and, after plaintively asking, 'No, no, where is the ball?' turned and ran for the hills with Jack bellowing after him.[36]

Even though there were times when he found things difficult, Miročević clearly adored Jack, his recollections punctured by outbreaks of laughter and shakes of the head at the chaotic absurdity of it all. 'Jack Charlton was a little eccentric,' he said. 'Football was not number one for him – he loved hunting and fishing, and he was like a world champion in dominoes. I stayed in his house for my first month in England. It was some kind of castle, with a snooker table and fishing rods everywhere. We would go fishing near Barnsley. I remember when I met Bobby Charlton the first time. I went to watch a game with Jack. We went to the main stand and there at the entrance were Bobby Charlton and Nobby Stiles, who was very short with big glasses – but a great player, very powerful. And Jack said, "You'll know Nobby, of course, but this is my brother Bobby."[37]

*

Freddie Pye, like Bobby, had been spotted by Joe Armstrong and signed by Manchester United while he was a teenager. But he had nothing like Bobby's talent and, after being released by the club, played for Accrington and Rochdale, later becoming manager of Altrincham. He never lost his love for football, but that was only one part of his life. After working as a butcher's boy and an apprentice engineer, he went into the scrap metal business, at which he was extremely successful.

Bobby knew him well and had briefly lodged with Pye and his wife. In 1974, Pye became joint chairman of Stockport. When Bobby lost his job at Preston, he offered him a role. But the Preston experience had hurt Bobby. Lower-league management, he decided, was not for him. Pye, recognising the benefits of being associated with somebody of Bobby's status and his organised mind, found him a role at Halba Travel, a company he co-owned with the future Chelsea and Leeds chairman Ken Bates, organising foreign tours for football clubs.

It seems to have been a job to which Bobby was well-suited and that he enjoyed. But he carried on training at United and playing for them in charity games. Fundamentally, he wanted to play football and nothing would ever change that. In 1975, he played a game for Stockport against United and the following year four matches for Waterford in the League of Ireland after an introduction made by Shay Brennan. George Best was playing for Cork Celtic, but Bobby withdrew from a game against them.

There was something vaguely absurd about a player of his abilities turning out in ramshackle stadiums and the incongruity wasn't lost on local observers: a piece in the *Irish Press*, under the headline 'Our Soccer Circus of One-Night Stands', pointed out that other players had to take a pay cut so the likes of Waterford and Cork could afford Bobby and Best – despite the fact that Bobby doubled Waterford's gate receipts. Within a month, with away sides reluctant to share their increased revenues (if they materialised; Bohemians saw no increase for a game at Dalymount Park because of doubts over whether Bobby would play), it became apparent that the financial terms of the deal were unsustainable.

Bobby played well enough, even at thirty-eight. He 'still retains the enthusiasm of a schoolboy for the game,' said the *Press*.[38] Certainly, he played better than Best, who was a huge disappointment at Cork. 'I cannot believe that a player of his calibre can go off so much. He doesn't get involved and he seems moody,' said manager Paul O'Donavan.[39]

There was a sadness, nonetheless, to Bobby's presence. As much as Best, although in a very different way, he was lost, fighting against the tide to recapture past glories. Bill Shankly, similarly bereft after retiring from Liverpool in 1974, used to haunt the training ground at Melwood until it was pointed out that he was undermining the authority of his replacement as manager, Bob Paisley. Shankly became a regular visitor at Bobby's house, talking endlessly about football. And if Bobby happened to be out, he'd stay anyway and talk at Norma. When your life has been football, what do you do when the game no longer has a role for you?

'In the physio room down at Hillsborough,' said Mark Smith, 'we had a brand-new ice machine which churned out ice into polythene bags so you could have a packet of ice to put on whatever injury. One day, the physio said to me, "Go and get some ice," so I got a bag, went over there, lifted the lid of the fridge and there were three fish looking up at me! Jack had obviously caught them in the morning and then was trying to keep them fresh, so he stuck them in the ice machine. I was there with three fish looking at me, thinking, My God, I wonder if this happens anywhere else?'[40]

*

At the end of February 1981, Wednesday were third in the Second Division and seemingly on course for a second successive promotion. But they only won twice more that season and ended up tenth. On the face of it, that represented a decent return to the second flight, but there was a distinct sense it could have been more.

The following season, they came far closer, missing out by a point to Norwich as they were undone by a defeat to Bolton on the penultimate weekend of the season. That was the first season in which three points were awarded for a win; under the old system, Wednesday would have pipped Norwich by a point. In that sense, they paid for drawing too many games.

That perhaps suggests Jack remained too defensive, too concerned with holding on to draws rather than pushing on for the three points. But there was another criticism to be made. 'He had a lot of other interests and I felt we probably missed out in two seasons,' said Mark Smith. 'He was into his fishing, into his shooting, that kind of stuff, or maybe filming a TV programme, Jack being Jack. He was quite a funny character, he loved working with kids and everything. He always seemed to be missing quite a bit. Going back and looking at it now I'm older, I think he could probably have got us into the First Division.'[41]

After breakfast and a team meeting, the midfielder Pat Heard and David Mills returned to the room they were sharing at a hotel in Hertfordshire. It was a big day: an FA Cup semi-final against Brighton. 'We came downstairs at the allotted time to leave to go to Highbury,' Heard said, 'and the coach had gone! I said to the receptionist, "Where are all the footballers?" She said, "Oh, they left fifteen minutes ago." The police had arrived and said that the traffic jams were too bad so they needed to leave as soon as possible. They left David Mills and me in the hotel. We had to get a taxi to Highbury. We got dropped off as close as we could get to the ground but, obviously, the police were delaying us along the way with barricades and stuff, so we had to walk the last quarter of a mile with our suit holders over our shoulders.

'We got to Highbury, walking along with all the fans, and arrived at the Highbury steps. The commissioner is stood on the door, which they used to have at Arsenal, and was like, "Who are you?"

'We had to say, "Well, we're playing this afternoon."

'He obviously didn't know who any of the Sheffield Wednesday players were. He said, "Oh, no, you're not coming in here! You can't come in, it's half past two now."

'I say, "Yeah, we're kicking off in half an hour!"

'In the end, Jack came to the door and said, "Bloody hell, where have you two been?" We said, "Jack, it's your fault! You left us in the bloody hotel!"[42]

Heard had joined Wednesday from Aston Villa in January 1983, as Jack sought to arrest a slump in form. His signing was typically chaotic. Heard and his wife went to Hillsborough to see Jack before an FA Cup replay against Southend, leaving their toddler with Ron Smith, a steward at Villa Park and the father of Dean Smith, the future Aston Villa and Norwich manager. After the game, Jack decided it was too late for negotiations so told Heard to come back the following morning. Heard explained that was impossible and, after calling Smith and making sure he and his wife could look after their child, made for Jack's house near Barnsley.

'Once we'd set off,' Heard recalled, 'Jack said, "We're not going home, we're going to the pub!" We went to a pub in Barnsley, which was closed, then we went to a fish shop to get some fish and chips, and that was closed too, so we ended up getting back to the house really late. Jack turned round and said we needed some sandwiches, so Pat and my wife were making sandwiches, I was talking to Jack in the living room and he was showing me the outtakes of that show he was on where he did all the wildlife stuff, shooting and fishing and so on. We got up the next day and Jack had already left for the ground. He said we should meet him there, so off we went. It was strange things like that with Jack. But he was great.'[43]

That season had begun well and, by the end of November 1982, Wednesday were well-placed in the promotion race. But they then won just one of their following thirteen games, a run from which they never really recovered.

The FA Cup run might have offered solace, but Brighton won the semi 2–1, Michael Robinson getting the winner after Miročević cancelled out Jimmy Case's opener. 'Afterwards we were all gutted,' said John Pearson. 'We'd played all right; I don't think we deserved to win, but we'd played all right – they were in the First Division then, as well. But Jack was absolutely gutted, he was absolutely distraught.

'I was there thinking, This is a man who's won all these trophies, this is a man who's won the World Cup, and he's devastated. It just showed to me how much he cared about and loved the club. So that stands out in my memories of Jack, because I think he loved being our manager and he loved Sheffield Wednesday. He wasn't there for any other reason than to make Sheffield Wednesday as good as they could possibly be. It's hard to forget that, how absolutely distraught he was. It meant so much to him. He was gutted for us, he was gutted for the supporters, he was gutted for everybody involved with the club.'[44]

The sense now is that the defeat came as the final straw. Jack was growing tired, frustrated by the repeated failures to earn promotion into Division One. He had been at Wednesday six years – two more years than he had ever intended to spend at any club. The minor irritations had begun to mount up.

In 1981, he had signed Gary Bannister, looking to change the shape to 4-3-3, with Bannister and Curran flanking

McCulloch. Bannister thrived, scoring twenty-two goals in his first season, but Curran resisted the move back to the flank and their relationship began to fray. Doubts began to spread among the squad about whether Jack could even take them the final step. 'All he was doing was trying to stop the opposition playing,' said McCulloch. 'Make no mistake, Jack has done well, but has he actually won anything?'[45]

At the end of the season, Jack resigned.

16

HIS OWN LAND

For Jack, 1983–84 was a season of great relaxation. He hunted and fished, he made money from his after-dinner speaking, public appearances and television work until, on 28 March, Malcolm Allison was sacked as manager of Middlesbrough, less because of results than because, as the *Middlesbrough Evening Gazette* had it, 'He refused to help the club survive by sanctioning the sale of players'.[1] Jack was appointed the following day, making clear he was doing a favour for the club chairman Mike McCullagh: he refused to take any pay and insisted he would leave at the end of the season.

Boro had gone six games without a win, but Jack abandoned Allison's high offside line, deployed the Dutch midfielder Heini Otto as a centre-forward and was rewarded with a 3–2 victory over Oldham that took Boro eleven points clear of the relegation zone. Nine further points in the final seven games of the season meant that survival was never really in doubt. True to his word, when McCullagh started to discuss transfer budgets for the summer with him, Jack walked out.

For Newcastle United, 1983–84 was a season of great attacking football. With a front three of Kevin Keegan, Chris Waddle and Peter Beardsley, they scored eighty-five goals in forty-two games to finish third in Division Two and secure promotion after six years out of the top flight. That season remains one of the most fondly remembered in the club's history, but off the pitch all was not well. The club was £700,000 in debt and the board was prepared only to authorise £200,000 of transfer spending. Aged thirty-three, Keegan had retired, leaving the St James' Park pitch in a helicopter after the final game of the season. It was presumably supposed to represent some sort of ascension into the pantheon, but rapidly came to feel like the fall of Saigon. The manager, Arthur Cox, frustrated by the financial restrictions and by his own contract, resigned as manager, moving to Third Division Derby County. The mid-fielder Terry McDermott, a few months younger than Keegan, rejected the terms of a new contract offer.

Jackie Milburn, who was working as a journalist in the North-East, was asked by the club to approach Jack. Thirty years earlier he had advised Bobby not to join Newcastle because they were so badly run; he extended no similar con-sideration to Jack. At first, Jack turned him down flat. He didn't like how club football was going, didn't like the growing involvement of agents in the game, didn't like the hooliganism and found the regular travel increasingly tiring. But Milburn was persistent – and there was a part of Jack that still missed the North-East. Eventually, he agreed to meet Newcastle's directors at a golf course near Darlington after he'd opened a double-glazing factory in Consett. Jack admitted he got the sense that they were desperate, but they offered him £35,000 a year, more than he had been on at Sheffield Wednesday and this was, after all, the club he had always supported.

'I have always had the feeling that one day I would manage Newcastle United ...' he said at his introductory press confer-ence. 'Theirs has always been the first result I have looked for on match days ... Now I want to stay here and make it my last managerial job. I want to stay here for ten years. If I can do that, I will have been wildly successful.'[2]

Although he took Maurice Setters with him, Jack followed his usual practice and kept on Colin Suggett and Willie McFaul as coaches. Almost immediately, though, there were tensions over contract negotiations. The twenty-seven-year-old John Trewick, at the time Newcastle's record signing, was surprisingly released after hesitating on a new deal – an indication of Jack's 'iron man' status, according to the *Newcastle Journal*[3] – and so too was the thirty-two-year-old David Mills, who had joined Newcastle from Wednesday the previous summer. David McCreery was given a take-it-or-leave-it offer and McDermott told that the financial position hadn't changed since Cox's departure; no improved contract would be available. Eventually, McDermott walked, joining Cork City in January 1985. Jack saw vindication in the fact no other league club came in for him; by then McDermott felt relieved to get away.

Summer 1984 was also a homecoming of a kind for Bobby, as he was invited to join the Manchester United board. The chairman Louis Edwards had asked him a few years earlier, but Bobby had demurred, feeling the time was not right; by 1984, though, he had nine years of experience working at Halba Travel and had for six years been running his Soccer Schools. The inspiration for the schools apparently came from filming he had done with gifted Argentinian children while working for the BBC at the 1978 World Cup. They became hugely successful, stretching from Old Trafford across the globe, to the USA, the USSR, Japan and Saudi Arabia. By 1990, 120,000 students had completed a course, including David Beckham.

To the surprise of those who saw Bobby as aloof, he had proved himself extremely adept in an ambassadorial role, even in his later days as a player. In the summer of 1971, for instance,

Bobby flew round Europe promoting a youth development pro-gramme sponsored by Ford, encouraging children, posing for photos and chatting to parents. Personal appearances became more and more a part of his life, to the point that in his autobi-ography, he expressed gratitude to Tommy Docherty for being so understanding when he needed to take a day or two off.[4] And he clearly relished the experience of working with children at the schools. David Sadler described him as a Pied Piper figure: 'He was so at ease in the middle of hundreds of screaming ten year olds,' he said. 'I wouldn't have thought that would be his cup of tea, but he obviously just loved working with them.'[5]

Although Bobby's accession to the board was simple enough – he and the lawyer Maurice Watkins replaced two long-standing directors who became vice-presidents – it was not a move without controversy. Matt Busby had yearned to be chairman and had become increasingly frustrated at the reluctance of Louis Edwards's family to elect his son, Sandy, to the board. It was his opposition to a rights issue to raise funds that had led the ITV current affairs programme *World in Action* to investigate. In January 1980, the show alleged that Louis Edwards's meat empire had been based on bribing local councils. He suffered a fatal heart attack shortly afterwards and was succeeded as United chairman by his son, Martin, who remained bitter towards Busby for, as he saw it, having instigated the chain of events that led to his father's death.[6]

By joining the board, Bobby was seen by some as having sided with the Edwards family against Busby. 'You have to be realistic in this day and age,' Bobby told Eamon Dunphy – sug-gesting a strikingly different attitude to business to that which he had shown to football. The experience of Preston, perhaps, had left him cynical. 'Oh, it's not the same game as it used to be, much as you might like to go back to the good old days. The only way you can have the same sort of feeling is to try and have the same kind of success.'[7]

Eventually that success came, although it would be nine years after Bobby joined the board and twenty-six years after their last league championship that Alex Ferguson led United to the inaugural Premier League title. Almost from the start, Bobby was sceptical of the abilities of Ron Atkinson, who had replaced Dave Sexton as manager in 1981. Atkinson brought United two FA Cups, and never finished outside the top four in the league, but he spent what at the time was a significant amount of money in doing so and allowed a drinking culture to flourish at the club. His love of champagne, jewellery and fancy cars, his quips and general flashiness meant he was never somebody to whom Bobby was likely to warm.

They clashed initially over Bobby's Soccer Schools, which Atkinson worried were a needless distraction for the coaching staff at Old Trafford: he didn't want them, he said, 'being bothered by a bunch of schoolteachers with big ideas'.[8] Then, in 1986, Atkinson wanted to use some of the money raised by the sale of Mark Hughes to Barcelona to sign Terry Butcher from Ipswich for £750,000. Bobby opposed the transfer, suggesting Butcher was no better than the central defenders already at the club. Perhaps unwisely, Atkinson replied that Butcher might have been good enough to keep Preston up.[9]

That summer, Bobby was working for the 1986 World Cup and, before Scotland's group game against Uruguay, spoke to Alex Ferguson, who was still at Aberdeen but had taken over as national manager following the death of Jock Stein. Bobby always insisted it was a casual chat, a version of events supported by Ferguson,[10] but Atkinson believed Bobby had been tapping him up as a potential successor.[11] Whatever the truth, when United, who were struggling in the league, lost 4–1 to Southampton in the League Cup in November that year, Atkinson was sacked and Ferguson appointed.

*

The full-back John Anderson had missed only one game for
Newcastle in 1983–84 and played in pre-season under Jack,
but the day before the opening league match, at Leicester,
Jack took him aside and told him he wouldn't be playing. His
place would be taken by Malcolm Brown, who had joined
from Huddersfield for £100,000 in 1983 but had snapped his
Achilles tendon almost immediately, an injury from which he
never fully recovered.

'"This club can't afford to pay that sort of money for a
player who isn't playing,"' Jack told Anderson. 'But Jack says,
"You can be on the bench if you want."

'I went, "Oh, all right, OK, fair enough." But after a few
games I was back in the team. But that's the way he was. He
said it how it was and if he upset you, he upset you. He upset
better players than me. But he was great for me really. He was
a great spotter of players; their strengths and their weaknesses.
He'd pull you to one side and tell you what your weakness was
and what you needed to work on, but also what your strengths
were. I don't think he ever got enough credit for that, people
just saw him as this big character.

'Tactically, as well, I think he was spot on. He got things
right, he got players right. I played right-back all through
the promotion season and, that first season back in the First
Division, I played quite a lot of games for Jack at centre-half.
He played me at right-back, centre-back, left-back, he even
played me as a holding midfield player. He said, "You can do
those jobs for me. I've got no qualms about it." He made you
feel good about yourself. He was great with the way he spoke to
you. It didn't matter whether you were royalty or sweeping the
streets. Jack had a word for everybody. He spoke to everybody
and he spoke to everybody exactly the same. When he walked
in he'd fill the room. He was such a big man anyway, but he had
a presence about him and an aura about him. Some didn't like
him because of his abrasiveness, but others did. Some managers

size players up and realise that one or two players need an arm around their shoulder or whatnot, while others need a kick up the backside. Jack wasn't into that. Everybody got tret exactly the same way, got spoke to exactly the same way. If you were a little bit fragile mentally, that wouldn't go down well. But that was the way that he was. He could cut you in half sometimes, but then all managers back then could.'[12]

Some players responded to that better than others.

Things began well enough. 'Pre-season training,' said Peter Beardsley, 'was lively, hectic, enjoyable and at times highly amusing.'[13] Newcastle won their first three games under Jack and lost the next three. Then they managed to compress the pattern into a single game, charging into a 4–0 half-time lead away at Queen's Park Rangers, only to draw 5–5. Jack raged in the dressing room. He grabbed the goalkeeper Kevin Carr by the throat and cursed Beardsley for having continued to hit crosses into the box, where the QPR keeper Peter Hucker would habitually claim possession and launch a counter-attack with a long clearance downfield. From then on, Jack's relationship with Beardsley was, as he put it, 'very tindery'.[14]

That was the first example of what would become a recurring theme, as some of Newcastle's squad objected to Jack's more pragmatic approach. With Keegan and Mills gone, there was need for a new centre-forward and Jack signed George Reilly and Tony Cunningham, two big, powerful players suited to the direct style he had used at Middlesbrough and Sheffield Wednesday. That meant Beardsley and Waddle being pushed out to the flanks. 'Peter and Chris would be stood out wide with the ball never even reaching them,' said Malcolm Brown, 'but that's the way he wanted to play. He was stubborn in what he wanted to do and that's the way it was.' Beardsley hated it. 'I got bored playing the way I did because it was just not my game,' he said. 'I needed to be more involved with the play.'[15]

Training was idiosyncratic. 'The coach would be there trying to plan what he was going to do,' Brown said, 'but we didn't know what time Jack was going to show up or whether he was going to show up for the session. We'd all be sat around, we'd start the session and then Jack would turn up halfway through and take over. But that was Jack. He seemed to do stuff however he wanted to, really.'[16]

Jack colour-coded exercises, shouting out 'red', 'green' or 'blue' to indicate what he wanted players to do. Once, he shouted 'Puce!' and everybody stopped, looking at him in bemusement. It was, he said, a 'test of improvisation'.[17]

He had Beardsley shaping in balls right-footed from the left side of the D, looking to hit the post. When he demonstrated, barefoot, wearing a sports jacket and flannels, he hit the post five times out of ten.

The striker Ian Baird joined Newcastle on loan from Southampton and remembers his first day of training. 'The session was going particularly badly,' he said, 'and the likes of Wes Saunders weren't putting it where Jack wanted it to be put. He walked on with a pair of wellies on and a sort of hunting-and-fishing suit, with a hat on. He just got hold of the ball and stuck it exactly where he wanted to put it.'[18] As Chris Turner had observed at Wednesday, Jack as a manager, in inappropriate clothing, seems to have been far more technically gifted than he was ever given credit for being as a player.

Waddle recalls he and the centre-back Steve Carney trailing in last in a cross-country run and being made to run around the training ground as punishment while Jack, coat flapping behind him, chased them on a child's bike.[19] As with so many football stories, how that is viewed is dependent on context: an eccentric manager trying to make his players fitter in a mildly comedic way doesn't necessarily sound like a bad thing – and

Jack, it should be remembered, had been a cross-country refusenik himself, before Revie persuaded him to take training more seriously. But Jack – or, more specifically, his football – was not popular with the players or fans. Waddle always said he enjoyed Jack's company, so long as he wasn't playing for him. He intervened in one early five-a-side after Waddle had exchanged passes with McDermott, saying, 'I don't want you playing one-twos on goal; I want you playing one-twos with God.' He then had the pair stand on benches at one end of the gym while players chipped balls to them: 'You can't get hurt so long as the ball's in the clouds.'[20]

The Northern Irish winger Paul Ferris remembers smashing a half-volley against the bar in training. 'He stopped training and just said, "I hate half-volleys. They're a crowd-pleaser. You hit that ball on the half-volley, nine times out of ten it's going to rise over the bar and go into the crowd. You'll get a big cheer but you haven't scored a goal." He had very clear ideas of how he wanted us to play. He'd look at great players like Peter Beardsley, who was a fantastic player, and he would think nothing of stopping everything and berating those skilful players for trying to be too skilful.'[21]

What Waddle and Beardsley objected to, others saw as lucidity. 'Of all the coaches I worked with, he was probably the best at putting his message across,' said the goalkeeper Martin Thomas. 'He was really clear with what he wanted. He had a really simple idea of how we were going to play in terms of shape, both in possession and out of possession. We were very, very well organised; we had good structure. The big thing with Jack was that he knew what his philosophy was and he knew how to put that across.'[22]

But that meant brooking no dissent. Jack didn't care what players or fans thought. 'He was very straightforward, had no airs and graces and was very clear about how we were going to do things,' said Anderson. 'It was, "Anyone who doesn't want to do it this way, there's the door, you can get up, walk out and leave now, no problem whatsoever." '23

That, perhaps, endeared Jack more to the back of the team than the front. 'He was a great fella,' Anderson went on. 'He was direct, to the point. We'd scored a lot of goals in the Second Division, but he came in and said, "If yous play the same way you're going to get relegated, so we're going to change the way we play." '24

Maybe he was right, but it does sound a lot like Jack's justification for how his Middlesbrough played: that he was forced into it by the quality of players available. But then if you're letting McDermott and Trewick go and bringing in the likes of Cunningham and Reilly, that surely is creating a squad to play in a direct way. And it does seem more than a coincidence that Jack ended up playing that direct style in all four of his managerial jobs. What's intriguing, though, is that a man usually thought of as being so blunt and thick-skinned felt the need to justify his approach at all – as though he had a sense, deep down, that it wasn't quite right, that he had to convince himself he was only playing that way because it was the only way for that side to play.

'In some ways he could be quite brusque, but in other ways he was a warm man,' said Paul Ferris. 'I hurt myself in a reserve game – I got a bang and I ended up in hospital. I was due to be involved with the first team over the Christmas period but it was clear there was no way I was going to be able to do that. So I was in the hospital ward in the RVI [Royal Victoria Infirmary] in Newcastle and, about eight o'clock at night, it was all dimmed lights and the door just opened. In steps Jack – I was only a young lad, obviously – he walked in with a huge bag of sweets, threw them and they landed on my bits they shouldn't have landed on. He says,

"Have a look in there." When I opened them, there was a plane ticket to go home [to Lisburn] for Christmas so I could see my family.'[25]

After those initial three victories, Newcastle won only two of the following sixteen league matches. When they lost 4–0 to the eventual champions, Everton, in January 1985, 'a complete utter embarrassment,' as the *Newcastle Journal* had it, Newcastle were seventeenth, six points above the relegation zone. For the first time, fans called for him be sacked, leaving Jack facing what the *Journal* referred to as 'the sternest test of his career'.[26] Questions were asked about the lack of time Jack spent on the training ground. Was the proximity of Northumberland – with its rivers and moors, its hunting and fishing – too much of a distraction?

Even when games were won, there was tension. Towards the end of February, Newcastle led Luton 1–0 with a minute to go when Beardsley, rather than taking the ball into the corner as instructed, turned infield and, with only Mal Donaghy between him and the box, made for goal. He lost control, squandering possession and, when Luton broke, only a goal-line clearance from John Anderson prevented an equaliser. Jack, perhaps remembering the vital goal his Middlesbrough had conceded to Derby in similar circumstances, was apoplectic, raging at Beardsley on the pitch and then complaining about his lack of discipline to the press. Beardsley pointed out he had nearly scored and objected to Jack berating him in public.

The following week, with Newcastle 2–1 up against Watford, Beardsley refused to take a free kick short so the ball could be taken into the corner to run down the clock. Instead, he crossed to the back post where Reilly headed in against his former club. Jack was nevertheless furious.

Beardsley, he said, was 'a good player' but 'he just doesn't listen or, if he does, he chooses to ignore what you say'.[27]

And that was not something Jack could tolerate.

Not surprisingly, perhaps, Beardsley soon began to suggest he might seek a move (he didn't actually leave until 1987, but it's odd how many of his coaches and teammates seem to have felt he was on the way as early as 1984–85) while, according to Jack, Waddle's head was turned after making his England debut against Ireland in March 1985. That summer, Waddle joined Tottenham for £590,000. Newcastle stayed up, finishing fourteenth, three points above the relegation zone. Fans may have hoped survival would lead to consolidation and a less cautious approach the following season, but Jack wasn't worried by the fifty-five goals scored; what concerned him were the seventy Newcastle had conceded.

Discontent had been mounting all summer. The Waddle money had been spent on Ian Stewart, a winger from QPR, and Alan Davies, a twenty-four-year-old centre-forward who had played just seven games for Manchester United. Neither had captured the imagination of fans. Jack also wanted to sign Eric Gates, a clever centre-forward who could drop off a front man – a signing which would surely have meant a slightly less direct approach. A fee was agreed with Ipswich but, shortly before Newcastle's final pre-season friendly, at home against Sheffield United, news broke that Gates had decided to sign for Sunderland, who had been relegated to the Second Division the previous season. Perhaps there simply was no more money available, perhaps Jack was being tight, perhaps Lawrie McMenemy's ultimately doomed project at Roker Park seemed more exciting, but a significant section of Newcastle's support was appalled.

Jack got the blame. There were fewer than five thousand fans at St James' Park that afternoon to see Cunningham score in a grim 1–1 draw and they booed and barracked Jack throughout, cheering whenever Sheffield United had the ball. For Jack this was too much; he couldn't stand being rejected by his own people. 'It wasn't a big deal, it wasn't a big protest, but there were chants against him,' said Ferris, who was sitting behind him on the bench. 'He just said, "Fuck this. I don't need this." He got up, walked off and we never saw him again!'[28]

As soon as the final whistle had blown, Jack went to the chairman's office and resigned. 'The first real demonstration against his managerial qualities,' noted John Richardson in the *Journal*, 'would be the last.' The tone of the report suggested he felt Jack had over-reacted, but it acknowledged how the fans' demands to buy had become 'an irritant': 'he didn't like the hypermarket type of football buying, tending to try and make do with the odd conventional purchase from the corner shop.'[29]

Pat Heard had followed Jack from Wednesday to Newcastle. 'I was driving home and it came on the radio that Jack had resigned,' he said. 'It was a bit of a shock but, to be honest, I think he'd just had enough of being badgered by the supporters. People would come up to him and ask, "Who are you going to buy?" He couldn't go out anywhere and have a quiet drink like he'd been able to do in Sheffield or when he lived in Barnsley. In those days, in terms of going out in public, it really wasn't that bad. When he got to Newcastle, he was pestered everywhere he went. "Who are you buying? What are you doing? Jack, Jack, Jack, Jack . . ." I think it got to him in the end.'[30]

Jackie Milburn was frustrated by Jack's decision, insisting 'it was only a few hooligans' who had turned on him. But the abuse was only the final straw, and perhaps not even that. Jack was wearied by modern football, wearied by the board, wearied by his squad and wearied by the constant sniping from the terraces and the newspapers. 'That whole episode,' he later admitted, 'provided me with the excuse I needed for getting away.'[31]

Typically, Jack didn't consider anybody else or how his snap decision would influence them. Maurice Setters was away scouting a player and only found out that Jack had quit when he saw it on the television news. 'Like many of the lads he had inherited,' Beardsley said, 'I thought – good riddance!'[32]

ANOTHER FAI MESS

Jack Charlton became manager of Ireland by mistake.

He would become the greatest manager in the country's history. He took them to their first major tournament finals and then to their first World Cup. He transformed the Football Association of Ireland (FAI) from a body teetering on the brink of extinction to one that was, at least temporarily, hugely profitable. He is widely credited with having helped shift perceptions and attitudes and, if some of the claims made about his influence are overblown, his symbolic importance was profound. And yet very few people in the FAI particularly wanted him to get the job, there was little support for him initially in Ireland and when he got the call to confirm the position, Jack had, at least by legend, forgotten being in the running. His appointment, frankly, was a fiasco of the sort only an FAI committee could ever have pulled off.

Football in Ireland was improving, but the base was so low that wasn't necessarily saying a lot. Despite the open hostility of the GAA (Gaelic Athletic Association), which ran Gaelic football and hurling and dismissed soccer as 'the garrison game', Ireland had always produced good players. But there weren't enough of them to create a critical mass and the FAI, even by the standards of international sporting bodies, was shambolic. John Giles made his international debut in 1959 and he acknowledged, 'It wasn't professionally good ... As a nation we didn't expect to win, the players didn't expect to win.'[1] Eamon Dunphy described playing for Ireland as 'a bit of a joke'.

For the FAI's executive, football rarely seemed the priority. When they found how good the hospitality was in Poland, Ireland started playing the Poles on such a regular basis that one director became an importer of Polish lingerie. As the Charlton Athletic forward Ray Treacy's famous quip had it, he won forty-two caps for Ireland, forty of them against Poland.

Things did begin to improve under John Giles, who was player-manager between 1973 and 1980, and then Eoin Hand. Only the mysterious decision to disallow a Frank Stapleton effort away against Belgium cost them a place in the 1982 World Cup.* An extremely tough draw that grouped them with Spain and the Netherlands effectively ended any hope of qualifying for Euro 84, after which the qualifying campaign for the 1986 World Cup was a major disappointment. Ireland didn't score in away games against Denmark, the USSR, Switzerland and Norway and, by the time of their final qualifier – at home against Denmark – they had long since been eliminated. Only twelve thousand turned out at Lansdowne Road and many of them were Danes celebrating their side's qualification. Ireland lost 4–1 and Hand's contract was not renewed.

The FAI was going broke. In 1984 it had made losses of

---

* The writer Paul Howard visited the Portuguese referee Raul Nazare in 2001 and watched the video of the game with him (Eoin Hand's copy, as a matter of fact) for the *Sunday Tribune*. Nazare, struggling to remember the incident, went through various contortions to try to justify his decision, suggesting it had been offside (it hadn't) or an indirect free kick (it wasn't, and Stapleton clearly touched the ball anyway). The kindest explanation is perhaps that Nazare was running backwards across the box as the free kick was taken, bumped into the central defender Walter Meeuws and, having hampered him, blew his whistle out of some guilty instinct.

IR£60,000, in 1985 of IR£30,000. They realised that belts were going to have be tightened and wastage cut, and recognised that the only way finances were going to improve was if the football team started attracting crowds back to Lansdowne Road. There was a movement among younger FAI directors to appoint a full-time manager, preferably one based in England, given that was where the vast majority of the best Irish players played. An advert was placed in the British and Irish press.

The FAI president Des Casey and a young official, Dr Tony O'Neill, were despatched to England to interview candidates. They spoke to Giles but he was cautious, having been bruised by experiences at Shamrock Rovers and Vancouver Whitecaps and by the way his 'square ball' football had been dismissed during his first spell in charge.

They spoke to Billy McNeill, then at Manchester City, who had won three league titles as manager of Celtic.

They tried to speak to Brian Clough but were denied permission by Nottingham Forest.

They spoke to Noel Cantwell, then manager of Peterborough United.

They spoke to the former Arsenal and Northern Ireland manager Terry Neill.

They spoke to the former Ireland right-back Theo Foley.

They spoke to the former Everton manager Gordon Lee.

They spoke to Pat Crerand, whose previous managerial experience comprised a miserable season at Northampton. 'It only took me weeks to realise that management wasn't for me,' he said.[2] His only real qualification was that his family was Irish, his desire for the job born of his overt republicanism.

And they approached Jack, who was recording a fishing programme for Channel 4 but said he could fit them in for an hour at the Crest hotel at Manchester airport. Jack admitted he had never seen Ireland play but felt that, with the talent they had produced over the years, they should have qualified for at least one major tournament. He at least gave a sense of being keen, even if he didn't know many specifics.

Three candidates were interviewed in Ireland: Shamrock Rovers manager Jim McLaughlin, the former international Paddy Mulligan and Liam Tuohy, who had been national manager before Giles, but had impressed with more recent work with the Ireland youth setup. When the Republic of Ireland Soccer Supporters Club was polled for its opinion, more than half favoured Tuohy, with McNeill second on 10 per cent. There were clear concerns about appointing an English manager.

After a series of leaks, Giles withdrew from the process. A shortlist of three was drawn up: McNeill, Tuohy and Jack, seemingly because there was a vague sense that what he had done with Middlesbrough and Sheffield Wednesday might transpose itself to Ireland. Dunphy, by then an outspoken columnist, worried that the candidates had become pawns in the FAI's politicking, with battlelines long since drawn between the general secretary, Peadar O'Driscoll, and modernisers, as represented by Casey and O'Neill.[3] He was troubled, too, by the insularity that led so many to favour Tuohy, 'for whom the gombeen press constitutes a noisy and persistent lobby'.[4]

The FAI council approved the list and passed it to the executive to make the final decision. Among journalists and officials, McNeill was the preferred candidate. 'He is a Celt,' wrote Gerry Callan in the *Sunday Tribune*, 'and would thus have a decided advantage in dealing with the Irish players in comparison to Charlton, who has spent his entire playing and managerial career in the north of England, an area where people are renowned for their dour and blunt attitude. Admirable qualities they may be, but ... they are nevertheless alien to the Irish temperament.'[5] George Best sneered that Jack was under consideration only because Irish officials must have been impressed by seeing him on television and suggested that, if that were the case, they should give the job to Terry Wogan.[6]

On 9 January, Casey went to Manchester to try to get McNeill on a part-time deal for between twenty and thirty days a year. City rejected the plan. And so that left just Jack and Tuohy, at that stage a clear favourite. Dunphy persuaded Giles to re-enter the race but, although he had some support among the FAI, it was by no means clear that the shortlist could be extended again. Jack, apparently having given up – if he was really bothered at all – went on holiday to his home in Altea near Benidorm.

At 8 p.m. on 7 February, all nineteen executive committee members met at the FAI headquarters in Merrion Square, Dublin, to decide. 'It is going to be a very close fight between Giles and Tuohy with Charlton in the role of outsider,' Charlie Stuart reported in the *Irish Press*, before noting that Jack 'may yet emerge as the compromise candidate between the power-hungry factions within the FAI.'[7]

First, there was the issue of whether the shortlist could be re-opened for Giles. For an hour they discussed the issue before deciding that, yes, it was legitimate to expand the list of candidates. But once that had been accepted, why not add more names? Some still wanted to try to entice Clough. And then Casey dropped his bombshell: he had been in touch with the former Liverpool manager Bob Paisley who, with seven league titles and three European Cups, was by some way the most successful manager in English history. Paisley was sixty-five and had retired in 1983 but yearned for a return to coaching and thought he could combine being a director at Liverpool with being Ireland manager; he was willing. There was uproar. Had Giles been a stalking horse all along? Had the whole process been a charade to normalise the idea of an English manager of Ireland, to let Jack take the personal hits, before the real candidate was unveiled?[8]

Paisley was added to the list. A candidate needed an absolute majority, that is ten votes, to win, with the lowest-scoring candidate being eliminated in each round. Casey, the president, would be involved only in the event of a tie. John Giles waited in the Berkeley Court hotel, about a mile away, ready to go on *The Late, Late Show* on RTÉ if he won.

The first ballots were cast: Paisley nine, Tuohy three, Giles three, Jack three. There was a run-off to determine who would be eliminated: Tuohy came third, prompting his joke that he had come fourth in a two-horse race.

The second ballot: Paisley nine, Jack five, Giles four. Although there was a clear faction opposed to Paisley being admitted so late in proceedings, the assumption then was that, even if all of Giles's backers switched to Jack, Casey's casting vote would win the day for Paisley.

The third ballot: Jack ten, Paisley eight. Someone had switched away from Paisley. Who it was has never been decisively confirmed. Charlie Stuart, writing in the *Irish Press*, named Colonel Tom Ryan, the army representative on the FAI board and the aide de camp to the president of Ireland, Patrick Hillery. Why he switched, if indeed he did, has never been explained, the whole issue complicated by the fact that, in time, almost everybody subsequently claimed to have backed Jack from the start.

At the Berkeley Court hotel, another round of drinks was ordered. Giles would not be going on television that night. On *The Late, Late Show*, a sheet of paper bearing the news was handed to the presenter Gay Byrne. He looked at it, sceptically and then said with barely disguised disdain, 'I've just been handed a piece of paper here,' he said, 'which says that Jack Charlton has been appointed manager of Ireland ... whatever that means.'[9] The audience responded with silence, broken by a solitary whoop.

And what did it mean? Casey hadn't spoken to Jack since 20

January. It wasn't entirely certain he still wanted the job. Casey rang Paisley to pass on the bad news. But nobody could get hold of Jack. He wasn't at home in Northumberland. Nobody seemed to know where he was. Was he filming the fishing show for Channel 4? Eventually, the following morning, it was the former Blackpool full-back Jimmy Armfield, who had been in England's World Cup squad in 1966 and was by then working as a BBC radio broadcaster, who got hold of him.

According to Jack, he was at a hotel after a speaking engagement in Birmingham when the phone rang. According to Rowan, Jack was hunting at Coverdale in North Yorkshire.[10]

'Congratulations,' said Armfield.

'For what?' asked Jack.[11]

He went on to explain, four days after his appointment, 'Because there was such a long time between the various interviews and the announcement, I was surprised to hear the news.'[12] Wherever he was, the point is that the process was chaotic and Jack was not anxiously waiting at the end of a phone or in a Dublin hotel, to find out whether he had got the job. 'Even by the abysmal standards set by the FAI,' wrote Stuart, 'last Friday night was their most shambolic hour.'[13]

And Jack was English. 'I was disappointed ...' said Paul McGrath. 'After all that's happened in this country, why would we have to have an Englishman, of all people, to run our soccer team?'[14]

Jack had only ever been to Ireland once before, on a pre-season tour with Leeds. He had tried to book an Irish fishing holiday, only to be thwarted by a strike among postal and telecommunications workers. This time he flew to Dublin and went straight to Merrion Square to negotiate his personal terms. As ever, Jack refused a contract. 'I'm not in it for the money,' he said, or at least that's how the much-told story goes, doubtless with embellishments justified by the success that followed. 'Give me whatever Eoin Hand was on. I'm doing it because it's an honour.'

Casey, supposedly, then wrote Hand's salary on a piece of paper and slid it over the desk.

Jack glanced at it. 'It's not that much of a fucking honour,' he said, and pushed the paper back.

A rise was negotiated, but only from IR£16,000 a year to IR£20,000.

That afternoon, Jack and the FAI hierarchy went to the races at Phoenix Park. People kept coming up to Jack and shaking his hand, wishing him well. He was struck by how little expectation people had.

A press conference was held at the Westbury hotel off St Stephen's Green. Or at least, that's the order of events Rowan gives; in his autobiography, Jack has the press conference coming before the negotiations. It probably doesn't much matter, but it is telling of how difficult it is even to pin down basic details about fairly major events; even in 1996, when Jack's autobiography was published, his memory was fading.

All nineteen members of the executive committee and Jack sat at a long table facing the press, as though parodying Leonardo da Vinci's *The Last Supper*. Everything seemed to be progressing smoothly and Jack gave his home number to everybody there to head off any potential accusations of being too distant. But then Peter Byrne from the *Irish Times*, who later ghosted Jack's autobiography, asked Casey about Paisley and his sudden introduction to the shortlist. Casey said that it was neither the time nor the place for such questions (which makes you wonder when would have been) and Jack dismissed the issue as 'irrelevant', claiming in his autobiography he couldn't answer as he knew nothing about it.[15]

But Dunphy backed Byrne, saying that the FAI was a national body and the matter was in the public interest. 'Public interest?'

Jack snapped. 'I know you. You're a fucking troublemaker, you are. I'm not going to argue with you. I'm bigger than you are. If you want to step outside, I'm ready now.' He then grabbed his cap from the table, stood up and marched off, to a ripple of applause from most of the assembled journalists. Even Dunphy wrote the following week, 'He made the assembled feel good about themselves, good about being Irish and optimistic about Ireland's football future.'[16]

Walking out as soon as he faced a tough question soon became a trait, evidence of what the writer Sean Ryan called Jack's 'paranoia and tactlessness'.[17] Dunphy spoke of Jack having 'a bully's attitude to life. He doesn't like being crossed'.[18] And Jack himself, in the notes he scribbled, many of which were collected for the remarkable documentary directed by Gabriel Clarke and Peter Thomas, *Finding Jack Charlton*, wrote, 'Be a dictator. But a nice one.' Those notes also refer to the need to establish a sense of 'fear' early on, when a manager is at his most influential. Wherever he was manager, Jack's way was the only way.

A little later, Jack had a drink with Peadar O'Driscoll, who suggested that the physio Mick Byrne should be released. Jack, though, wanted to maintain his policy of keeping on as many of the existing backroom staff as possible and refused on principle. Byrne would become a key part of the group that achieved success.

The FAI thought that Tuohy would make a good assistant. Jack was sceptical but met him and agreed that Tuohy should oversee the two games that remained in qualifying for the European Youth Championship, after which a long-term decision would be taken. The first of those games was against England in Sheffield. It was a foggy, bitterly cold day, which led to the match being switched to Elland Road, where visibility was a little better. Jack had intended to go and watch the Milk Cup tie between Aston Villa and Oxford, but when it was called off because of the weather, he turned up at the team hotel and queried both the steaks the players ate as a pre-match lunch and the team selection.

Before kick-off, Jack popped into the dressing room – even though he had always been strongly against any interference when he was coaching. Tuohy suggested he should come back at half-time. By then, though, Ireland were 2–0 down. Jack, in a fury, laid into the team, insisting they should abandon their neat passing approach for something more direct. Ireland were tighter in the second half and the game finished 2–0 but Tuohy felt he had been undermined and resigned on his return to Dublin, along with his assistants, Brian Kerr and Noel Reilly. Jack believed he had merely done as Tuohy asked and offered some advice at half-time. And the second half *had* been better than the first.[19]

Maurice Setters was appointed as Jack's number two amid widespread sympathy for Tuohy. Niall Quinn always spoke of how important the youth coach had been in his development[20] and, even a decade later, it was still Tuohy's players who formed the bedrock of the national side. (Of the eleven who started against England in Stuttgart, eight had been regulars before Jack, and it would have been ten but for the injuries to Liam Brady and Mark Lawrenson.)

That controversy was part of wider teething problems. Jack found that, when he rang the FAI to give them his squad, O'Driscoll – who had been general secretary nearly twenty years – would add a couple of names. Jack took to calling at lunchtime, when O'Driscoll was away from his desk, and delivering his squad to a commercial manager who would follow his instructions. O'Driscoll soon retired, replaced by Tony O'Neill, who was instrumental in getting Jack the job. He persuaded Jack to go through him and him alone; Jack agreed, so long as O'Neill did what Jack wanted.

Jack getting his own way became a theme. When the FAI director Louis Kilcoyne suggested an end-of-season tour to South America, claiming it could raise as much as fifty thousand pounds, Jack refused out of hand. He knew it would be extremely difficult to get clubs to release players and he preferred to fight those battles for more consequential games.

Having dealt with the press, the FAI and the youth team manager who was a potential rival, the next step was to sort out the players. Jack rang Eoin Hand to ask who were the players to watch, who were the players to 'fucking not watch'. Hand gave his advice 'and it's amazing,' Jack said, 'how what he said was almost certainly a hundred per cent right.'[21]

Like everything else, Ireland's first training session under Jack bordered on the shambolic. Snow meant they couldn't train outside and instead had to use an Aer Lingus gym near the airport. It was small and, according to McGrath, had the feel of a church hall. Jack did his old trick of shouting out colours that corresponded to exercises, amusing the players with an unconventional selection of shades.

In time, though, McGrath began to realise at least some of the eccentricity was put on and that beneath the bluster and the confusion there was a calculating mind at work.[22] When Jack turned up before a game against Latvia and began to read out notes on the opposition scribbled on a fag packet, only to give up because he couldn't read his writing, was that real confusion? Or was that him relaxing his players, ensuring they weren't worried about their opponents? McGrath was too shy even to complain when Jack called him 'John', seemingly mixing him up with the former Newcastle centre-half, but he also remembered the jolt of pride when, in a meaningful chat about his importance to the team, Jack suddenly called him

'Paul'. Chance, or brilliant psychology? It was never easy to tell; Jack, like his football teams, was adept at creating chaos and capitalising from it in unexpected ways.

Ireland's first game under Jack was a friendly against Wales. A banner in the sparse crowd read, 'Go home, Union Jack'. Jack, feeling he didn't really know the players, had Mick Byrne pick the team. They lost 1–0, leading to widespread criticism. In the *Evening Press*, Con Houlihan referred to Jack as 'the manager who should never have been appointed'.[23] Jack's biggest concern was the performance of the Arsenal central defender David O'Leary, who liked to drop off a forward and use his pace to beat him. Jack blamed him for losing Ian Rush for the game's only goal. That game and the subsequent 1–1 draw against Uruguay attracted such low gates that it cost the Irish Football Association (IFA) thirty thousand pounds to stage them.[24]

The consequence was that O'Leary was dropped for a triangular tournament in Iceland to celebrate the two-hundredth anniversary of the foundation of Reykjavik – the first time in ten years that he had been left out; and when Jim Beglin, Ronnie Whelan, Mark Lawrenson and Kevin Sheedy all then withdrew, Jack rang O'Leary to call him up. O'Leary, who was irritated by the fact he had only found out about his omission from press reports, said he had booked a holiday to Portugal and was not prepared to change plans. It would be three years before Jack recalled him. Yet Whelan, Beglin and Lawrenson were on a club holiday with Liverpool to celebrate their double and none of them were ostracised in the same way, seemingly because their club manager Kenny Dalglish told Jack that if he took any action he would withhold all Liverpool players. Given Ireland had depth at centre-back, O'Leary was perhaps a useful sacrifice *pour encourager les autres*. Jack, though, always maintained his problem with O'Leary was stylistic.[25]

O'Leary's absence provided an opportunity for Mick McCarthy, then a twenty-seven-year-old at Manchester City. He was notoriously slow, to the extent that when the heavily built John O'Shea of the *Evening Press* challenged him to a race he only just won, but he pushed out and encouraged others to do the same and that made him valuable to Jack.

McCarthy had been born in Barnsley and spoke with a broad Yorkshire accent, but his father was Irish and he had been an Irish citizen since birth. Still, his accent made him unmistakably an "Anglo". The drive to find Ireland-qualified players outside of Ireland had started before Jack, under Eoin Hand, who had given debuts not only to McCarthy but also to Tony Galvin, Kevin Sheedy and Tony Cascarino.*

Jack identified two areas in which Ireland were deficient: up front and on the right side of midfield. So he went out to find suitable candidates who had Irish relatives that would qualify them. He found both at Oxford United. John Aldridge was a prolific goalscorer and had a great-grandmother who came from Athlone, and he pointed out that Ray Houghton, who had been born in Glasgow, had an Irish father. Neither had been to Dublin before making their debuts in the defeat to Wales.

It was that tournament in Iceland, though, that marked the real start of Jack's reign. He wanted the ball worked to the full-back and then played down the line behind the opposing full-backs; if the centre-backs tried to play those passes there was a risk the ball simply ran out for a throw in. After the ball had been played into the corner, Ireland squeezed up, looking to force mistakes. There were complaints about a supposed

---

* Cascarino, it subsequently turned out, because of confusion over his mother's parentage, did not even have an Irish grandparent.

lack of sophistication but from the start Jack's methods were effective. A late Gerry Daly goal gave Ireland a 2–1 victory over the hosts and they sealed the tournament two days later with victory over Czechoslovakia, Frank Stapleton getting the only goal with eight minutes remaining. It might only have been the Iceland Triangular Tournament, but Ireland had never won anything before.

Jack went to Mexico for the World Cup. For many that was a tournament of brilliant goals and brilliant individuals, played in vivid sunshine that gave everything a distinctive look. It was the tournament of Gary Lineker, Josimar, Vasily Rats and, most of all, of Diego Maradona. But Jack wasn't impressed. He felt international football had slipped into a rut and that there was an opportunity for Ireland if they were prepared to be different, to challenge teams in ways they weren't used to being challenged.

'Nearly all the countries in the 1986 World Cup were like peas in a pod and most of the matches were boring as hell,' he said. Teams played through one playmaker, occasionally pushing the full-backs up, 'building in tight little areas until they feel sufficiently comfortable to commit men forward.'

Ireland, he determined, would not play like that. While they certainly had players capable of patient, technical football, Jack argued that they did not have enough. To play other teams in that style was to engage in a form of the game at which Ireland would be beaten – as Giles's reign had proved. And so they would play on their own terms. 'Ours is basically a hustling game,' Jack explained before the 1990 World Cup. 'We play the ball in behind people, aiming to turn them all the time. We prefer to play the game in the other team's half of the field. If we get the ball behind full-backs, into the holes, one of our fellas will try to reach it first and if he does, we'll support him wide and support him deep, creating productive angles. Once we're in those hurtful positions there's nothing cut and dried – our fellas can be as imaginative as they like.

'The idea is to go towards the corner flags first, which draws the sweeper out, and then move the ball in from there to the goal-scoring areas ... Whenever things get tight in the midfield build-up, you stop passing the ball to people and get it behind their defenders so we are facing the right way and they aren't.'

He was happy enough to tell everybody what his plan was. As he saw it, there was no point trying to disguise it. 'I want managers of other countries to know how we play because there is bugger all they can do about it,' he said. 'And the more they try to cater for what we are doing, the more likely they are to interfere with their basic approach and misuse their strengths.'[26]

But his changes weren't only tactical. Eoin Hand had moved the team base to the Dublin airport hotel, which seemed to make sense, given how many flew in. But Hertz had provided cars and so players would fly in on a Sunday and those who had relatives in Ireland would drive off to visit them, leaving the likes of McCarthy, Galvin and Chris Hughton sitting around, bored in the hotel.

Jack cancelled the cars and insisted players had to get permission to leave the hotel. Any requests for public appearances, to visit hospitals or draw raffles, had to go through him and he ensured many were rejected, so players could focus more on winning football matches. Although there was initial frustration, as the players spent more time together, a routine developed: they had coffee in the city on a Sunday, cinema on a Monday, usually followed by a pint of stout. Slowly, a formidable team spirit was forged.

18

YEARS OF GLORY

Ireland were used to failure, used to events conspiring against them. Yes, if Scotland won in Bulgaria, Ireland would qualify for Euro 88 and play at a major tournament for the first time, but how likely, really, was that? Scotland couldn't qualify: what had they to prove against a Bulgaria side who had already drawn 0–0 at Hampden? Why should they give their all? And Bulgaria had won all three previous home games, including a 2–1 win over Ireland secured with an eighty-second-minute penalty.

And besides, qualifying just wasn't something that happened to Ireland. They all knew what had happened in Brussels in 1981 – that and the whole litany of near misses and mysteriously disallowed goals. In the days leading up to Scotland's game in Sofia, more in Ireland seemed more exercised by the death of Eamonn Andrews, the presenter of *This Is Your Life,* than by the possibility of reaching the Euros.

Scotland, with nothing to play for, started slowly, sitting deep, content to frustrate Bulgaria. They also frustrated Maurice Setters, who was doing co-commentary on RTÉ and was critical of Andy Roxburgh's negativity. Jack was shooting on a farm in Shropshire and had managed to set up a system to watch the game but, unbeknown to him, it was on a half-hour delay.

Just before the hour, Roxburgh took off Paul McStay and sent on the young Hearts midfielder Gary Mackay for his debut. Two minutes remained when, with Bulgaria's defence perhaps wrongfooted by an advantage played after a foul on the right touchline, Mackay ran into the right side of the box and clipped a neat finish just inside the far post. From nowhere, Scotland had scored and Ireland had qualified for the Euros. Somebody phoned Jack, who initially didn't believe the news; on his screen there was still thirty minutes to go. When he finally did, he said, nothing in football had ever given him more pleasure.[1]

Ireland had been drawn in a Euro qualifying group that was awkward rather than intimidating. Jack took a major gamble and asked the FAI when negotiating the fixtures to try to arrange as many away games as possible first. That meant that Ireland might have the advantage of playing decisive games at home, but there was also a risk that those games would be dead rubbers and would be played in front of meagre crowds, something the FAI could not afford.

They began with the toughest game, away against the World Cup semi-finalists Belgium. They were one of the few sides who had impressed Jack in Mexico; their use of Jan Ceulemans, he said, was similar to his use of Alan Foggon at Middlesbrough. He had Liam Brady shut down Eric Gerets, which worked to a point, but Ireland were trailing 2–1 going into the final minute when the Belgian keeper Jean-Marie Pfaff gave away a penalty. Brady converted; Ireland's luck, perhaps, was turning. A 0–0 draw at home to Scotland, though, was a grim trudge, exactly what Jack's critics had feared Ireland would look like under him.

There was a big improvement away to Scotland. Mark Lawrenson started at the back of midfield and scored from an early free kick. Ireland then controlled the game to win 1–0.

Defeat away to Bulgaria, though, left Ireland as outsiders – before they concluded their campaign with two decisive home games either side of perfunctory wins over Luxembourg. The first, against Belgium, was drawn, which seemed to have effectively ended their hopes. But then Belgium lost in Bulgaria which meant there was just a chance. Scotland did Ireland a huge favour by beating Belgium 2–0 on the same day they faced Bulgaria at Lansdowne Road. Goals from McGrath and Kevin Moran completed a 2–0 win of their own.

It had not been in any sense a spectacular campaign: just four wins from eight games. But Ireland had also lost only once and, thanks to Mackay's goal, that was enough.

For those who were minded to see it, qualification for the Euros was part of a wider pattern. To claim that Jack and his team were responsible for the transformation of Ireland in the early nineties would be too much, but they became a potent symbol of the changes. Not that they were alone: the late eighties were also the time of Stephen Roche's and Sean Kelly's successes in cycling, of the Pogues, U2 and Sinéad O'Connor, and of Daniel Day-Lewis and *My Left Foot*. Ireland generally was going through a period of cultural and sporting vibrancy, set against a rather bleaker social picture.

The seventies had seen some liberalisation, but in the eighties the Catholic church and the forces of conservatism fought back, winning referendums on abortion and divorce in 1983 and 1986. But the liberals still existed, which was why Joe Lee's book *Ireland 1912–85: Politics and Society* – essentially an account of why and how everything had gone wrong – became a surprise bestseller.

For Declan Lynch in *Days of Heaven*, his book on the Charlton years, the 'moral civil war' was the main reason the majority of Ireland fans were so welcoming to those who qualified to play for the team through a grandmother: 'We were sick men,' he wrote. 'Anyone who had made it out of here had made it despite all the bullshit, driven by a desperate desire to be free of the bullshit.'[2] There was no sense that the diaspora had betrayed Ireland by leaving; rather Ireland had betrayed the diaspora by forcing them to leave. Jack was smart enough to pursue that line of thought. 'You've always exported people,' he said in 1987, 'and it's nice of them to come back and help you out now and again.'[3]

And in that dynamic, football played a very specific role. The church backed the GAA and refused to allow football to be played in any of its facilities. The likes of Ray Treacy and Eoin Hand had been beaten by the Christian Brothers who ran their schools for playing football.[4] In that context, simply playing the game could be seen as an act of resistance against oppressive conservatism. 'We were always struggling for acceptance ...' said Brian Kerr, the long-time St Patrick's Athletic coach who would succeed Mick McCarthy as national manager in 2003. But Jack changed that. 'It became acceptable for trenchant Gaelic people to be OK with supporting the soccer team. It was no longer a mortal sin.'[5]

Then there were the Troubles. In the March between Scotland's win over Bulgaria and Ireland's first game at the Euros, SAS operatives in Gibraltar shot and killed three unarmed members of the IRA. At their funeral, the UDA member Michael Stone attacked mourners with hand-grenades and pistols, killing three and injuring sixty. He claimed he was exacting revenge for a bomb attack on a Remembrance Day service in Enniskillen that had left eleven dead; that had taken place three days before the game in Sofia. At the funeral of Stone's victims, two out-of-uniform British Army corporals were dragged from their car and beaten to death. For an Englishman – a former guardsman at that – to be manager of Ireland at that time could have been extremely awkward.

That it was not was largely because Jack was unprecedentedly successful and because of that very northernness that had so worried Gerry Callan. Jack was laidback and forgetful, he liked a pint and he liked to fish. There was a straightforwardness to him: he was quick to anger and quick to move on. He was nothing like the cold, uptight, duplicitous Englishman of stereotype – and that meant allowances could be made. 'We told ourselves,' Lynch wrote, 'what we wanted to hear, that this was the sort of Englishman we could take orders from, a rough-hewn individual, a plain fellow whose tastes were not unlike our own.'[6]

Still, whatever impact Jack may have had on perceptions, there was an undeniable frisson when the draw determined that Ireland's first game at a major tournament would be against England – and an England that, after suffering elimination in the World Cup quarter-final to Maradona's Hand of God goal, had gone unbeaten through Euro qualifying.

In front of fifteen thousand of their own fans in Stuttgart, Ireland were ahead inside six minutes with a goal that seemed the very essence of Jack: a long ball down the line from the left-back Chris Hughton, confusion between the defenders Mark Wright and Gary Stevens, gifting possession to Tony Galvin, a hooked cross, a miscued clearance from Kenny Sansom and a clever header from John Aldridge to Ray Houghton, who shaped a header back across a flat-footed Peter Shilton and in at the far post. It was about the creation of chaos and then making the most of it, and what was baffling was that England, whose players were hardly unfamiliar with direct football, should have proved susceptible to it. Jack stood up sharply in celebration and banged his head on the dugout. As Mick Byrne hugged him, he turned away from the pitch, right hand clamped to his by-then substantial bald patch in a mix of pain and delighted disbelief.

Although Ronnie Whelan later hit the bar – from a partially cleared free kick, naturally – Ireland did not play particularly well. England had chances, but Packie Bonner was inspired. On RTÉ Kevin Moran described it as the 'hardest ninety minutes' he'd ever played. But Ireland hung on: they would always have Stuttgart.

That was the start: a win in their first game at a major tournament, and against England to boot. Did anybody think then about reaching the semi-final? Perhaps not, but they were thinking about it seven minutes before half-time in Ireland's second game, against the USSR, as Whelan, tumbling backwards, met a long throw on the edge of the box with a chest-high volley that flashed into the top corner. Ireland were playing well: could they get through the group? But reality began to dawn sixteen minutes from full-time as Ireland were themselves undone by a long ball before Oleh Protasov clipped his finish between Bonner's legs to equalise.

Still, a draw against the Netherlands – who had lost against the USSR in their opening game before beating England 3–1 with a Marco van Basten hat-trick – would have been enough. The Dutch were by far the better side on the day. For eighty-two minutes, they held out. Then a headed clearance from McGrath fell for Ronald Koeman. His volley was driven into the ground and bounced up so loaded with spin that when Wim Kieft got a head to it, the ball arced in the air, around Bonner's dive and just inside the far post. It was a luckless goal generated from getting the ball into the box, Ireland again undone by the sort of goal they were used to scoring.

Ireland were eliminated, but they had proved they belonged at that level – and in those days, with just eight sides qualifying for the finals, the Euros represented an extremely high level. And more than that, the nation had come to understand what being part of a tournament could mean: the sense of togetherness and community, both in Germany and at home, in the stadiums and in bars, the feeling that normal life stopped and everything was focused on a handful of matches. Football, in that regard, offed a universality of experience that other sports could not. It promoted Ireland – and a form of drunken but good-humoured Irishness – to a mass global audience that was inaccessible to the GAA. Quarter of a million people turned out to welcome the squad home from Germany; suddenly the national football team was something people wanted to support and that made them attractive to sponsors. In a little over two years, the FAI's financial problems had disappeared.

Jack had done that. And yet the odd sense after the Euros was that his side might have done more. In the World Cup, they did.

First, they had to get there. Jack again asked for the away games first and this time it seemed a miscalculation. They drew in Northern Ireland, lost in Spain and drew in Hungary – and didn't score a goal in any of them. John Aldridge, who went on a run of just one goal in twenty-three games for Ireland while he remained prolific for Liverpool, complained about the amount of running he had to do and a lack of opportunities in front of goal. Jack began to doubt the fitness of Galvin, Stapleton (whom he had quickly marked down as a moaner) and Brady, who had chafed against the restrictions Jack placed on him before grudgingly accepting their effectiveness. Brady had played all eight games in Euro qualifying but was sent off in the win over Bulgaria and would have missed two group matches at the Euros even if he hadn't then gone down with a knee injury.

And then came Spain at home. The pitch at Lansdowne Road had long been a source of contention. The stadium was owned by the Irish Rugby Football Union, who took 15 per cent of gate receipts when the football team played, but always left the grass at a length appropriate for rugby. For Jack, that was ideal. The ball held up in the corners and more sophisticated sides couldn't get their passing game going. Spain certainly couldn't and were defeated by a Michel own goal. Two–nil wins over Malta and Hungary followed. With two to qualify and Hungary and Spain yet to play each other, Ireland were suddenly in an extremely strong position.

Jack took full advantage; the sense of confusion he exuded often disguised a canniness. In September 1989, he picked all three of Brady, Galvin and Stapleton, all of them by then thirty-three, for a friendly against West Germany. He knew that Irish fans were often slow to accept their heroes were beginning to decline and so decided to 'put them on display'[7] to prove that they were no longer fit enough. Stapleton rather scuppered the plan by opening the scoring after ten minutes, but the West Germans, who would win the World Cup the following year, dominated and levelled on the half hour. Jack, by then, was rattled and took off Brady for Andy Townsend three minutes later. That stabilised matters and the game finished 1–1, but Brady felt humiliated and promptly retired from international football.

Stapleton's position would remain a source of contention. He was on the bench as Ireland sealed qualification by beating Northern Ireland 3–0, and then was left out entirely as Ireland beat the Soviets 1–0 in a friendly in April 1990. But then he came off the bench to score in a 3–0 win away to Malta in Ireland's last friendly before the World Cup. Jack, knowing that, barring injuries, he was unlikely to be included in the match-day sixteen, included Stapleton in his twenty-two-man squad and regretted it. 'Frank is critical of everybody,' he said. 'He's a begrudger.'[8]

With injuries before the tournament, Jack brought in Swindon's Alan McLoughlin as cover for Ray Houghton, which meant leaving out Gary Waddock, who was 'a smashing lad'. It was, Jack said, 'the biggest fuckin' mistake I ever made'. Stapleton 'never stopped moaning and groaning ... he could have helped and joined in with the training, instead of which he carried on like a spoilt kid.'[9]

Jack banned the players from leaving the hotel without permission and warned them about the dangers of talking to the British media. Only Stapleton and John Byrne disobeyed, their boredom after a week of being cooped up while on the fringes of the squad leading them to go and take out a boat – 'no hat, no fuck all'. Jack later said he should have sent Stapleton home there and then.[10]

The hotels themselves were an issue. Ireland stayed largely in cheaper places, although whether because of disorganisation, a conscious plan to build spirit through adversity (a reversal of Revie's policy at Leeds of insisting on good quality hotels to make players feel valued) or Jack's instinctive parsimony was never clear. In Malta, Ireland had booked a hotel where Jack and Pat had stayed several years previously, discovering only when they arrived and saw the pool empty and the furniture draped in dustsheets that it had apparently been closed for years and was being reopened only for them. Entertainment consisted largely of games of Trivial Pursuit – at which Jack was characteristically competitive, forever disputing the answers on the cards or berating his team.

In Sardinia, Mick Byrne saw a group of players sitting bored in reception. The physio was an amusing and popular member of the backroom staff, who had thoroughly vindicated Jack's decision to keep him on. He decided to break the air of lethargy by performing the Lambeth Walk, but in so doing he danced backwards into one of a number of magnificently detailed model boats that dominated the lobby. It teetered briefly on its stand then crashed onto the tiled floor, shattering into tiny pieces.

The hotel owner came rushing out. Mortified, Byrne apologised profusely. The hotel owner, gesturing furiously, shouted in distress to his wife. 'I'm very sorry,' Byrne repeated. The hotel owner kept shouting. Byrne kept apologising. Eventually, Byrne decided he had had enough; there was only so much apologising he could do. As the owner kept ranting, he interrupted him.

'I no sorry any more,' he said in his thick Dublin accent. 'Fuck you and fuck your boat.'

While Jack achieved a level of success and fame he could never have anticipated when he took the Ireland job, Bobby continued in the shadows, a face at functions, an occasional television presence, but as reticent as ever.

And yet he too, in situations in which he felt comfortable, had the same common touch as Jack. A journalist tells the story of Bobby coming down to London in October 1987 to judge a competition to design a United kit. Realising that it was not merely Bobby's birthday, but his fiftieth, the journalist bought a cake as a gesture of thanks. Bobby arrived, spent about half an hour sifting through the entries and chose his favourites, at which the journalist produced the cake. Bobby was embarrassed but clearly touched, and stayed for another half hour, chatting happily. There are countless similar stories: Bobby behind the scenes conscientiously doing his duty, being decent, being pleasant.

In June 1988, he stood for election to the Football League board. There were four places available, but he came fifth in the voting, seemingly because there was a fear that he would simply be a mouthpiece for United and so entrench even further the dominance of the Big Five (United, Liverpool, Everton, Tottenham and Arsenal, the clubs who would lead the break-away to the Premier League four years later). Four months after that, two more vacancies emerged on the committee; Bobby was defeated by John Smith of Liverpool and Robert Chase of Norwich City.

There was a time when it was fashionable to decry the dearth of former high-level players involved in the administration of English football, as though the ability to read a game or lash a shot into the top corner had anything to do with directing commercial operations or negotiating the politics of sport. The corruption allegations against Michel Platini and Franz Beckenbauer have, at least for a time, quelled that argument. That's not to say Bobby might not have been good at the job, and it's certainly not to say he would have been corrupt, merely that it's a strange notion that former players would necessarily make good administrators.

Jack had given up cigarettes two years earlier but when he saw a man behind the dugouts in Genoa he couldn't help himself. 'Giz a tab,' he said. The man, an Italian, was initially bewildered, then realised what Jack was looking at. He reached in his pocket, took out a packet, lit one and passed it through the security fence. There was nothing unusual about Jack cadging cigarettes, but there was something extraordinary about the circumstances: managers in penalty shoot-outs in World Cup knockout games didn't usually beg for fags from random fans.

He lit up and turned back to the pitch, watching as the first eight penalties were scored. Then Packie Bonner saved from the Romanian substitute Daniel Timofte. That left the thirty-two-year-old David O'Leary, a player Jack had never entirely trusted, a player he had left out of the side for almost three years, with the chance to win it. As Silviu Lung fell to his right, O'Leary side-footed the ball calmly into the vacant half of the goal. At their first World Cup, Ireland had reached the quarter-final, and the party went on.

The group had been very similar to two years earlier. Ireland began, again, against England and ended, again, against the Netherlands. The only difference was that Egypt had replaced the USSR as the second opponent. This time, perhaps, there was, if not an expectation then at least a thought that, with the four best third-placed teams going through, Ireland had a chance.

What was certainly different was that, following the scenes in Stuttgart, Hanover and Gelsenkirchen, vast numbers of the Irish decided they didn't want to miss out. Loans were taken out as an estimated thirty-thousand fans made their way to Italy, and that became a social phenomenon in itself. As the feminist writer Nell McCafferty pointed out, for many this was a first experience of abroad – at least, beyond the confines of a package trip. Having to book hotels, arrange trains, handle foreign currencies and interact with locals inevitably gave them new perspectives, weakened some of the instinctive ties to the old Ireland.[11]

And yet, for all that, there was a sense that the real event was happening back home, in the mass gatherings in pubs. The streets were deserted and Dublin Bus stopped running services during games. Mick Jagger and Prince both had concerts at Lansdowne Road cancelled. On match days, and often the day after, people didn't turn up to work and nobody seemed to care. Normal life effectively stopped for the duration of the tournament. As Con Houlihan's famous quip had it, 'I missed the World Cup. I was in Italy at the time.'

*

England, inevitably, meant apprehension. Ireland had been lucky in Stuttgart and there was the clear danger of an England backlash, even if the sense in the build-up to the tournament had been of chaos and decay, with Bobby Robson deciding to quit the job after the tournament. Like Revie he had been panned by the press; like Revie he was then denounced as a traitor for having agreed a deal to take over at PSV Eindhoven – although results meant that the hostility he had faced has largely been erased from the popular memory.

As rain lashed down and thunder rumbled overhead, it seemed initially that Jack's luck might have run out. The match was awful. Ireland didn't press England as they had in Stuttgart, trying to encourage them to play across the back four rather than forward to Chris Waddle and John Barnes on the flanks. They largely stopped England playing, or perhaps England stopped Ireland, or perhaps neither side much wanted to play. *Corriere della Sera*'s headline, 'No Football Please, We're British', may have been politically suspect, but the sentiment was true enough. But this time, that was a problem for Ireland, because England scrambled an early goal as an Irish throw-in was kept in play by Chris Waddle and lofted into the box, where Gary Lineker chested it past Bonner and then bundled it over the line, despite Mick McCarthy's desperate slide. Yet again, it felt, Ireland had conceded the sort of goal in which they specialised.

But the equaliser, scored after seventy-three minutes, was rooted in the Jack method. Bonner's long kick came down about thirty yards from the England goal. Terry Butcher's header went sideways and landed at the feet of Kevin Sheedy, who miscontrolled it to Steve McMahon. But then McMahon miscontrolled it back to him and Sheedy drove a low shot into the bottom corner. It was a dreadful mess of a goal, but nobody Irish was complaining. A draw wasn't the start Ireland had managed two years earlier, but it didn't matter. Egypt, the team everybody expected Ireland to beat, were next.

As England fans were involved in numerous incidents with Italian police, Ireland seemed a welcome counter-example. Yes, they got drunk, but they seemed able to do so without belligerence. If they invaded squares in unsuspecting towns, it was with bonhomie rather than boorishness. And a reputation like that becomes self-perpetuating. Irish fans enjoyed being popular and so policed themselves.

There was a clear sense of a country taking a step outside itself, liking what it saw and being liked in return. 'This is for the whole country,' Eamon Dunphy said on RTÉ before the Egypt game, 'and the team is a catalyst. The character of our people out there, the team ... they haven't had one yellow card. And the way we've celebrated the whole thing is glorious and golden.'[12]

Two and a half hours later, his tone was very different. Ireland had enough good players to beat most sides, and their method made them extremely effective at beating better teams. But Egypt were stubborn, as they had proved in drawing their opener against the Dutch. There was no space behind their full-backs for Ireland to hit. And the result was a grim stalemate. Dunphy was not impressed. 'Anybody who sends out a team to play like that should be ashamed of themselves,' he said. 'When we got the ball we were cowardly.'[13]

That was not what the majority of people wanted to hear. RTÉ was inundated with complaints. Perhaps it was Dunphy speaking in his role as professional contrarian, but he had highlighted a key line of division. Jack had popularised football in Ireland to an unprecedented degree – IFA figures from 1990 showed the number of registered players had increased from 80,000 to 140,000 over the course of Jack's reign – and the new audience were happy enough to go along with the craic that came with success without asking too many questions (and 'crack', as Dan Jackson has pointed out, was a word in common currency in North-East England long before its appropriation by Irish theme pubs in the early nineties,[14] perhaps partially fuelled by the fun that Irish fans seemed to have). But parts of the football establishment – some of the football men who had always loved the game and kept it going in the dark days – looked at Jack's approach, compared it to the teams produced by Eoin Hand and John Giles and, wondering whether something might not have been lost along the way, found themselves alienated by his pragmatism. (An echo of that distrust of the nouveau fan and their focus on the party rather than performances perhaps lingers in the resentment some League of Ireland fans still exhibit towards the national team).

In turn, that reflected a more general shift in Irish society towards the harder, more cynical, results-driven mentality that would characterise the years of the Celtic Tiger. As Declan Lynch had it, Jack represented a liberation 'from all that bullshit of ours about the great poets and the great patriots and the great saints.'[15] Who cared if some of the soul had been lost when you were reaching the quarter-final of the World Cup?

After offering him outside at his first press conference as Ireland manager, Jack had got on quite well with Dunphy; holding a grudge was never his style. One night at the Euros, Jack had insisted Dunphy should join the squad for dinner, something that so disgusted Stapleton and McCarthy that they had walked out, at which Dunphy had also left. But when Dunphy then hammered McCarthy in his column in the *Sunday Independent*, Jack broke off relations. When he saw Dunphy sitting in his press conference to preview the game against the Netherlands, Jack told him to leave. Dunphy refused and was supported by a number of British journalists, at which Jack stormed off, saying he would speak to five senior journalists at the team hotel.

There was a danger then that this could be the end. Dunphy was an unlikely emblem of reaction – and Jack an unlikely revolutionary – but it seemed at that moment that the World Cup adventure could end in frustration against a backdrop of squabbling about style. And, of course, if Ireland had lost to the Netherlands, their exit would have been blamed, quite reasonably, on their failure to beat Egypt, a team who hadn't played at the World Cup in fifty-six years.

Jack made a change up front, preferring Niall Quinn to Tony Cascarino. When Cascarino asked why he had been left out, Jack replied, with the directness that made players feel they could trust him, 'You were fucking crap.'[16]

Ireland went behind after eleven minutes, Ruud Gullit playing a one-two with Wim Kieft before slotting calmly past Bonner – the first goal of aesthetic quality Ireland had conceded at a major tournament. On the touchline, Jack pointed at the failure to track Gullit's run, before flapping his hands down and turning away in an inverted shrug of disgust. Just before the hour, news came through that Mark Wright had scored for England against Egypt. Ireland were going out unless they scored, and there had seemed little chance of that.

Jack threw on Cascarino and Ronnie Whelan for John Aldridge and Kevin Sheedy. And then, at seventy-one minutes, Bonner launched another long kick downfield. It dropped over Cascarino, level with the edge of the D. Berry van Aerle, cutting in from right-back, got a foot to it, skewing the ball into the box. Hans van Breukelen should have gathered comfortably. It was a simple catch and he was under no pressure. But inexplicably, the ball slithered from his grasp and Niall Quinn slid in to turn the ball over the line. Gullit looked to the heavens, perhaps tracing the trajectory of Bonner's clearance. Ireland celebrated.

'I was glad I was Irish,' wrote Roddy Doyle. 'I'd never felt that way before.'[17]

On commentary, George Hamilton announced that Ireland would be facing West Germany in the last sixteen, but it was not so simple as that. Ireland and the Netherlands had finished with identical records and so had to draw lots. Ireland won to take second place in the group, a technicality that meant they would not be playing West Germany in Milan, but Romania in Genoa.

It was another grindingly dull game, two sides intent on not losing in very different ways, Romania all about technical ability and the retention of possession, Ireland all about whacking it clear, putting it in the corners and pressing them when they turned. But Timofte missed and O'Leary didn't and so Ireland were in the quarter-final.

Jack had promised the players that if they reached the last eight, he would be able to secure an audience with the pope. And, somehow, he did. The players, in their green-and-white tracksuits, trooped through St Peter's Square and had a few minutes with John Paul II, who wished them luck for the game against Italy, referred to Jack as 'the boss' and then asked who the goalkeeper was. Packie Bonner raised his hand and the pope said he would be paying him special attention as he'd been a goalkeeper in his youth in Poland.

Ireland's luck ran out eight minutes before half-time, as Bonner parried Roberto Donadoni's fierce strike and then stumbled to his right, leaving the way open for Toto Schillaci to knock in the rebound. A 1–0 defeat against the host was no disgrace, but the party was over at last. There was a moment at the final whistle, as Jack waved to the crowds, that he seemed on the verge of tears but, by the time he'd reached the dressing room, he was reconciled to their exit. He sat smoking, a broad grin on his face and, as Bonner passed him on the way to the shower, he turned to Andy Townsend. 'The fucking pope would have saved that one,' he said.

The return home was euphoric. The Aer Lingus plane was renamed St Jack for the day and deviated from its usual route to salute the crowds who had gathered on O'Connell Street. An estimated quarter of a million people turned out to welcome the squad home, packing the streets to the extent that Jack was terrified a child would be swept under the wheels of the bus. It was a strange triumph – Ireland's only win had been on penalties and they had scored only two goals, both the result of long clearances from Bonner – but a triumph it assuredly was.

Five months later, the impeccably liberal Mary Robinson became the first woman to be elected president of Ireland, promising to tap into the 'vitality and energy that was there in Italy during the World Cup.'[18]

19

AFTER THE PARTY

Where could Ireland go after the highs of Euro 88 and Italia 90? The first time is always the best; the sense of disbelief and wonder as your team reaches heights that had previously seemed impossible can never be replicated, perhaps particularly not when they seem to go hand in hand with a social or cultural revolution.

A lot of Ireland fans enjoyed trying to keep the party going, and there were, certainly, highlights between Rome 1990 and Anfield 1995, but doubts began to encroach on the euphoria. As Declan Lynch wrote, 'It would dishonour the memories of Euro 88 and Italia 90 to say it was still the same after that.'[1]

There was, for a time at least, an attempt to make Ireland more than just a team who were hard to beat. 'Moral victories like participation and the avoidance of humiliation or mass arrests were no longer sufficient,' wrote Tom Humphries. There was a perceived need 'to move beyond the gallant under-dog image'.[2]

It's not a transition that has been easily managed. In 1991, on a tour of the US, a young Roy Keane turned up late for a bus to the airport, wearing a 'Kiss Me Quick' hat.

'You call yourself a professional?' asked Mick McCarthy.

'You call what you have a first touch?' Keane replied.[3]

Eleven years later, though, in Saipan, it was Keane's frustration at the disorganisation around the team – the seeming acceptance of being plucky outsiders, there for the craic – that led to his public row with McCarthy, by then the manager, and his departure from the World Cup. There is still tension between those Ireland fans who just want to have a good time and will do so whatever the result or the performance and those who wish they could just be a normal football team, unburdened by the relentless bonhomie of their celebrated support.

In 1989, Martin Edwards decided to sell his 50.2 per cent share in Manchester United. For a time, it seemed he would be bought out by a consortium led by Michael Knighton, a former headmaster turned property magnate whose great-grandfather had won the league and FA Cup with Sheffield United. According to his fellow board member, Mike Edelson, Bobby played a key role in undermining that bid,[4] which eventually fell apart when his two backers pulled out in the face of an intense media campaign.*

A year later Bobby was part of the consortium led by Amer Al Midani, the son of a Lebanese millionaire, that considered buying Edwards out, only to be put off by the thirty-million-pound asking price. Their plans had included a public flotation, which Edwards went ahead with in 1991. Bobby, to his annoyance, was left off the PLC board, seemingly because he lacked a legal or business background.

*

---

* When it looked as though he would be taking over at United, Knighton performed keepie-uppies on the Old Trafford pitch before the opening game of the 1989–90 season, a 4–1 win over Arsenal. He has since become rather more circumspect about self-promotion, refusing numerous interview requests over the years. After a time as owner (and manager) of Carlisle United, he became an artist, with his depictions of the crucifixion displayed at the chapel of King's College, Cambridge, while hinting that he was the victim of a campaign against him by the Murdoch press.

Ireland's qualifying games for Euro 92 brought a minor tactical adjustment with the deep-lying midfielder sometimes given a little more licence. The result was goals – thirteen scored in six qualifiers for Euro 92, but also six conceded. There were a pair of 1–1 draws against England, but what cost Ireland was a pair of draws against Poland, 0–0 at Lansdowne Road and then 3–3, having been 3–1 up in Poznań.

Ireland went into their final game needing to win away against Turkey and hoping that England would lose in Poland. Jack had always been a lucky coach for Ireland, but that night in November 1991 his fortune began to turn. Ireland did their bit, winning 3–1 while England struggled, falling behind after thirty-two minutes. Poland were then denied a fairly obvious penalty before, with thirteen minutes to go, Lineker scored the equaliser that took England to the finals at Ireland's expense.

The Euros were an eight-team tournament, hard to qualify for, particularly with a draw as tough as the one Ireland had been given. Far more significant was the 1994 World Cup: who wouldn't want a trip to the US, to revel among the great diaspora? But the draw was testing: two to qualify from a seven-team group that included Spain and the European champions Denmark.

Albania turned up for the first qualifier with half a team and no kit. Adidas stepped in to provide shirts, while the FAI provided their Albanian counterparts with a loan, underwritten by Fifa, that allowed them to pay for the travel of the players who had found themselves stranded in Athens. Ireland had their own problems, the first hints of the disquiet that would grow. Kevin Moran was dropped, having returned late from a round of golf on a tour of the US, while Townsend played, despite being fatigued having played three games for Chelsea the previous week on a post-season tour of Canada. Jack could, under FIFA regulations, have demanded he missed the third match to report for his national side, but he preferred not to pick fights with English clubs. For somebody so belligerent in certain circumstances, he was oddly keen to avoid confrontation in others. Nevertheless, Ireland won 2–0.

There was a straightforward win over Latvia, then a 0–0 in Copenhagen, Denmark's third successive goalless draw since winning the Euros, a hangover that would, ultimately, cost them. Ireland drew in Spain, then beat Albania in Tirana, a result due in no small part to Jack's preparation. He had accompanied Northern Ireland's squad on their trip to Albania. They found a country on its knees after the collapse of communism. Jack had taken his own food in the form of some salmon and a chicken-and-game pie and insisted on using the stairs to reach his tenth-floor room, a decision that was vindicated when Alan McDonald got stuck in the lift. When Ireland went there, they flew in and out in a day, and took their own chefs with their own pots and pans, cooking oil and washing-up liquid, while each player was provided with a pack containing a toilet roll, a candle, a towel, a bar of soap and a bottle of mineral water.

Relations with the Northern Ireland manager Billy Bingham, though, soured as Ireland beat the north 3–0 in Dublin and fans sang, 'There's only one team in Ireland.' Jack hadn't helped with some injudicious comments about the standard of the Northern Ireland squad. That would have consequences.

Ireland beat Latvia away and Lithuania home and away, which meant they topped the group with two games remaining. A draw at home to Spain would almost certainly have been enough. Jack was unusually indecisive about his tactics and settled late on a 4-5-1. It didn't work and Spain were 3–0 up inside twenty-five minutes, eventually winning 3–1. Suddenly, Ireland were a point behind Denmark and level with Spain with an inferior goal difference to both. A win away to Northern Ireland would secure qualification, as would a draw, provided Spain's match against Denmark did not also finish level.

It was Bingham's last game as manager of Northern Ireland after fourteen years and, seething at what he saw as Jack's presumptuousness, he was determined to mark it by stopping Ireland. His side, he pointed out, were all 'homegrown' as opposed to the 'mercenaries' on whom Jack relied.[5]

Bingham insisted his comments were 'anti-Jack' not 'anti-republican',[6] but their antipathy was set against wider political concerns. There had been an escalation in violence in the weeks before the game. The IRA blew up a fish-and-chips shop in the Shankill Road area of Belfast, killing eight civilians and a UDA member and in reprisal loyalists shot fourteen Catholics around Northern Ireland, including eight in a pub in Greysteel, County Derry. For a time there was talk of moving the game from Belfast to England before it was decided security could be guaranteed at Windsor Park stadium.

Ireland stayed, as usual, at the Nuremore hotel, Monaghan, but rather than taking the short bus ride to Belfast, they returned to Dublin and flew. The atmosphere was tense, hostile.

'The venom in their eyes shocked me,' said Alan McLoughlin.[7]

'I can remember ... coming into Windsor Park and seeing a crowd of very, very young boys – no older than ten – all pointing to us with imitation guns and pretending to shoot,' said Niall Quinn. 'Then this man, this grotesque man, got them all to kneel down and another group stood up behind them and did the same thing.'[8]

Terry Phelan and Paul McGrath were racially abused. Alan Kernaghan, who had grown up in Bangor and played for Northern Ireland at youth level, was jeered as a 'traitor' (he was born in Otley, West Yorkshire and an agreement between the four UK football associations meant he could not have played senior international football for Northern Ireland). He chatted with an RUC officer, who soon realised a photograph of them together could put either in danger.

The game was scrappy. At half-time it was 0–0, which was also the score in Seville, although Andoni Zubizarreta, Spain's goalkeeper, had been sent off. At that point, it seemed, Ireland were going out and Jack was probably coming to the end of his time as manager. But eighteen minutes into the second half, Fernando Hierro scored for Spain. Ireland were going through. And then Jimmy Phillips, with a majestic, leaping volley, put Northern Ireland ahead with sixteen minutes remaining. Bingham danced a jig on the touchline as the crowd rejoiced, 'There's only one team in Ireland'.

Jack needed one more moment of inspiration, and it came through Alan McLoughlin, who had come on for Houghton in the second half to make his first competitive appearance in two years. Jack had told him to play behind the front two, to pick up the scraps if crosses were cleared. But he needed more. Having gone behind, he called on Tony Cascarino, who peeled off his tracksuit top to realise, to his horror, he was wearing just a plain, white T-shirt. Jack was apoplectic. 'You fucking idiot,' he screamed. Kit man Charlie O'Leary was sent to the dressing room to find Cascarino's shirt and he had just returned when Ireland won a free kick on the right. Gerry Taggart headed clear, but the ball came to McLoughlin, who chested it down and stroked it, with incongruous calmness, into the bottom corner. With twelve minutes to go, Ireland had the goal that took them to the US.

After the final whistle, as anger roiled around the stands, Alan McDonald came into the Ireland dressing room and wished them all the best, saying they would have the support of the north at the World Cup. But as Ireland played Italy in their first game at the World Cup, UVF gunmen burst into a pub in Loughinisland, County Down, and fired at customers watching the match on television. Six were killed and five wounded.

*

One night in January 1994, at his holiday home in Altea, Spain, Jack found himself unable to remember the name of the former Arsenal midfielder Graham Rix. He had a reputation for forgetting names, or for referring to players by the names of players with similar names from the sixties, but this was different and that troubled him. That night, he couldn't sleep. His frenzied brain kept presenting him with images and asking him to name what he saw.[9] His ear began to throb and by the time he saw a doctor, his head and throat were sore as well.

The initial diagnosis was that wax had become compacted in his ear, but Jack was concerned and had a series of tests. His schedule had been hectic as media and speaking events piled up and it was decided he was stressed, although given what subsequently happened it's impossible not to wonder if that was the first sign of the Alzheimer's that would later overwhelm him. Doctors advised him to ease back so he took four weeks off, missing a February meeting for World Cup coaches. Perhaps an assistant should have gone, but Jack insisted it was a waste of time, that he'd played at two World Cups and managed in one: what more was there to learn? But when the heat and the humidity became a major issue during the group stage, FIFA could say that Jack had had the chance to raise his concerns and had not turned up.

And Jack perhaps did still have things to learn. Football was changing. The negativity of the 1990 World Cup, to which Ireland had made a hearty contribution, had prompted FIFA into a series of law changes, outlawing the backpass and the tackle from behind – both of which affected how Ireland played – and adopting a system of three points for a win. Bingham pointed out that Jack's instinctive caution, and his preference for full-backs in midfield, might count against them now draws were worth less than they had been.[10]

*

Shortly before the squad left for the US, Tony Cascarino smuggled a woman he'd met at a bar in Church Street into the team hotel in Dublin. Police were notified when security cameras picked up an intruder. The next day, Jack called together the squad and asked who was responsible. Initially, everybody denied it, but Cascarino then privately owned up. Jack raged that he should expel him from the squad before finally calming down and saying, 'Well, I hope she was worth it.'[11]

Perhaps it wasn't significant. Breaches of discipline happen in most squads most of the time, even if the temptation is to contrast Jack's response to that of Alf Ramsey when he found members of his England squad had been out drinking. Perhaps it shows nothing more than the laddish humanity that always lay just below the surface of Jack's leadership. But for those who believed that Ireland, with a little more application, could be more, there was no shortage of attack lines.

Then again, Ireland was fun. Players enjoyed being part of it, to the extent that Kevin Sheedy joined a tour of the US despite having a calf injury that meant he was unable to play. A stricter regime might easily have destroyed the team spirit that was such an essential part of Jack's Ireland.

Ireland under Jack were probably the hardest-drinking national team in the world. The stories of how the players would chant 'We love you, Jackie, we do,' whenever they wanted the bus to pull over at the next pub added to their charm. But the dreadful irony was that their best player across the decade of Jack's reign was an alcoholic and, in the later years, had to be prevented from joining his teammates.

Paul McGrath was a brilliant centre-back or holding midfielder. He was physically imposing, good on the ball and read the game as well as anybody, one of those calm, commanding presences from whom others draw strength. Off it, he was a mess. He had grown up in a brutal orphanage. He was in constant pain from his knees. He suffered from a crippling sense of insecurity. And he drank – at times, for days on end. Twice he tried to take his own life. He would go missing. His teammates were constantly having to cover for him. On occasions he played drunk. But Jack loved him. Whenever McGrath erred, Jack would tell him off, 'gruff and hostile and – in spite of himself – ever so slightly paternal'.[12]

Matters reached a head late in 1990 when McGrath, having been on a bender and suffering from the DTs, was unable to play in a European Championship qualifier against Turkey. Jack initially tried to persuade him at least to get off the bus at the stadium so they could claim he was struggling with the knee problems that everybody knew about. But McGrath couldn't. He was taken back to the hotel alone, thinking his international career might be over. That night, he was sitting on the floor in a terrible state when Jack came into his room. He sat down next to him, put an arm round his shoulders and said, 'Sorry, son. I didn't realise how bad you had it.'

From then on, Jack was consistently supportive. 'I loved him,' said McGrath.[13]

The most moving moment of the very moving documentary *Finding Jack Charlton* shows Jack, desperately confused by dementia near the end of his life, suddenly illuminated by a shaft of understanding as he sees a photograph on the screen of his laptop. As a smile breaks across his face, he says, 'Paul McGrath.' It might have been only the second time he ever got his name right.

Ireland had hoped to be drawn in either Boston or Chicago, the centres of the diaspora. Instead, they were drawn in New York and Orlando. There were plenty of Irish in New York, of course, but there were more Italians and Ireland were grouped

with Italy. They'd feared being outnumbered by Italians at their
first game, but as the coach eased through a sea of green shirts,
Jack turned to Cascarino and said, 'You're the only fucking
Italian here.'

This was the final great high and it began with familiar
chaos as Ireland left their dressing room wearing white shirts
only to be told that Italy were already in the tunnel, also wearing white. That not only meant a rapid change into their home
strip, but as only one set of green shirts had been brought, that
there was no dry kit to change into at half-time.

With Niall Quinn ruled out of the tournament with ruptured
knee ligaments, Stapleton retired and Cascarino ageing, Jack
had no real target man and was forced to modify his approach,
using Tommy Coyne as a willing runner in behind the full-
backs with Ray Houghton as the most advanced of a five-man
midfield. But the goal was very familiar. A long ball caused
chaos, Franco Baresi's clearing header was weak and Houghton
gathered just outside the box, his mis-hit shot floating over
Gianluca Pagliuca to give Ireland a twelfth-minute lead.

McGrath was magnificent as Ireland held out. With sec-
onds to go, Andy Townsend intercepted a pass from Roberto
Donadoni and broke forward. Suddenly, he was alone in the
Italy half, bearing down on Pagliuca. He had time to think
and what came to mind was not the possible glory of adding a
second but of watching the end of the 1988–89 league season
at an Ireland get-together at the Finnstown Castle hotel, as
Arsenal pinched the title with a late goal against Liverpool.
As everybody else marvelled at Arsenal's dramatic 2–0 win,
Jack had blamed John Barnes for darting into the box when a
1–0 defeat would have been enough for Liverpool. Barnes had
lost possession, leading to Arsenal's second goal. So Townsend
changed course and headed for the corner. He had learned the
lesson that Peter Beardsley would not and it secured Ireland's
first win in a World Cup finals.[14]

At the final whistle, Jack, in a white shirt and tie topped with a white baseball cap that sat awkwardly on his head, raised his fists in celebration, walking briskly towards the mass of Ireland fans behind the goal in which Houghton had scored. Red-faced, hair soaked, Steve Staunton wrapped an iced towel around his neck. The camera lingered briefly on Terry Phelan, his face oddly blank as his eyes soaked in the mass of waving tricolours. 'I couldn't believe I was on the green grass, playing for my country in the Giants Stadium,' he said. 'I could have stood there for ninety minutes more and just looked at it and soaked it in again.'[15]

That was true for many of the Ireland squad. For all the frustration Roy Keane subsequently felt – that they could have done more – for all the quality they undoubtedly had, there were also several players from lower mid-table sides and worse. But Jack had put them in a World Cup and made them into a team that could beat Italy.

And given what then happened, it's possible Phelan had a sense that this was the pinnacle, that it was never going to be this good again. A couple of hours later came a reminder that this was still Ireland. The plane they'd chartered to take them back to Florida hadn't arrived and so, exhausted, the players sat for hours on a bus by a customs gate round the back of Newark airport.

Noon in Orlando for the game against Mexico was monstrous. It was hot and humid, the air so still that a couple of seconds after the crowd had roared the players could smell the beer and hot dogs from their breath. Jack raged against the conditions and FIFA, in the end, agreed that bags of water could be thrown on during games, but still Ireland suffered. They went 2–0 down to a pair of Luis García goals and then, as Jack tried to make a double substitution in response to the second, confusion with a FIFA official led to John Aldridge's entrance being delayed so Ireland played for a couple of minutes with ten men. Aldridge and Jack, his face beetroot beneath his cap, raged, and Jack called the official 'a fucking cheat'. Aldridge eventually got on and pulled one back, but he was fined £1,250 for his conduct. Jack's sanction was worse: a seven-thousand-pound fine and a one-game touchline ban, which he put down to FIFA getting their own back for his complaints over the temperature.

It was decided that Jack would sit in the stand wearing a headset to communicate with Maurice Setters, but first the technology needed to be tested. Jack, pushing his finger into his ear, bellowed into the microphone. 'Maurice,' he shouted. 'Maurice. Can. You. Hear. Me?'

Setters was standing no more than two feet away.

Aldridge's goal against Mexico was crucial because it meant that every team in the group had three points and a level goal difference, but that Ireland had scored a goal more than Norway and so needed only a draw to secure their place in the last sixteen. They got it, with a turgid 0–0 that was almost as bad as the Egypt game four years earlier.

All four teams finished on four points. Mexico were top because they had scored three and conceded three, Norway bottom because they had scored one and conceded one. And Ireland were placed second, above Italy, because of their victory in New York, which meant a return to Orlando to face the side that won Group F, rather than taking on Nigeria in Foxborough.

Would it have made a difference? Perhaps not. But the return to Orlando was undertaken with a sense of fatalism. It didn't help that, because Belgium had beaten the Netherlands, Jack had assumed they would top the group and went to watch them play Saudi Arabia in their final group game. But they lost and Ireland instead faced the Dutch. They were familiar enough opponents, but perhaps one last look would have given Jack a fresh idea of how to stop them.

Ireland had beaten the Netherlands in a friendly in Tilburg two months before the World Cup, but the heat and humidity meant it was impossible to press Ronald Koeman in the same way; he was able to dictate the game from the back. 'We maybe needed to adapt our game a little,' Phelan said, 'but we didn't.'[16]

It was a Koeman ball over the top that led to the weak back-header from Phelan that let Marc Overmars in to cross for Dennis Bergkamp to open the scoring. Then a long-range drive from Wim Jonk squirmed through Bonner's arms. Two–nil down at half-time, an exhausted and despondent Jack could barely give a team talk. Townsend urged him to throw Cascarino on to force Frank Rijkaard back and at least end the Dutch control of midfield, but he was reluctant to open up and risk a hammering.[17] There were no further goals.

In the US, fans partied and mingled with players; it was all still a laugh. But subtly the mood had changed. McGrath spoke of how 'so much of the innocence is gone'.[18] In Dublin, Women's Aid had already begun to report that incidents of domestic violence rose whenever Ireland lost, and that night there were dozens of arrests as brawls broke out in pubs. A welcome home party had been arranged for Phoenix Park. Initially, Jack had turned down his invitation, preferring to stay in the US to work as a pundit on ITV. He was eventually persuaded to return, but the event was a damp squib with only around ten thousand turning out. He himself admitted Ireland had 'underachieved' in the US.[19]

'I don't know if I want to go through this again,' Jack wrote in his column in the *Sunday Press*. 'Maybe I'm getting a little bit weary over the whole business, maybe my thoughts are not as clear as they should be, maybe I'm not as sharp as I was.'[20]

The best book on the Charlton years and how they revolutionised Irish football is Paul Rowan's 1994 work *The Team that Jack Built*. It includes lengthy passages from a forthright interview Jack gave the author while driving to Sligo that became a slightly baffling *cause celêbre*. Rowan himself was surprised Jack gave him such access when he had signed a deal to write his autobiography for what was, at the time, the highest advance ever given to a British sportsperson.* That night at dinner, Jack and his agent asked for money. Rowan refused, pointing out payment had never been mentioned before.

Perhaps Jack was just annoyed at missing out on the cash – and he always made sure he capitalised on his popularity, which is why Sean Ryan could refer to him as 'the ultimate grasper'[21] – or perhaps he realised he had been indiscreet, as, amid other attacks, he accused Rowan of having turned off one tape recorder after quarter of an hour while secretly keeping another one rolling. Rowan reluctantly released a section of the interview in which it is clear that Jack knew the whole thing was both being recorded and on the record.[22]

Most anecdotes about Jack focus on the sense of chaos that surrounded him alongside his basic straightforwardness and sense of decency. But he could be hard when he needed to be, and he was as capable as anybody of lying when under pressure, even when it led to serious unpleasantness. The instincts of Tanner Milburn were always there.

*

* Taking the record jointly held by Ian Botham and George Graham.

During the World Cup, Rowan bumped into Jack in the lobby of the Sheraton in New Jersey. 'I'm sorry for shouting at you the other day,' Jack said. 'I thought you were somebody else.'

But Jack hadn't shouted at Rowan the other day. 'I think I am that somebody else,' Rowan replied.

As they stepped into the lift together, Jack grinned broadly.[23] Even when he was angry with somebody, he had a charming sense of the absurdity of life – and his shambolic approach to it only made it more absurd.

The lure of playing a tournament in England was too much. Jack stayed on.

Qualifying began well enough. Latvia and Liechtenstein were dismissed, Northern Ireland thrashed 4–0 in Belfast. But things began to go wrong in February 1995, as England fans rioted in Dublin, forcing a friendly to be abandoned. It was not Jack's fault, of course, and if there had been some naivety on the part of the authorities about the impact of the peace process on the mentality of the worst of England's support it was perhaps an understandable flaw. But that night introduced a note of sourness that never entirely went away.

The following month Northern Ireland came to Dublin, dug in as Jack's side itself so often had, and pinched an equaliser when a misplaced McGrath pass allowed Keith Gillespie to cross for Iain Dowie. Jack, slightly bafflingly, then withdrew the forward David Kelly for the midfielder Jason McAteer, as though happy with the point. Bingham's observation about the declining value of draws suddenly seemed very relevant. In his post-match interview with RTÉ's Ger Canning, Jack was oddly snappish.

But it was only later that game came to feel significant. Ireland were very good in beating Portugal 1–0 and at that point, the halfway stage, Ireland led the group by a point. And then they went to Liechtenstein.

The game was played in June, long after many players' seasons had finished. Keane and Townsend were injured. Quinn and Aldridge missed early chances. The home keeper, Martin Heeb, had an inspired game. Ireland could not score. At half-time, Jack, again, seemed to surrender responsibility. 'There's nothing I can do for you,' he said. 'You'll have to work this one out for yourselves.'[24] They could not, and drew 0–0.

The University of Limerick had given Jack an honorary doctorate, so as a gesture of appreciation, Jack had the squad spend the week between Liechtenstein and a home game against Austria there. For reasons that he never explained, he took twenty-four players, most of whom, knowing they would not be involved, were bored and resentful. McGrath's room was guarded, but he managed to smuggle booze in by calling somebody he'd spoken to at a supporters' function a few weeks earlier. 'By 1995,' he said, 'we had all become comfortable and a little bit careless.'[25]

Jack went to Belfast for a couple of days to watch Northern Ireland play Latvia. With Setters in Dublin with the under-twenty-ones, for a spell Jack's son, John, was in charge. Discipline unravelled. 'Our drinking was so bad,' said Niall Quinn, 'that even I couldn't take any more.'[26]

The night before the Austria game, there was a training session at Lansdowne Road. But first there was a charity function at a community centre in Ballyfermot, Dublin. The players got out of the bus and wandered around, but nobody seemed to know what they were doing there. They got back on the coach and stopped off at the Harry Ramsden's restaurant on Naas Road, in which Jack happened to own shares. Although Jack defended the decision afterwards, pointing out the protein content of fish and insisting nobody had had soup or a pudding[27] (a curious echo of his own argument over starters with

Bill Lambton when he was at Leeds), it didn't suggest hyper-professionalism and made training a farce.[28] Ireland went 1–0 up after sixty-five minutes, but then let in three. Suddenly, their campaign was collapsing.

Ireland lost 3–1 in Austria and although they beat Latvia 2–1, there were more reports of players staying out late. A win away to Portugal would still have secured top spot in the group, but that never seemed plausible. As Ireland lost 3–0, they were reliant on Northern Ireland beating Austria, which they did, 5–3, to remain second and take a play-off slot. But Ireland never looked like beating the Dutch in Liverpool. In those final six months, as Jack seemed unable to retain control, everything had fallen apart remarkably quickly.

Bobby had none of Jack's reputation for liking money and being canny with it, yet in April 1994 *Business Age* put Jack's assets at two million pounds and Bobby's at £6.5 million, a difference that could only in part be explained by the fact that Jack's wealth was far harder to calculate.

A large of part of Bobby's wealth came from his Soccer Schools, part of Bobby Charlton Enterprises, which also had interests in corporate entertainment, security and consultancy. In 1991, it was bought by the textile firm Conrad International, although Bobby retained a stake and various directorships. Manchester United's flotation that same year led to some questions about why the club used Conrad and Halba but it wasn't until 1997 that Bobby began to sell up, concerned by a potential conflict of interest as Conrad invested in Sheffield United.

Although never as regular a presence as Jack, Bobby also dabbled in television. He was an occasional co-commentator, particularly on England matches, although he was neither as charismatic nor outspoken as his brother. Then there were eighty-six episodes of *Bobby Charlton's Football Scrapbook*, in which Dickie Davies would lead Bobby and a guest in discussing an old game. While it could never be said that Bobby was a natural on television, he was by the nineties far more comfortable in front of a camera than he had been, particularly when he was doing something as uncontroversial as recalling old footballers.

That ongoing preference for avoiding public confrontation was a major factor in the deep ambivalence many United fans felt towards Bobby the director. Right from the start, his reserve made him a slightly awkward boardroom figure, with players chanting 'Bobby, Bobby, give us a smile,' on the team bus. Some fans dismissed him as a cold fish, an establishment figure with little concern for their interests. Critically, he did not speak out publicly against either Sky's attempted takeover in 1998 or the Glazer takeover in 2005.

His last major act as a United director was to veto the potential appointment of José Mourinho to succeed Alex Ferguson when he retired in 2013, seemingly because he felt he did not represent the values of the club. Mourinho's eventual appointment in 2017 was an indication of Bobby's declining influence and, although he never formally ceased to be a director, the club's announcement in November 2020 that he had dementia effectively marked the end of his involvement.

Almost all footballing lives end in failure. Bobby's had at Preston and, ultimately, Jack's did with Ireland. His final game, a play-off against the Netherlands at Anfield, seemed entirely fitting. Ireland fought gamely but were outplayed, losing 2–0. As he walked around the pitch after the final whistle, applauding the fans who applauded him, there were echoes of that evening in 1969 when the same stands had saluted him and his Leeds teammates as they were crowned champions. Some in the dressing room may already have been wondering if giving it a go were good enough, with their status as – to use Niall Quinn's phrase – 'beautiful, skilled losers',[29] a tension within Irish football that would spill over in Saipan in 2002. For most, though, gallant failure was enough to justify more booze and more revelling in the fact of being Irish in a major stadium abroad. And nobody – whatever doubts may have begun to crystallise in the final couple of years – could seriously doubt the enormous strides Ireland had made under Jack.

But was it the end? The FAI expected Jack to confirm his retirement, but it didn't come. Jack himself later claimed, somewhat implausibly, that he was waiting for February 1996, the tenth anniversary of taking the job, as though such landmarks had ever meant anything to him before, as though giving his successor only a month before his first games in charge were in any way reasonable. Others wondered if he were having second thoughts. He was only sixty; could he leave behind a sport that had been his life for forty-five years?

Quinn had been suspended for that play-off and Roy Keane and Steve Staunton injured. Perhaps he was wondering what might have happened had he not been so cautious against the Dutch, had he not fielded a side with four full-backs.[30] Maybe they hadn't been so far off. And the draw for World Cup qualifying looked favourable.

But for the FAI, the time had come. Joe Delaney, the treasurer, told Jack to make an announcement before the end of the year or they would make one for him. He agreed to meet them at Merrion Square on 21 December. He was emotional, knew his time was up, and asked each of the four FAI executives present in turn if they thought he should go.

All of them said, 'Yes.'

But nobody was unaware of what Jack had done. He had taken Ireland into their first three major tournaments and, in so doing, had transformed perceptions of football in a country in which it had always faced suspicion and hostility. And the

Ireland he left was very different from the Ireland that had appointed him; more liberal, more outward-looking. The years of the Celtic Tiger had just begun; between 1995 and 2000, the economy grew by between 7.8 and 11.5 per cent per year.[31]

The talks that would lead to the Good Friday Agreement in 1998 were well underway. Jack's role in that process was, at best, indirect, but it didn't hurt to have a popular Englishman in a high-profile position. 'Jack showed that you can be English and be loved in Ireland,' said Niall Quinn. 'He opened a little window of opportunity. Great political leaders could come in then to bring an end to the violence.'[32]

In 1996, Jack was still only sixty-one. But he was tired and felt he was done with football. And football, perhaps, was done with him.

20

CURTAIN

There is a clip of an interview with Jack in the early seventies in which he describes what a 'terrible fisherman' Bobby was. He is sitting on a sofa, wearing a collar and tie with a V-neck jumper, hair brushed forwards to disguise his baldness. Alongside him sits his mother in a brown polo neck and heavy-rimmed glasses. Jack describes how he had to put the worm on the hook for Bobby – 'a right chicken he was'. Only once, Jack says, did Bobby catch a fish. 'He bent over, and he had hold of the line – and he'd picked a nice trout, it was about a pound – and he picked it out of the water and he said, "Look at that!" And it dropped off. And he was shouting at me, "But it counts, doesn't it?" and I said, "No."'[1]

What's striking is not so much the story itself as Cissie's reaction. Perhaps she is just nervous being on television – although, as Tommy notes in the same documentary, she relished the limelight – but through what is, at best, a routine anecdote, she emits a high-pitched giggle. It feels forced, unnatural, as though she is rather too keen to enjoy a story about her second son being discomforted. Or perhaps the exaggerated laughter is intended to show how supportive she is of Jack, as if to emphasise that the rift with Bobby is not the result of any parental failing.

But a rift there was and it was to do with Bobby's wife.

Norma's relationship with Cissie, he said, 'started badly and ...
never recovered',[2] and that put a strain on his own relationship
with his mother. 'She fought for us and made sacrifices for
us ...' he said. 'The tragedy ... was that in the end she could
not give me what I wanted most. She couldn't love my wife.'[3]
And that, in turn, affected Bobby's relationship with Jack, who
said, 'Aside from the way he treated our mother, I don't hold
any bad feeling towards him.'[4]

Cissie died in 1996. Bobby hadn't visited in a number of
years, but he was a pallbearer at her funeral and it seemed
perhaps that, with their parents gone, there was the possibility of reconciliation. But a few months later Jack released his
autobiography, which exposed the tensions within the family.
Bobby was mortified to have such personal details revealed and
'deeply offended by the picture he painted of my wife'.[5]

Tommy, the youngest brother, agreed that perhaps it might
have been better had Jack not been so public about such personal details, but he acknowledged the basic truth of Jack's
account. 'I would have liked it to have been different to that,'
he said. 'But it wasn't. It's a fact.'[6]

'Maybe,' Jack told Sue Lawley on *Desert Island Discs*, 'if we'd
had something in common, like the problems of being a manager over a period of twenty-odd years, maybe we'd have been
better friends.'[7]

Yet his favourite was 'Day In, Day Out' by Frank Sinatra, a
choice of which Bobby would surely have approved.

His luxury item was a fishing rod.

Bobby never appeared on *Desert Island Discs*.

Don Revie coached the UAE for three years and the Dubai club
Al-Nasr for four. After a brief spell in Cairo with Al Ahly, he

returned to Britain in 1984. He lived in Surrey for two years then moved to Kinross in Scotland. A year later, he was diagnosed with motor neurone disease. He died in Edinburgh in May 1989, aged sixty-one.

Matt Busby was made president of Manchester United in 1980 and continued to live in Manchester. He was admitted to hospital with a blood clot in his leg in January 1994. Surgery appeared to have gone well, but his condition suddenly deteriorated and he died later that month, aged eighty-four.

United beat Bayern Munich in the Champions League final in Barcelona in 1999 to complete the treble on what would have been his ninetieth birthday.

After being sacked by England, Alf Ramsey took a break from football, before an uncomfortable four-month spell in charge of Birmingham City. He resigned after the board overruled his decision to place Trevor Francis on the transfer list. He had a brief stint in Athens as technical director of Panathinaikos, then retired to Ipswich, where he played a lot of golf and watched a lot of westerns. He suffered a stroke in June 1998 and was then hospitalised with Alzheimer's and cancer. He died following a heart attack in April 1999, aged seventy-nine.

Jack kept hunting and fishing, living in his cottage in Northumberland.

Bobby continued to live in Cheshire. He remained on the board at Manchester United, a face in the directors' box, wheeled out whenever they needed somebody with stature and gravitas to say something diplomatic. He was devoted to his wife and daughters, and played a lot of golf.

*

George Best died in the Cromwell hospital in South Kensington, London, on 25 November 2005 from complications with the immunosuppressants he had had to take following a liver transplant three years earlier. By the end, the slight grace of his youth had gone, and so too had the bloatedness of drink. Photos taken by his agent showed him thin and frail, the hospital gown sliding from his shoulder, his skin parchment yellow, his cheeks sunken, his beard a sooty white. He was fifty-nine, just a year old than his mother when she died, the same age Busby had been when he first retired. He looked much, much older.

Shortly before Best's death, Bobby Charlton met Denis Law at Stockport station and they travelled together to London to visit, the three greats who had never really got on, reunited once more. The acrimony of the early seventies, trivial in the face of mortality, fell away. 'The time for judgement had long passed,' said Bobby. 'I whispered to him, as I had to Duncan Edwards and Matt Busby all those years before in Munich.'[8]

The following Saturday, before Manchester United's game at West Ham, Bobby put on the dark suit and the black tie again and took his sombre place in a brief ceremony by the side of the pitch at Upton Park. Another hospital, another commemoration, more duty to be done.

Finding Jack Charlton is a brave and beautiful documentary. It is unflinching about showing Jack in his later years, when dementia had claimed him, when only glimpses of the man he had been remained. He is frail, struggling with his balance. He is surprised by his World Cup winner's medal, by photographs of himself playing football, by the documentaries he made about the North-East. He is often obstreperous – 'I don't want to go and see the ducks' – but as he jokes with people at a fishing competition, his basic humanity is obvious. His eyes are often baffled, his speech slightly slurred. The lop-sided grin that once suggested canniness denotes only confusion. The support Pat provided is clear. She comes across as being just as tough, clear-sighted and blunt as Jack; you see how their marriage functioned for sixty-two and a half years, how she was able to deal with somebody even his own friends admitted was habitually pig-headed.

There are numerous, desperately poignant shots of him sitting in his kitchen, watching clips of his former self. He is thinner than in his time as Ireland manager and the effect is, in profile, to make him resemble even more closely his younger brother.

Footballers, we now know, are around 3.5 times more likely to die from dementia than the average person.[9] Ray Wilson, Martin Peters and Nobby Stiles, who had won the World Cup in 1966, all died with dementia. So did Jeff Astle, who had played in 1970.

Heading the ball is bad for you, and Jack headed a lot of balls. 'He's enjoyed his football,' said Pat. 'Would you take that away from him? I don't think so.'[10] He had escaped the noise and danger and confusion of the pit as a young man, but in the end a different darkness would claim him. No amount of bluff good sense could avert that – and neither could caution. The darkness would claim Bobby as well.

Jack died in July 2020. Ill health prevented Bobby from attending the funeral. That November, it was confirmed that he too was suffering from dementia. They had done so much. Bobby had been perhaps the best player in England's history, he had suffered the agonies of Munich and returned at who knew what cost to win the European Cup. Jack had helped transform Leeds as a player and had transformed Ireland as a manager. Together, they had won the World Cup and together,

England's greatest footballing brothers, so different in life, had been claimed by the same awful disease.

Image shouldn't matter, but it does. Ask somebody to describe Bobby Charlton the footballer and the vast majority will mention early on the comb-over, that absurd scrape of half a dozen strands of muddy blond hair across his scalp which, far from masking his baldness, served only to accentuate it. The effect is unfortunate because, perhaps allied to his reserve and conservatism, it emphasises the feeling that he was of another age, gives the sense he was perpetually middle-aged. In terms of attitude, that may not be entirely untrue, but it detracts from what an extraordinary footballer he was.

He was thirty when Manchester United won the European Cup in 1968 but, even though he scored twice and was probably the most effective player on the pitch, he seemed old, constantly shoving his hair back into place, his cheeks haggard. It's perhaps not unreasonable to highlight the toll of Munich but, despite all that he suffered in its aftermath, he was a great player. That final was not an aberration. There's a reason why, until Wayne Rooney took both records, Bobby was the leading scorer for Manchester United and England, despite rarely playing as an out-and-out forward.

Look back at the handful of clips that exist of him in his earlier days, before his hair drew the attention, and what stands out is his combination of power and grace. He had the build of a middleweight boxer, stocky but lean with it, and was capable of bursts of explosive pace. But there was also an elegance to him. He ran with his head up; even he came to accept that there was a time when he tried glory balls too often, but he had to be able see his team-mate before attempting to pick him out with a long cross-field pass, even if the pass itself was ill-conceived. That awareness, that poise, that mastery of his environment, is why Matt Busby compared him to a pianist.

It can be difficult in histories to reflect how great a player was. To speak of all the goals scored, all the passes made, all the inspirational performances, quickly becomes repetitive. It's the nature of both reporting and drama that it is in flaws that the interest lies. And it is intriguing that, although he had so many attributes, a sense lingered – and was arguably borne out by his management – that he did not quite understand the game so well as his brother. But even if he did at times feel like a relic of a previous age, preserving a style and an attitude out of keeping with the increasing stridency of the sixties, nobody should be in any doubt that Bobby Charlton was an exceptional footballer, quite possibly the best England has ever produced.

Jack's reputation too suffered from his image. He was tall and gangling. His height helped define him as a central defender and also made him a potent attacking threat: he scored seventy times for Leeds, a remarkable figure for a defender, and got six goals in thirty-five appearances for England. From child-hood he was the less gifted brother and that, along with his ungainliness, his bluff manner and the direct approach of the teams he managed, perhaps meant there was a tendency to see his destructive rather than his technical qualities. And yet a series of players who played under him tell stories about how talented he was with a ball. Jack was probably a rather better footballer than people gave him credit for, than even he gave himself credit for.

He was somebody it was easy to get a rise out of, an amus-ing target for dressing-room banter because it clearly annoyed him in the moment without having longer-term repercussions. Perhaps his Leeds teammates were right that the footballer of the year award he won in 1967 derived in part from sentimen-tality, but there were other World Cup winners the English press could have rewarded if that was their motive. At the very least, Jack was effective, charismatic and well-liked enough to win the vote. There was a time in the mid-sixties when the two brothers were among the most famous half-dozen sportspeople in Britain. They remain the most famous siblings in British sporting history.

In 2008, at the BBC Sports Personality of the Year Awards, Bobby Charlton was honoured with a lifetime achievement award. It was presented to him by his brother. They were never fully reconciled, but there was at last enough love and respect to appear on the same stage together.

'When we were kids,' Jack said, his voice thick with emotion, the tears glinting in Bobby's eyes, 'and we used to go to the park and play, I would go home for dinner and he'd stay on and play.

'Bobby Charlton was the greatest player I've ever seen. He's me brother.'[11]

ACKNOWLEDGEMENTS

Books are always collaborative exercises and this could not have been written without the help of many others, not least the dozens of players, managers, journalists, fans and historians who agreed to be interviewed on or off the record.

For their help in arranging, conducting and (most important) transcribing interviews, I thank Will Magee, Richard Jolly, Vladimir Novak, Martín Mazur and Aleksandar Radović.

Huge numbers of people provided documents and offered their thoughts, ideas and advice: I thank Phil Shaw, whose scanning of old magazines and programmes went above and beyond, John Brewin, Miguel Delaney, Paul Fraser, Dan Jackson, David Owen, Jack Pitt-Brooke and Mike Walters. I also thank Miguel's dad, Robert, for sending over loads of books about Ireland, and the staff at the British Library. And thanks to Ruth Dunleavy for all the lifts.

At Little, Brown, I thank Richard Beswick (who was perhaps unduly impressed by my uncharacteristic 31 off 26 balls in an Authors v Publishers cricket match), Zoe Carroll and Lucian Randall.

I thank my agent, David Luxton.

For her stern eye and sterner eyebrows in reviewing the text, I thank Kat Petersen.

And thanks, especially, to Nicola Cowen for all her patience and support.

ENDNOTES

Preface

1. www.dmm.org.uk/colliery/l012.htm

Introduction

1. Jack Charlton, *The Autobiography*, p.93
2. Bobby Charlton, *My England Years*, p.289
3. J. Charlton, *The Autobiography*, p.93
4. Ron Atkinson, *Big Ron*, p.10

1

1. John Seymour, *The Coast of North-East England*, p.89
2. Cited in Daniel Finkelstein, 'Money changes sport for the better, not worse', *The Times*, 14 July 2020 www.thetimes.co.uk/article/ money-changes-sport-for-better-not-worse-g0mm98md6#:~:- text=Yet%20ten%20years%20later%20he,forward%20 %E2%80%94%20that%20was%20Jack%20Charlton.
3. Speech given 24 September 2019 https://industrialstrategycouncil. org/ashington-speech-andy-haldane. I'm grateful to the historian Dan Jackson for bringing it to my attention and for his moving piece on Jack's death, locating him within a Northumbrian framework, 'Jack Charlton's Vanished World' https://unherd. com/2020/08/jack-charltons-vanishing-england/
4. Mike Kirkup, *Coal Town: Growing Up in Ashington: 1934–54*, pp.1–2
5. *Big Jack's Other World*, Tyne Tees, 1971, https://www.youtube. com/watch?v=1NlnXq0QmLM

6. Martin Wainwright, 'A village in a million', the *Guardian*, 26 August 1999, www.theguardian.com/theguardian/1999/aug/26/features11.g24

7. Dan Jackson, *The Northumbrians*, p.90

8. This is partly explained in this brief but fascinating clip from the chair of German studies at the University of Newcastle, Professor Henrike Lähnemann, although she is talking more generally about why, because the area was never settled by the Vikings, the North-East accent in general has more in common with Germanic language groups than Scandinavian. www.youtube.com/watch?v=ETS33IJrGJ8

9. *Big Jack's Other World*, 17m 30s

10. See, for instance, Tom Humphries, *The Legend of Jack Charlton*, p.20

11. Jackson, *The Northumbrians*, pp.88–9

12. Robert McManners and Gillian Wales, *The Quintessential Cornish*, p.10

13. Graham Robb, *The Debatable Land*, p.244

14. Jackson, *The Northumbrians*, p.3

15. C. H. Hunter-Blair, 'Wardens and Deputy Wardens of the Marches of England towards Scotland in Northumberland,' *Archaeologia Aeliana*, fourth ser., xxviii, 1950, p.32, cited in Jackson, p.37

16. *Itinerarium Curiosam; Or An Account of the Antiquities and Remarkable Curiosities observed in Mature and Art observed in Travels through Great Britain*, cited in Jackson, p.55

17. Robb, *The Debatable Land*, p.3

18. Cissie Charlton, *Cissie*, p.63

19. ibid. p.64

20. Quoted in Leo McKinstry, *Jack & Bobby*, pp.6–7

21. C. Charlton, *Cissie*, p.73

2

1. C. Charlton, *Cissie*, p.69

2. Norman Harris, *The Charlton Brothers*, pp.15–16

3. McKinstry, *Jack & Bobby*, p.8

4. DIED BECAUSE THEY WANTED TO KEEP THEIR SHOES CLEAN, *Blyth News*, 26 February 1948

5. C. Charlton, *Cissie*, p.69

6. ibid. p84
7. B. Charlton, *My Manchester United Years*, p.162
8. ibid. p.163
9. In *Football Stories: The Charlton Brothers*, Hotshot, 2001
10. B. Charlton, *My Manchester United Years*, p.27
11. Harris, *The Charlton Brothers*, p.28
12. B. Charlton, *My Manchester United Years*, p.39
13. C. Charlton, *Cissie*, p.84
14. BBC radio interview 1989, cited in Colin Young, *Jack Charlton*, p.23
15. In *Football Stories: The Charlton Brothers*, Hotshot, 2001
16. C. Charlton, *Cissie*, p.96
17. Harris, *The Charlton Brothers*, p.8
18. From 'Jack Talking', an interview with Don Warters in the programme for Jack's testimonial, 7 May 1973
19. Warters, 'Jack Talking'
20. Gordon Burn, *Best and Edwards*, p.35
21. Bobby Charlton, *Forward for England*, p.15
22. ibid. p.15

3

1. J. Charlton, *The Autobiography*, pp.29–30
2. Warters, 'Jack Talking'
3. See https://www.theguardian.com/uk/2003/jun/03/monarchy.martinwainwright
4. Quoted on The Mighty Mighty Whites website, www.mightyleeds.co.uk/seasons/195253.htm
5. Burn, *Best and Edwards*, p.55
6. McKinstry, *Jack & Bobby*, p.66
7. *Manchester Evening Chronicle*, 1 November 1953
8. Interview in the *Sun*, 1975
9. B. Charlton, *My Manchester United Years*, p.93
10. Burn, *Best and Edwards*, p.223
11. Tom Jackson, 'Charlton back in reserves – he won't mind', *Manchester Evening News*, 8 October 1956

4

1. John Charles, *King John*, p.73
2. Rob Bagchi, *Leeds United*, p.115

3. Cited in Bagchi, *Leeds United*, p.115
4. C. Charlton, *Cissie*, p.100
5. J. Charlton, *The Autobiography*, p.43
6. ibid. p.43
7. McKinstry, *Jack & Bobby*, p.45
8. *The Times*, 22 September 1956
9. J. Charlton, *The Autobiography* p.54
10. Richard Sutcliffe, *Revie: Revered and Reviled*, p.54
11. Eric Todd, 'Leeds United's Play Conforms to No Logic', the *Guardian*, 4 April 1960
12. Colin Young, *Jack Charlton: The Authorised Biography*, p.49
13. J. Charlton, *The Autobiography*, p.51
14. ibid. p.53

5

1. 'Silchester', 'Arsenal Go Down Bravely', the *Guardian*, 3 February 1958
2. 'Magnificent Arsenal's Rally Defied', *The Times*, 3 February 1958
3. Harry Gregg, *Harry's Game*, p.26
4. B. Charlton, *Forward for England*, p.31
5. ibid. pp.26–27
6. Henry Rose, 'The Greatest Victory in Soccer History', *Daily Express*
7. Burn, *Best and Edwards*, p.66
8. Interview, March 2016
9. Bill Foulkes with Ivan Ponting, *United in Triumph and Tragedy*, p.82
10. B. Charlton, *My Manchester United Years*, p.6
11. ibid. p.6
12. Interview, March 2016
13. David Rayvern Allen, *Arlott*, p.235
14. Burn, *Best and Edwards*, p.62
15. Foulkes, *United in Triumph and Tragedy*, p.95
16. B. Charlton, *My Manchester United Years*, p.1
17. BBC interview with Hunter Davies, 1991
18. Foulkes, *United in Triumph and Tragedy*, p.104

6

1. Jeff Powell, 'Revie Quits Over Aggro', *Daily Mail*, 12 July 1977
2. Brian Clough, *Clough: The Autobiography*, p.7
3. See Jonathan Wilson, *Nobody Ever Says Thank You*

4. *This is Your Life*, Thames Television, 1974
5. Don Revie, *Soccer's Happy Wanderer*, p.25
6. Sutcliffe, *Revie: Revered and Reviled*, p.29
7. Roger Hermiston, *Clough and Revie*, p.150
8. J. Charlton, 'I was a one-man awkward squad', *Leeds United Book of Football*, 1970
9. Revie, 'From awkwardness to greatness', in Jack Charlton's testimonial programme, 7 May 1973
10. Warters, 'Jack Talking'
11. Peter Lorimer, *Leeds and Scotland Hero*, p.28
12. Hermiston, *Clough and Revie*, p.197
13. Christopher Evans, *Don Revie: the Biography*, pp.87–88
14. J. Charlton, *The Autobiography*, p.65
15. Interview with Eddie Gray, May 2021
16. Revie, 'From awkwardness to greatness'
17. Interview with Eddie Gray, May 2021
18. Hermiston, *Clough and Revie*, p.165

7

1. 'Leicester for Cup!', *Daily Mirror*, 23 January 1961
2. Eamon Dunphy, *A Strange Kind of Glory*, pp.252–3
3. Iain McCartney, *Rising from the Wreckage*, p.119
4. Matt Busby, *Soccer at the Top*, p.46
5. John Roberts, *The Team that Wouldn't Die*, pp.182–83
6. McKinstry, *Jack & Bobby*, p.98
7. B. Charlton, *My Manchester United Years*, p.174–5
8. Busby, *Soccer at the Top*, p.47
9. B. Charlton, *Forward for England*, p.43
10. Heward Aimes, 'Quiz Show Worse than a Cup Final', *Leicester Evening Mail*, 5 February 1959
11. John Harding, 'When Bobby Charlton Doubled His Money', *When Saturday Comes*, Issue 320, October 2013
12. McKinstry, *Jack & Bobby*, p.104
13. Paddy Crerand, *Never Turn the Other Cheek*, p.57
14. Patrick Barclay, *Sir Matt Busby*, p.230
15. Dunphy, *A Strange Kind of Glory*, p.262
16. John Giles, *A Football Man*, p.109
17. Malachy Clerkin, 'Glory Days: How Eamon Dunphy brought Matt Busby to book', *Irish Times*, 30 January 2021

18. James Lawton, 'Duncan Edwards: the greatest footballer who ever lived?', the *Independent*, 6 February 2008
19. B. Charlton, *My Manchester United Years*, pp.169–70
20. ibid. p.162
21. ibid. p.159
22. ibid. p.160
23. ibid. p.87
24. Jonathan Wilson, *The Anatomy of England*, pp.65–107
25. Geoffrey Green, *There's Only One United*, p.82
26. Wilson, *The Anatomy of England*, pp.65–106
27. Ray Simpson, *The Clarets Chronicles*, p.295
28. Dave Bowler, *Winning Isn't Everything*, pp.126–40
29. McKinstry, *Jack & Bobby*, p.141
30. Dunphy, *A Strange Kind of Glory*, p.257
31. McKinstry, *Jack & Bobby*, p.141
32. Charles Korr, *West Ham United*, pp.107–8
33. Crerand, *Never Turn the Other Cheek*, pp.59–60
34. Gregg, *Harry's Game*, p.143
35. McKinstry, *Jack & Bobby*, p.141
36. Giles, *A Football Man*, p.135
37. ibid. p.110
38. McCartney, *Rising from the Wreckage*, pp.146–7
39. Busby, *Soccer at the Top*, pp.51–4
40. Dunphy, *A Strange Kind of Glory*, p.255
41. Wilf McGuinness with Ivan Ponting, *Man and Babe*, p.149
42. Dunphy, *A Strange Kind of Glory*, p.257
43. Gregg, *Harry's Game*, p.96
44. Dunphy, *A Strange Kind of Glory*, p.271
45. ibid. p.265
46. ibid. p.277
47. B. Charlton, *My Manchester United Years*, p.171
48. ibid. p.168
49. McCartney, *Rising from the Wreckage*, p.132
50. B. Charlton, *My Manchester United Years*, p.182
51. McKinstry, *Jack & Bobby*, p.136
52. Gregg, *Harry's Game*, p.142
53. ibid. p.142
54. Dunphy, *A Strange Kind of Glory*, p.216
55. McKinstry, *Jack & Bobby*, p.142
56. Alex Stepney, *Alex Stepney*, p.34

57. Dunphy, *A Strange Kind of Glory*, p.285
58. Crerand, *Never Turn the Other Cheek*, p.58
59. Dunphy, *A Strange Kind of Glory*, p.267
60. Busby, *Soccer at the Top*, p.42
61. Busby, *Soccer at the Top*, p.46

8

1. Ken Jones, 'Moment Of Soccer shame ... Off Go Twenty-two Players!', *Daily Mirror*, 9 November 1964
2. Jack Archer, 'Police Put Guard on Riot Ref', the *People*, 8 November 1964
3. Sun Says, 'Well played, the Ref', the *Sun*, 9 November 1964
4. Bryon Butler, 'FA Promise War on Hooliganism', *Daily Telegraph*, 9 November 1964
5. Colin Wood, 'Blame Players, not Referee Stokes', *Daily Mail*, 9 November 1964
6. Butler, 'FA Promise War on Hooliganism', *Daily Telegraph*, 9 November 1964
7. Brian Crowther, 'Manners and Tempers Lost at Goodison Park', the *Guardian*, 9 November 1964
8. Sun Says, 'Well Played, The Ref', the *Sun*, 9 November 1964
9. Dunphy, *A Strange Kind of Glory*, p.292
10. Ken Jones, 'I Won't Allow Our Name to be Smeared', *Daily Mirror*, 14 November 1964
11. Charles Summerbell, 'Raw Tangle in Which Only Revenge Counted,' *Daily Mirror*, 29 December 1963
12. Eric Sanger, 'Plenty of Time for Leeds United to Make More Club History', *Yorkshire Evening Post*, 30 December 1963
13. *FA News*, August 1964
14. Phil Brown, 'United Aim to Get Rid of "Dirty" Label', *Yorkshire Evening Post*, 11 August 1964
15. J. Charlton, *The Autobiography*, p.65
16. Hermiston, *Clough and Revie*, p.201
17. Giles, *A Football Man*, p.135
18. Hermiston, *Clough and Revie*, p.185
19. Phil Brown, '"Our Conscience is Clear," says United Chairman', *Yorkshire Evening Post*, 9 November 1964
20. Phil Brown, 'United Explode', *Yorkshire Evening Post*, 10 November 1964

21. Phil Brown, 'United Showed Leaders the Way in Gaining "Summit Win"', *Yorkshire Evening Post*, 5 December 1964

22. ibid.

23. Steve Richards, 'Hooligans: And They Dare to Call Themselves Sportsmen', the *Sun*, 29 March 1965

24. Roy Peskett, 'The Most Shameful Semi-Final', *Daily Mail*, 29 March 1965

25. Richards, 'Hooligans: And They Dare to Call Themselves Sportsmen', the *Sun*, 29 March 1965

26. R. H. Williams, 'A Brawl that Should Have Been Prevented', *Daily Telegraph*, 29 March 1965

27. 'Sad Distortion of the Game of Football: Ill-Starred Coterie Poison Whole Atmosphere,' *The Times*, 29 March 1965

28. Phil Brown, 'Cup Day Again – And The Tip is Still Leeds United', *Yorkshire Evening Post*, 31 March 1964

29. 'Sad Distortion of the Game of Football: Ill-Starred Coterie Poison Whole Atmosphere', *The Times*, 29 March 1965

30. Donald Saunders, 'Rowdyism Threatens Cup's Reputation: Lack of Sportsmanship On and Off Field', *Daily Telegraph*, 29 March 1965

31. Peskett, 'The Most Shameful Semi-Final', *Daily Mail*, 29 March 1965

32. Richards, 'Hooligans: And They Dare to Call Themselves Sportsmen', the *Sun*, 29 March 1965

33. Brian James, 'Ref May Be Dropped,' *Daily Mail*, 29 March 1965

34. Frank Taylor, 'I Want None of It', the *Sun*, 31 March 1965

35. Phil Brown, 'Wembley Here We Come! And We'll Win, Say Revie's Men', *Yorkshire Evening Post*, 1 April 1965

36. Busby, *Soccer at the Top*, pp.51–4

37. J. Charlton, *The Autobiography*, p.72

38. Dunphy, *A Strange Kind of Glory*, p.296

39. David Meek, 'Gay United Find Way to Goal!', *Manchester Evening News*, 5 April 1965

40. Phil Brown, 'United Forwards Seemed to be Up Against "A Brick Wall"', *Yorkshire Evening Post*, 19 April 1965

41. ibid.

42. B. Charlton, *My Manchester United Years*, p.193

43. Ken Jones, 'The Final that Rose from the Dead', *Daily Mirror*, 3 May 1965

44. Peter Wilson, 'This Method Madness Made Me Sad for Soccer', *Daily Mirror*, 3 May 1965
45. 'Goodbye, Mr Clough', *Calendar*, Yorkshire TV, 13 September 1974

9

1. J. Charlton, *The Autobiography*, p.74
2. In an interview with Joan Seddon, 'If Only My Husband Would be Wrong – Just Once', the *Sun,* 13 December 1965
3. David Downing, *The Best of Enemies: England v Germany*, p.118
4. Footage can be seen from 0:54 here: www.youtube.com/watch?v=CudemgNQqMs
5. Patricia Keighran, 'The 1980s House', *Daily Mail*, 2 March 1956
6. Jonathan Meades, 'Pomo's Greatest Hits' (2016), in *Pedro and Ricky Come Again*
7. For far more on this, see Jonathan Wilson, *Inverting the Pyramid*
8. Jonathan Wilson, *The Anatomy of Liverpool*, pp.42–43
9. Ben Highmore, *The Art of Brutalism*, p.9
10. Barnabas Calder, *Raw Concrete*, p.10
11. Jonathan Wilson, *The Names Heard Long Ago*, pp.304–321
12. Wilson, *The Anatomy of England*, pp.65–106
13. Calder, *Raw Concrete*, p.10
14. Elaine Harwood, *Space, Hope and Brutalism*, pp.v–xix
15. In an interview with Joan Seddon, 'If Only My Husband Would be Wrong – Just Once', the *Sun,* 13 December 1965
16. B. Charlton, *My England Years*, p.149
17. ibid. pp.146–7
18. ibid. p.160
19. ibid. p.160
20. ibid. p.166
21. J. Charlton, *The Autobiography*, p.73
22. B. Charlton, *My England Years*, p.166
23. Peter Lorenzo, 'A Night of Shame', the *Sun*, 21 October 1965
24. Donald Saunders, 'England Lead Twice Then Go Down,' *Daily Telegraph*, 21 October 1965
25. Quoted in B. Charlton, *My England Years*, p.223
26. Albert Barham, 'Apathetic Display by England Ends in Defeat', the *Guardian*, 21 October 1965

27. David Miller, 'Ramsey: I Am Not Very Disappointed', *Daily Express*, 21 October 1965

28. Brian James, 'Fans Mock England', *Daily Mail*, 21 October 1965

29. Donald Saunders, 'England Lead Twice Then Go Down', *Daily Telegraph*, 21 October 1965

30. Brian James, 'Fans Mock England', *Daily Mail*, 21 October 1965

31. Albert Barham, 'Apathetic Display by England Ends in Defeat', the *Guardian*, 21 October 1965

32. Peter Lorenzo, 'England Wonders Crush Spain', the *Sun*, 9 December 1965

33. Bowler, *Winning Isn't Everything*, p.186

34. Donald Saunders, 'Injured Baker's Goal Begins a Triumph', 9 December 1965

35. B. Charlton, *My England Years*, p.167

36. Brian James, 'Great New England', *Daily Mail*, 9 December 1965

37. 'Ramsey's Case Rests on Sound Evidence', *The Times*, 6 July 1966

38. B. Charlton, *My England Years*, p.191

39. Brian James, 'Angry, Baffled, Goalless England', *Daily Mail*, 12 July 1966

40. Quoted in Bowler, *Winning Isn't Everything*, p.201

41. J. L. Manning, 'What Is Fascinating the Senior Gnats?', *Daily Mail*, 15 July 1965

42. B. Charlton, *My England Years*, pp.226–27

43. Peter Lorenzo, 'England Wonders Crush Spain', the *Sun*, 9 December 1965

44. Peter Lorenzo, 'England Must Recall Luxury Goal Ace', the *Sun*, 10 December 1965

45. 'Ramsey's Case Rests on Sound Evidence', *The Times*, 6 July 1966

46. B. Charlton, *My England Years*, p.236

47. Bowler, *Winning Isn't Everything*, pp.187–88

48. Interviews with Antonio Rattín, November 2007 and April 2014

49. B. Charlton, *My England Years*, p.244

50. J. L. Manning, 'What Has Happened to Sport is What Already Has Happened to People', *Daily Mail*, 25 July 1966

51. Interview with Silvio Marzolini, April 2014

52. Brian James, 'World's best non-losers', *Daily Mail*, 25 July 1966

53. Brian James, 'Ramsey Must Gamble on Greaves', *Daily Mail*, 26 July 1966

54. Quoted in Roy Peskett, 'World's Press Agree Super Soccer', *Daily Mail*, 27 July 1966

55. B. Charlton, *My England Years*, p.271

56. ibid. pp.269–70

57. In *Finding Jack Charlton*, dir. Gabriel Clarke and Pete Thomas, 2020

58. In *Football Stories: The Charlton Brothers*, Hotshot, 2001

59. 'Ramsey Proved Right in World Cup,' *The Times*, 1 August 1966

60. 'The World Says "Well Done"', *The Times,* 1 August 1966

61. Michael Williams, 'I lift my hat to Ramsey', *Sunday Telegraph*, 31 July 1966

62. Stephen Fay, 'Rebirth of English Football', *Sunday Times*, 31 July 1966

63. Tony Pawson, 'Tony Pawson comments …', the *Observer,* 31 July 1966

64. Dominic Sandbrook, *White Heat*, p.288

65. ibid. p.304

66. 'London Goes Wild After England's 4–2 Cup Triumph', *Sunday Telegraph*, 31 July 1966

10

1. Busby, *Soccer at the Top*, p.56

2. Crerand, *Never Turn the Other Cheek*, p.120

3. Foulkes, *United in Triumph and Tragedy*, p.129

4. ibid. p.128

5. B. Charlton, *My Manchester United Years*, p.221

6. Interview, March 2016

7. Miguel Delaney, 'The Story of Manchester United's 1966 European Cup Semi-Final That Brought Sir Matt Busby to Tears', the *Independent*, 24 October 2019

8. Interview, March 2011

9. B. Charlton, *My Manchester United Years*, p.223

10. Interview, March 2011

11. Delaney, 'The Story of Manchester United's 1966 European Cup Semi-Final That Brought Sir Matt Busby to Tears', the *Independent*, 24 October 2019

12. Norman Wynne, 'United Wall Stops Hunt', *People*, 27 March 1967

13. Busby, *Soccer at the Top*, p.57
14. Dunphy, *A Strange Kind of Glory*, p.314
15. Busby, *Soccer at the Top*, p.57
16. B. Charlton, *My Manchester United Years*, p.246
17. Foulkes, *United in Triumph and Tragedy*, pp.135–6
18. Albert Barham, 'Attacking Defenders Take United to European Cup Final', the *Guardian*, 16 May 1968
19. B. Charlton, *My Manchester United Years*, p.256
20. Dunphy, *A Strange Kind of Glory*, p.317
21. B. Charlton, *My Manchester United Years*, p.260
22. ibid. p.259
23. Burn, *Best and Edwards*, p.8
24. Duncan Hamilton, *George Best: Immortal*, pp.176–8

11

1.   Sutcliffe, *Revie: Revered and Reviled*, p.85
2.   Giles, *A Football Man*, pp.212–3
3.   In *Finding Jack Charlton*, dir. Gabriel Clarke and Pete Thomas, 2020
4.   Quoted in Hermiston, *Clough and Revie*, pp.196–97
5.   A radio interview from the 1980s cited in Hermiston, *Clough and Revie*, p.195
6.   Pathé News, 1968 League Cup final, www.youtube.com/watch?v=maoQkoADBVo
7.   '1968 League Cup Final Win Carried Leeds United Into Era Among the Elite', *Yorkshire Evening Post*, 2 March 2018
8.   Phil Brown, '"The Worst Decision I Have Ever Seen," says Revie', *Yorkshire Evening Post*, 19 April, 1971
9.   Sutcliffe, *Revie: Revered and Reviled*, pp.142–43

12

1.   B. Charlton, *My England Years*, p.331
2.   See Matt Dickinson, *Bobby Moore*, p.167
3.   Ronald Ricketts, 'Bobby: This is the Girl Who Has Accused Him of Stealing a Bracelet', *Daily Mirror*, 27 May 1970
4.   B. Charlton, *My England Years*, p.307

13

1. Hamilton, *Immortal*, p.186
2. Crerand, *Never Turn the Other Cheek*, pp.174–75
3. Barclay, *Sir Matt Busby*, p.298
4. Stepney, *Alex Stepney*, p.68
5. McKinstry, *Jack and Bobby*, p.259
6. Stepney, *Alex Stepney*, pp.72–73
7. Barclay, *Sir Matt Busby*, p.304
8. McGuinness, *Man and Babe*, p.200
9. B. Charlton, *My Manchester United Years*, p.280
10. Busby, *Soccer at the Top*, pp.69–70
11. Denis Law and Bernard Bale, *The Lawman*, p.161
12. Dunphy, *A Strange Kind of Glory*, p.336
13. McKinstry, *Jack and Bobby*, p.216
14. Dunphy, *A Strange Kind of Glory*, p.335
15. Burn, *Best and Edwards*, p.117
16. Hamilton, *Immortal*, p.223
17. McKinstry, *Jack and Bobby*, p.261
18. Sutcliffe, *Revie*, p.67
19. Hamilton, *Immortal*, p.224
20. Cited in Burn, *Best and Edwards*, pp.80–81
21. Hamilton, *Immortal*, p.314
22. ibid. p.315
23. Burn, *Best and Edwards*, p.16
24. Law, *The Lawman*, p.167
25. Hamilton, *Immortal*, p311
26. ibid. p.299
27. ibid. p.311
28. ibid. p.315
29. ibid. p.102
30. B. Charlton, *Forward for England*, p.10
31. McKinstry, *Jack and Bobby*, p.270
32. Hamilton, *Immortal*, p.315
33. Harry Pearson, 'Brother World,' *When Saturday Comes*, issue 188, October 2002
34. Hamilton, *Immortal*, p.318
35. Tommy Docherty, *The Doc: My Story*, p.398
36. Hamilton, *Immortal*, p.315
37. Dunphy, *A Strange Kind of Glory*, p.357

38. Hamilton, *Immortal*, p.315
39. Stepney, *Alex Stepney*, p.80
40. George Best, *Blessed*, p.163–66
41. Hamilton, *Immortal*, p.278
42. Dunphy, *A Strange Kind of Glory*, p.357
43. ibid. p.358
44. Gregg, *Harry's Game*, p.139
45. J. Charlton, *The Autobiography*, p.118
46. Leo McKinstry, 'The Truth About the Bitter Feud Between Jack and Bobby Charlton', *Daily Mail*, 28 August 2007
47. B. Charlton, *My Manchester United Years*, pp.157–58
48. Hamilton, *Immortal*, p.319
49. ibid. p.320
50. Burn, *Best and Edwards*, p.179
51. ibid. p.222
52. ibid. p.20
53. B. Charlton, *My Manchester United Years*, p.290

14

1. Interview with Jim Platt, October 2021
2. Jonathan Wilson, *The Names Heard Long Ago*, p.365
3. Interview with Jim Platt, October 2021
4. *The Boss*, BBC TV, 1974
5. Shelley Rohde, 'Jackie Charlton's Secret', *Daily Mail*, 1 December 1973
6. Interview with David Mills, January 2022
7. Jack Charlton, 'Don't Blame Me for the System', *Daily Mail*, 2 November 1973
8. Bill Mallinson, 'Charlton Learned from Two Masters', *Daily Mail*, 15 August 1974
9. Geoffrey Green, 'Praiseworthy Approach Suffers Through Faulty Planning', *The Times*, 30 September 1974
10. See Wilson, *The Anatomy of Liverpool*, pp.117–148
11. Jack Charlton, 'It's the Fans who Destroy Our Chance in Europe', *Daily Mail*, 9 Nov 1973
12. B. Charlton, *My Manchester United Years*, p.295
13. Interview with Mike Elwiss, March 2021
14. Jack Charlton, 'Too Soft? Our Kid is Hard as Nails', *Daily Mail*, 5 October 1973

15. Interview with John Bird, March 2021
16. Interview with Mike Elwiss, March 2021
17. Interview with John Bird, March 2021
18. Interview with Mike Elwiss, March 2021
19. In *Finding Jack Charlton*, dir. Gabriel Clarke and Pete Thomas, 2020
20. ibid.
21. McKinstry, *Jack & Bobby*, p.304
22. Brian Madley, 'Charlton: My Future', the *People*, 3 August 1975
23. J. Charlton, *The Autobiography*, p.151
24. ibid. p.153
25. Interview with John Bird, March 2021
26. Interview with Mike Elwiss, March 2021
27. Gerry Harrison, 'Lone Middlesbrough Goal Stands Out in a Sea of Effort and Attack', *The Times*, 14 January 1976
28. Interview with David Mills, January 2022
29. Paul Fitzpatrick, 'City's Final Flourish', the *Guardian*, 22 January 1976
30. Interview with David Mills, January 2022
31. Interview with John Bird, March 2021
32. ibid.
33. Bobby Charlton, 'Why I Quit', *Daily Mirror*, 22 August 1975
34. Bob Russell, 'We Back Bobby', *Daily Mirror*, 22 August 1975
35. ibid.
36. Interview with John Bird, March 2021
37. ibid.
38. McKinstry, *Jack & Bobby*, pp.306–7
39. Interview with John Bird, March 2021
40. Interview with Mike Elwiss, March 2001
41. Brian Madley, 'Charlton: My Future', the *People*, 3 August 1975
42. Interview with John Bird, March 2021
43. B. Charlton, *My Manchester United Years*, p.294
44. ibid. p.295
45. ibid. p.294
46. Interview with Jim Platt, October 2021
47. Interview with David Mills, January 2022

15

1. J. Charlton, *The Autobiography*, p.156
2. Jack Charlton, 'Revie, Greenwood and Me', *News of the* World, 22 August 1977
3. J. Charlton, *The Autobiography*, p.156, confirmed by Casey in *Finding Jack Charlton*
4. Jack Charlton, 'Get Off My Back: I'm Not a Bore – Just a Realist', *News of the* World, 29 August 1977
5. Jack Charlton, 'That Wembley Win Makes It More Difficult', *Daily Mail*, 28 September 1973
6. Nigel Clarke, 'Chelsea's New Star Steps Up', *Daily Mirror*, 8 October 1977
7. J. Charlton, *The Autobiography*, p.162. In his autobiography he says it was a 2–1 win over Brighton, but it's almost certain that it's the Chesterfield game he was referring to; Brighton didn't play Sheffield Wednesday that season and the Chesterfield game is the only win that fits the timeframe even if it did finish 1–0. Bob Bolder remembers it being Chesterfield.
8. 'Big Jack and the Big Test', *Liverpool Echo*, 15 October 1977
9. 'Big Jack and the Big Test', *Liverpool Echo*, 15 October 1977
10. Interview with Rodger Wylde, October 2021
11. ibid.
12. J. Charlton, *The Autobiography*, p.161
13. Interview with Chris Turner, October 2021
14. Interview with Bob Bolder, October 2021
15. Daniel Gordon, *Blue-and-White Wizards*, p.193
16. Interview with Bob Bolder, October 2021
17. ibid.
18. Interview with Chris Turner, October 2021
19. Interview with Rodger Wylde, October 2021
20. ibid.
21. ibid.
22. *Finding Jack Charlton*, dir. Gabriel Clarke and Pete Thomas, 2020
23. Interview with Mark Smith, October 2021
24. ibid.
25. Interview with Chris Turner, October 2021
26. Interview with Bob Bolder, October 2021
27. Interview with Rodger Wylde, October 2021
28. ibid.

29. ibid.
30. Gordon, *Blue-and-White Wizards*, p.197
31. ibid. p.201
32. Paul Brown, *Savage Enthusiasm*, p.201
33. Interview with John Pearson, October 2021
34. Interview with Ante Miročević, October 2007
35. J. Charlton, *The Autobiography*, p.168
36. McKinstry, *Jack & Bobby*, p.322
37. Interview with Ante Miročević, October 2007
38. Jimmy Meagan, 'Classy Charlton', *Irish Press*, 19 January 1976
39. Mel Moffat, 'Best Will Have to Improve', *Irish Press*, 23 January 1976
40. Interview with Mark Smith, October 2021
41. ibid.
42. Interview with Pat Heard, October 2021
43. ibid.
44. Interview with John Pearson, October 2021
45. Gordon, *Blue-and-White Wizards*, p.204

16

1. Paul Daniel, 'Big Mal Sacked!', *Middlesbrough Evening Gazette*, 28 March 1984
2. Martin Howey, 'United We Stand or Fall – Charlton', *Newcastle Journal*, 21 June 1984
3. John Richardson, 'Iron Man Jack Cracks Whip!', *Newcastle Journal*, 27 June 1984
4. B. Charlton, *My Manchester United Years*, p.288
5. McKinstry, *Jack & Bobby*, p.348
6. ibid. p.348
7. Dunphy, *A Strange Kind of Glory*, p.393
8. Ron Atkinson, *Big Ron*, p.11
9. ibid. pp.7–8
10. Alex Ferguson, *Managing My Life*, p.233
11. Atkinson, *Big Ron*, pp.2–12
12. Interview with John Anderson, November 2021
13. Peter Beardsley, *My Life Story*, p.75
14. J. Charlton, *The Autobiography*, p.179
15. Beardsley, *My Life Story*, p.77
16. Interview with Malcom Brown, November 2021

17. Beardsley, *My Life Story*, p.75
18. Interview with Ian Baird, November 2021
19. Mel Stein, *Chris Waddle: the Authorised Biography*, p.113
20. McKinstry, *Jack & Bobby*, pp.333–34
21. Interview with Paul Ferris, October 2021
22. Interview with Martin Thomas, November 2021
23. Interview with John Anderson, November 2021
24. ibid.
25. ibid.
26. John Richardson, 'Wrong: Miser's Route to Newcastle Misery', *Newcastle Journal*, 14 January 1985
27. J. Charlton, *The Autobiography*, p.179
28. Interview with Paul Ferris, October 2021
29. John Richardson, 'Jack and the Inglorious Tenth', *Newcastle Journal*, 12 August 1985
30. Interview with Pat Heard, October 2021
31. Mike Kirkup, *Jackie Milburn In Black and White*, p.163
32. Beardsley, *My Life Story*, p.87

17

1. Paul Rowan, *The Team that Jack Built*, p.37
2. Crerand, *Never Turn the Other Cheek*, p.227
3. Eamon Dunphy, 'Soccer Side Play', *Sunday Tribune*, 26 January 1986
4. Eamon Dunphy, 'FAI Still Want McNeil', *Sunday Tribune*, 12 January 1986
5. Gerry Callan, 'Lost in the Muddle', *Sunday Tribune*, 2 March 1986
6. 'The Best Verdict', *Irish Press*, 11 February 1986
7. Charlie Stuart, 'D-Day for Irish Manager', *Irish Press*, 7 February 1986
8. The detail of this meeting is taken from Rowan, *The Team that Jack Built*, pp.65–92
9. *The Late, Late Show*, RTÉ, 7 February 1986
10. Rowan, *The Team that Jack Built*, p.95
11. J. Charlton, *My Autobiography*, p.197
12. Charlie Stuart, 'Charlton Takes Up His Duties', *Irish Press*, 11 February 1986
13. ibid.

14. *Finding Jack Charlton*, dir. Gabriel Clarke and Pete Thomas, 2020
15. J. Charlton, *My Autobiography*, p.198
16. Eamon Dunphy, 'The No-Messing Manager', *Sunday Tribune*, 16 February 1986
17. Sean Ryan, *The Boys in Green*, p.164
18. *Finding Jack Charlton*, dir. Gabriel Clarke and Pete Thomas, 2020
19. J. Charlton, *My Autobiography*, p.209
20. Ryan, *The Boys in Green*, p.166
21. Rowan, *The Team that Jack Built*, p.105
22. Paul McGrath, *Back From The Brink*, pp.202–03
23. Con Houlihan, 'New Irish Ship Becalmed!', the *Evening Press*, 27 March 1986
24. Ryan, *The Boys in Green*, p.164
25. J. Charlton, *My Autobiography*, p.204
26. Hugh McIlvanney, 'Ireland's Honest Hustler', the *Observer*, 25 February 1990

18

1. Young, *Jack Charlton: The Authorised Biography*, p.189
2. Declan Lynch, *Days of Heaven*, p.18
3. In *Finding Jack Charlton*, dir. Gabriel Clarke and Pete Thomas, 2020
4. Rowan, *The Team that Jack Built*, p.149
5. Michael Walker, *Green Shoots*, p.153
6. Lynch, *Days of Heaven*, p.43
7. Rowan, *The Team that Jack Built*, p.121
8. ibid. p.122
9. ibid. p.123
10. ibid. p.124
11. ibid. pp.136–44
12. Eamon Dunphy, *Ireland v Egypt*, RTÉ, 17 June 1990
13. ibid.
14. Jackson, *The Northumbrians*
15. Lynch, *Days of Heaven*, pp.131–32
16. Tony Cascarino as told to Paul Kimmage, *Full Time*, pp.107–08
17. Roddy Doyle, 'Republic Is a Beautiful Word', *My Favourite Year*, pp.9–28
18. *Wogan*, BBC, 28 November 1990

19

1. Lynch, *Days of Heaven*, p.213
2. Tom Humphries, *The Legend of Jack Charlton*, pp.15–17
3. Niall Quinn, *The Autobiography*, p.81
4. McKinstry, *Jack & Bobby*, p.357
5. Rowan, *The Team that Jack Built*, p.163
6. ibid. p.167
7. Miguel Delaney, *Stuttgart to Saipan: The Players' Stories*, p.112
8. *Ceasefire Massacre*, ESPN, 2014
9. J. Charlton, *My Autobiography*, p.280
10. Ryan, *The Boys in Green*, p.201
11. Cascarino and Kimmage, *Full Time*, pp.109–10
12. McGrath, *Back From The Brink*, p.200
13. *Finding Jack Charlton*, dir. Gabriel Clarke and Pete Thomas, 2020
14. Andy Townsend and Paul Kimmage, *Andy's Game*, p.103
15. Delaney, *From Stuttgart to Saipan*, p.146
16. ibid. p.159
17. Townsend and Kimmage, *Andy's Game*, p.182
18. McGrath, *Back From The Brink*, p.362
19. J. Charlton, *My Autobiography*, p.295
20. Cited in Ryan, *The Boys in Green*, p.205
21. Ryan, *The Boys in Green*, p.181
22. Rowan, *The Team that Jack Built*, pp.191–204
23. ibid. p.194
24. Ryan, *The Boys In Green*, p.29
25. McGrath, *Back From The Brink*, pp.251–52
26. Quinn, *The Autobiography*, p.214
27. Interview with Eoin McDevitt, c.2006, clipped on *Second Captains*, 2020
28. Quinn, *The Autobiography*, p.216
29. ibid. p.93
30. Ryan, *The Boys in Green*, p.211
31. IMF Staff Country report No. 02/170
32. *Finding Jack Charlton*, dir. Gabriel Clarke and Pete Thomas, 2020

20

1. In *Football Stories: The Charlton Brothers*, Hotshot, 2001
2. B. Charlton, *My Manchester United Years*, p.164
3. ibid. p.166
4. J. Charlton, *The Autobiography*, p.311
5. B. Charlton, *My Manchester United Years*, p.158
6. In *Football Stories: The Charlton Brothers*, Hotshot, 2001
7. *Desert Island Discs*, BBC, 25 October 1996
8. B. Charlton, *My Manchester United Years*, p.199
9. 2021 report by the University of Glasgow, cited in www.alzheimersresearchuk.org/career-length-linked-with-increased-dementia-risk-in-ex-professional-footballers/
10. *Finding Jack Charlton*, dir. Gabriel Clarke and Pete Thomas, 2020
11. *Sports Personality of the Year 2008*, BBC, 2008

BIBLIOGRAPHY

Allen, David Rayven, *Arlott* (Aurum, 2014)

Atkinson, Ron and Peter Fitton, *Big Ron* (Welbeck Publishing, 1999)

Bagchi, Rob, *The Biography of Leeds United* (Vision, 2021)

Bagchi, Rob and Paul Rodgerson, *The Unforgiven* (Aurum, 2011)

Barclay, Patrick, *Sir Matt Busby* (Ebury, 2018)

Beardsley, Peter, *My Life Story* (CollinsWillow, 1995)

Best, George, *Blessed* (Ebury, 2012)

Bowler, Dave, *Winning Isn't Everything* (Gollancz, 1998)

Brown, Paul, *Savage Enthusiasm* (Goal Post, 2017)

Burn, Gordon, *Best and Edwards* (Faber and Faber, 2006)

Busby, Matt, *Soccer at the Top* (Weidenfeld & Nicolson, 1974)

Calder, Barnabas, *Raw Concrete* (Cornerstone, 2016)

Cascarino, Tony and Paul Kimmage, *Full-Time* (Simon & Schuster, 2013)

Charles, John, *King John* (Headline, 2014)

Charlton, Bobby, *The Autobiography: My England Years* (Headline, 2008)

Charlton, Bobby, *The Autobiography: My Manchester United Years* (Headline, 2008)

Charlton, Bobby, *Forward for England* (Sportsman's Book Club, 1969)

Charlton, Cissie and Vince Gledhill, *Cissie* (Independent, 2019)

Charlton, Jack, *The Autobiography* (Partridge Press, 1996)

Clough, Brian, *Clough* (Corgi, 1995)

Crerand, Paddy, *Never Turn the Other Cheek* (HarperSport, 2007)

Delaney, Miguel, *Stuttgart to Saipan* (Mentor, 2010)

Docherty, Tommy, *My Story* (Headline, 2006)

Downing, David, *The Best of Enemies: England v Germany* (Bloomsbury, 2000)

Dunphy, Eamon, *The Rocky Road* (Penguin, 2013)

Dunphy, Eamon, *A Strange Kind of Glory* (William Heinemann, 1991)

Evans, Christopher, *Don Revie: the Biography* (Bloomsbury, 2021)

Ferguson, Alex, *Managing My Life* (Hodder & Stoughton, 1999)

Foulkes, Bill, *United in Triumph and Tragedy* (Know the Score, 2008)

Giles, John, *A Football Man* (Hodder & Stoughton, 2010)

Gordon, Daniel, *Blue and White Wizards* (Mainstream, 1999)

Green, Geoffrey, *There's Only One United* (Coronet, 1979)

Gregg, Harry, *Harry's Game* (Mainstream, 2002)

Hamilton, Duncan, *Immortal* (Century, 2013)

Harris, Norman, *The Charlton Brothers* (Stanley Paul, 1971)

Harwood, Elain, *Space, Hope and Brutalism* (Yale University Press, 2015)

Hermiston, Roger, *Clough and Revie* (Mainstream, 2011)

Highmore, Ben, *The Art of Brutalism* (Yale University Press, 2017)

Hornby, Nick (ed), *My Favourite Year* (Witherby, 1993)

Humphries, Tom, *The Legend of Jack Charlton* (Weidenfeld & Nicolson, 1994)

Jackson, Dan, *The Northumbrians* (Hurst, 2021)

Kirkup, Mike, *Coal Town: Growing Up in Ashington: 1934–54* (Woodhorn, 1995)

Kirkup, Mike, *Jackie Milburn, In Black and White* (Stanley Paul, 1990)

Korr, Charles P, *West Ham United* (Duckworth, 1986)

Law, Denis, *The Lawman* (Andre Deutsch, 1999)

Lynch, Declan, *Days of Heaven* (Gill Books, 2010)

McCartney, Ian, *Rising from the Wreckage* (Amberley, 2013)

McGrath, Paul, *Back from the Brink* (Arrow, 2007)

McGuinness, Wilf, *Man and Babe* (Know the Score, 2008)

McKinstry, Leo, *Jack & Bobby* (CollinsWillow, 2002)

McManners, Robert and Gillian Wales, *The Quintessential Cornish* (Gemini, 2009)

Meades, Jonathan, *Pedro and Ricky Come Again* (Unbound, 2021)

Quinn, Niall, *The Autobiography* (Headline, 2002)

Revie, Don, *Soccer's Happy Wanderer* (Museum, 1955)

Robb, Graham, *The Debatable Land* (Picador, 2019)

Roberts, John, *The Team that Wouldn't Die* (Littlehampton, 1975)

Rowan, Paul, *The Team that Jack Built* (Mainstream, 1994)

Ryan, Sean, *The Boys in Green* (Mainstream, 1997)

Sandbrook, Dominic, *White Heat* (Little, Brown, 2006)

Seymour, John, *The Coast of North-East England* (Collins, 1974)

Simpson, Ray, *The Clarets Chronicles* (Burnley Football Club, 2007)

Stein, Mel, *Chris Waddle, the Authorised Biography* (Cockerel, 1989)

Stepney, Alex, *Alex Stepney* (Barker, 1978)

Sutcliffe, Richard, *Revie* (Great Northern Books, 2010)

Townsend, Andy and Paul Kimmage, *Andy's Game* (Tiger, 1994)

Walker, Michael, *Green Shoots* (DeCoubertin, 2017)

Wilson, Jonathan, *The Anatomy of England* (Orion, 2010)

Wilson, Jonathan, *Inverting the Pyramid* (Orion, 2008)

Wilson, Jonathan, *The Names Heard Long Ago* (Blink, 2020)
Wilson, Jonathan, *Nobody Ever Says Thank You* (Orion, 2011)
Young, Colin, *Jack Charlton: The Authorised Biography* (Hero Books, 2019)

INDEX

Adamson, Jimmy 11, 105
Ainsley, George 62
Aldridge, John 289, 296, 298, 321, 325
Allison, Malcolm 106, 263
Anderson, John 268–9, 271–2, 273
Anderson, Stan 220
Angus, John 121
Archer, Jack 114
Arlott, John 76–7
Armfield, Jimmy 283
Armstrong, David 224
Armstrong, Joe 36, 37, 214, 257
Ashington 1, 9–13, 21–2
   football club 3, 14–15, 30
   Pit 9–10, 17–18, 21
   YMCA 3, 34, 43
Ashurst, Len 243, 245
Astle, Jeff 183, 192, 334
Aston, John 107, 172, 195
Atkinson, Ron 6–7, 267

Baird, Ian 270
Baker, Joe 141
Ball, Alan 141, 142, 143, 155, 185
Ball, Norma see Charlton, Norma (née Ball – Bobby's wife)

Banks, Gordon 137, 139, 142, 153, 154, 192–3
Bannister, Gary 262
Barham, Albert 140, 141
Barnes, John 304, 319
Barnes, Ken 86
Bates, Ken 257
BBC Sports Personality of the Year Awards 337
Beardsley, Peter 264, 269–70, 271, 273–4, 276, 319
Beckenbauer, Franz 153, 187, 193, 302
Beckham, David 265
Bedlington football team 32
Beglin, Jim 288
Bell, Colin 187, 193, 199, 232
Bell, Willie 114
Benson, George 32
Bent, Geoff 68, 77
Berry, Johnny 51, 67, 102
Best, Ann 208–9
Best, George 45, 121, 162–4, 165, 168, 169, 170, 172, 194, 198, 199–213, 218–19, 257–8, 280–1, 333
Big Jack's Other World 11–12, 14, 21, 242
Bingham, Billy 313, 314, 315, 316, 324

Bird, John 227–8, 231, 233–5, 236

Blanchflower, Jackie 46, 65, 70, 72, 102

Bobby Charlton Enterprises 326

Boersma, Phil 238

Bolder, Bob 245–7, 251, 252, 253

Bonetti, Peter 187, 193

Bonner, Packie 297, 302, 304, 307, 308–9, 322

Bowen, Robert 19

Bowler, Dave 147

Boxing Day Massacre 253

Bradshaw, Paul 251–2

Brady, Liam 293, 298, 299

Bremner, Billy 87–8, 92–3, 95, 114, 118, 125, 173, 181

Brennan, Shay 98, 106, 162, 165, 167, 257

Bridges, Barry 140

Briggs, Ronnie 96

Brown, Alan 87

Brown, Malcolm 268, 269–70

Brown, Phil 119, 122, 125

Brown, Tony 183

Bruce, Alec 233

brutalism 132–4, 157, 225

Buchan, Martin 213

Buckley, Major Frank 41–3, 53, 88

Burden, Tommy 55, 60

Burns, Francis 227

Busby, Matt 36–7, 46–7, 49–50, 65, 94–8, 100–2, 105–9, 111–12, 120–2, 125, 131, 138, 161–2, 164–5, 167–72, 196–7, 205–9, 211, 213–15, 237, 266, 336
  death 332
  Munich air disaster 71–2, 76, 78, 98
  retirement 194–5, 207, 219

Butcher, Terry 267, 304

Butler, Bryon 115

Butler, Ernie 84

Byrne, Gay 282

Byrne, John 137, 300

Byrne, Mick 285, 288, 296, 300–1

Byrne, Peter 284

Byrne, Roger 68, 70, 71, 72, 77, 214

Cable, Tom 78

Calder, Barnabas 134

Callaghan, Ian 146, 165, 166

Callan, Gerry 280

Canning, Ger 324

Cantwell, Noel 97, 98, 106–7, 108, 110, 111, 112, 156, 195, 227, 279

Carman, George 202–3

Carney, Steve 270

Carr, Kevin 269

Carter, Raich 53–5, 56, 57–8, 59, 85, 88

Cascarino, Tony 289, 307, 315, 317, 319, 322

Casey, Des 240, 279, 280, 281–3, 284

Catterick, Harry 92–3

Cavan, Harry 149

Charles, John 42, 43, 53, 54–5, 56, 58, 95

Charles, Mel 41

Charlton, Bob (father) 20–2, 26, 33–4, 74, 78, 151–2, 155, 217

Charlton, Bobby 3, 23, 62, 187
  and Alf Ramsey 135–9, 142
  autobiography 7
  BBC Sports Personality of the Year Awards 337
  and Best 201–2, 206, 207–8, 210, 212–14, 333
  childhood 9, 11–12, 23–4, 26–31

dementia 327, 334–5
Double Your Money 98–100
England Schoolboys 32
European Cup 6, 162–72
family tensions 216–17, 331
fishing 24, 330
Football League board 301–2
greatest goal 7
Halba Travel 257, 265
jewellery store incident
    189–91
Manchester United 36–8,
    44–52, 64–73, 96–8, 102,
    106–7, 109–13, 121–4,
    126–7, 162–72, 195–9,
    206, 209–15, 311–12,
    335–6
Manchester United director 6,
    265, 266–7, 326–7, 332
meets Norma 103, 104
Mexico 188–92
Munich air crash 6, 70–4,
    77–81, 98, 113
national service 65–6, 80
press-ups 196
Preston North End 226–30,
    231, 232–7
Soccer Schools 265–6, 267,
    326
television work 326–7
Waterford 257–8
wedding 104–5
1966 World Cup 5–6, 145–7,
    148–53, 155–6, 158–60
1970 World Cup 192–3
Charlton, Cissie (née Milburn -
    mother) 14, 15, 18, 19–23,
    27–9, 31–3, 35–6, 38, 49,
    55, 78–9, 216–17,
    330–1
death 331
Munich air crash 73, 74
World Cup 155, 159

Charlton, Gordon (brother) 22,
    25, 155
Charlton, Jack 78–9
autobiography 7
BBC Sports Personality of the
    Year Awards 337
Big Jack's Other World 11–12,
    14, 21, 242
'black book' 215–16
childhood 3, 9, 11–12, 23–6,
    27–9, 31–2, 33
death 334
dementia 316, 318, 333–5
Desert Island Discs 331
England manager job 240–1
England selection 125, 138–9
family tensions 216–17, 331
Finding Jack Charlton 285,
    318, 333–4
fishing 3, 24, 25, 26, 223, 242,
    256, 259, 263, 273, 279,
    283, 296, 330, 331, 332,
    333
footballer of the year 175,
    336–7
Ireland team 240, 277–326,
    327–9
Leeds United 3, 33, 35–6,
    40–4, 53–61, 63, 89–95,
    118–19, 121–2, 124–7,
    173–5, 178–80, 181–6
Maple Clothes 183
meets Pat 61–2
Middlesbrough 220–6, 228–
    30, 231–2, 238–9, 241
mines 2–3, 35
Munich air crash 73–4
national service 55–6
near-post corners 179
Newcastle United 264–5,
    268–76
newspaper columns 225, 228,
    241–2, 243

Charlton, Jack – *continued*
  public speaking 7, 175, 263
  Sheffield Wednesday 243–57,
    259–62
  television work 11–12, 14, 21,
    241, 242–3, 259, 263
  1966 World Cup 5–6, 146,
    148–9, 151, 153–9
  1970 World Cup 193
Charlton, John (Jack's son) 325
Charlton, Norma (née Ball -
  Bobby's wife) 103, 104–5,
    158, 159, 171, 216–17, 258,
    330–1
Charlton, Pat (Jack's wife) 61–2,
    73, 158, 159, 183, 220, 243,
    249, 261, 334
Charlton, Peter (Jack's son)
    248–9
Charlton, Tommy (brother) 14,
    21, 22, 29, 33, 331
Charlton, Tommy (uncle) 26–7,
    31
Chilton, Allenby 51
Clarke, Alf 70, 78
Clarke, Allan 184, 185
Clarke, Gabriel 285
Clarke, Jean 99
Clough, Brian 54, 62, 83, 121,
    128, 186, 241, 279, 281
Cockburn, Ted 73
Cocker, Les 90–1, 115
Cohen, George 139, 142, 149,
    151
Coleman, David 152
Collins, Bobby 92–3, 114, 122,
    173
Colman, Eddie 45, 47, 67, 70,
    77
Connelly, John 126, 140, 143,
    162
Conrad International 326
Cooper, Eric 74

Cooper, Terry 180, 230, 231
Cox, Arthur 264
Coyne, Tommy 319
Crawford, Ernie 115
Crerand, Paddy 100–1, 106,
    110, 112, 161, 162, 163,
    164, 165, 168, 194, 198–9,
    202–3, 211, 213, 279
Crickmer, Walter 77
Crompton, Jack 96, 107, 111–12,
    195, 227
Cross, David 238
Crowe, Chris 60
Crowther, Arthur 43, 73
Crowther, Brian 116
Crowther, Mary 40
Crowther, Stan 80
Cullis, Stan 42
Cunningham, Tony 269, 275
Curran, Terry 249–50, 252,
    253–4, 255, 262
Curry, Tom 46, 77
Cusack, Sinéad 206
Cush, Wilbur 60
Cussins, Manny 92

Dalglish, Kenny 288
Dalton, Ted 50
Daly, Gerry 290
Davidson, Andy 85
Davies, Alan 274
Davies, Barry 183, 185
Davies, Dickie 326–7
Davies, Donny 77, 78
Davies, Hunter 81
Dawson, Alex 68, 72
Delaney, Joe 328
Desert Island Discs 331
Docherty, Tommy 123, 211, 219,
    225, 266
Doherty, John 49, 50
Double Your Money 98–100
Dowie, Iain 324

Downing, David 130
Doyle, Roddy 308
Duncan, Johnny 85, 90
Dunne, Pat 165
Dunne, Tony 165, 167
Dunphy, Eamon 101–2, 106, 109, 111, 112, 117, 266, 278, 280, 281, 284–5, 305–7

Eastham, George 137, 158
Edelson, Mike 311
Edwards, Duncan 44, 45, 51, 64, 66, 69–70, 78, 79, 102, 152–3
Edwards, Louis 102, 213, 265, 266
Edwards, Martin 311
Elleray, David 182
Elwiss, Mike 226, 227, 228, 231, 235
England
    Ireland matches 296–7, 304
    see also European Championships; World Cups
England Schoolboys 32, 87
Eskenazi, Jean 152
European Championships 82, 136, 181, 188, 192, 292–8, 312, 318
European Cup 6, 161–72, 182, 243

FA Cup finals 42, 86, 96, 120, 134, 145, 176, 182, 186, 221
    1948 37
    1949 84–5
    1951 16
    1957 65
    1972 184, 185
    1979 249
FAI see Football Association of Ireland (FAI)

Fairs Cup 173–5, 181, 184
Fay, Stephen 156
Fear, Nancy 23
Ferguson, Alex 267
Ferris, Paul 271, 272–3, 275
Finding Jack Charlton 285, 318, 333–4
Foggon, Alan 224, 238
Foley, Theo 279
Follows, Denis 114, 120
Follows, George 78
Football Association of Ireland (FAI) 277–87, 293, 298, 312, 328
Forrest, Bobby 58–9, 73
Foulkes, Bill 70, 71, 72, 80, 81, 106, 109, 113, 161, 162, 164, 165, 168–9
Fox, Peter 245
Fuego Verde 189–91

Galvin, Tony 289, 296, 298, 299
Gates, Eric 274
George, Alma 75–6
Gibson, Archie 56
Gibson, Don 97
Giles, John 46, 95, 101, 107, 112, 114, 119, 120, 125, 173, 175, 185, 186, 204, 278–82
Gillespie, Keith 324
Glass, Jackie 172, 202
Goodwin, Freddie 91, 94
Grady, Mike 174
Graham, Robert 25–6
Gray, Eddie 93, 94, 179, 180–1, 183
Greaves, Jimmy 137, 139–40, 141, 142, 143, 146–7, 151, 179
Green, Geoffrey 65, 105, 143, 147, 156, 225

Greenwood, Ron 240, 241
Gregg, Harry 64, 65, 71, 72, 76,
    80, 106–7, 109, 110, 111,
    162, 163, 164, 217
Guttmann, Béla 222

Hair, Grenville 60
Halba Travel 257, 265, 326
Haldane, Andy 10
Hamilton, George 308
Hamilton, James 31
Hand, Eoin 278, 284, 287, 289,
    291, 295
Haraldsted, Eva 202
Hardman, Harold 68
Harewood, Lord 119
Harmison, Steve 11
Harris, Norman 25, 183
Harrison, Gerry 232
Harrop, Bobby 80
Harwood, Elaine 134–5
Haynes, Johnny 101, 136
Heard, Pat 259–61, 275
Hemingway, Stuart 36
Herd, David 97, 162, 165,
    166
Herd, George 122
Hickton, John 224, 231, 238
Highmore, Ben 133
Hill, Jimmy 140
Holland, Reg 80
Hornsby, Brian 245
Houghton, Ray 289, 296, 300,
    319, 320
Houlihan, Con 288, 303
Hughes, Mark 267
Hughton, Chris 296
Humphries, Tom 310
Hunter, Norman 90, 116, 117,
    118, 139, 141, 175, 183
Hunter, Reg 80
Hunt, Roger 7, 141, 142, 143,
    145, 146, 147, 151

Hurley, Charlie 101
Hurst, Geoff 5, 146–7, 149, 151,
    153–5

Ideal Home Exhibition 132
Inglis, Bill 74–5
Ireland team 240, 277–326,
    327–9
    England matches 296–7, 304
    Euro 88 292–8
    Euro 92 312
    World Cup 277, 278, 290,
        298–9, 302–9, 310–11,
        312–26

Jackson, Dan 13, 18–19, 306
Jackson, Reverend 176
Jackson, Tom 78
James, Brian 42, 140, 141, 144,
    150, 151
Jennings, Eric 183
John Paul II, Pope 308
Johnson, Frederick 1
Johnson, Jeff 245, 251
Jones, Alan 235
Jones, June 75
Jones, Ken 117, 127
Jones, Mark 44–5, 68, 70, 71,
    75, 77
Jones, Mick 178, 180, 185

Kanhai, Rohan 10, 11
Keane, Roy 310–11, 320, 325,
    328
Keating, Frank 54
Keegan, Kevin 263–4
Keighran, Patricia 132
Kelly, David 324
Kemp, Pat see Charlton, Pat
    (Jack's wife)
Kerfoot, Eric 44
Kernaghan, Alan 314
Kerr, Brian 286, 295

Kidd, Brian 168, 169, 170
Kilcoyne, Louis 287
King, Jeff 253
Kirkup, Mike 10–11
Knighton, Ken 245–6
Knighton, Michael 311
Koeman, Ronald 297
Kreitlein, Rudi 147–8, 149

Labone, Brian 188, 191, 192
Lambton, Bill 59–60, 87, 89
Lavery, Ian 10
Law, Denis 97, 107, 109–10,
    112, 120, 122, 124, 127,
    165, 166, 197–8, 207, 209,
    211, 219, 333
Lawrenson, Mark 229, 288, 293
Ledbrooke, Archie 78
Leeds United 3, 15, 33, 35–6,
    40–4, 53–61, 63, 73, 87–95,
    114–20, 121–8, 173–86,
    203–4
  1968 League Cup final 180–1
  FA Cup final 182, 185, 186
Lee, Francis 199
Lee, Gordon 233, 279
Lee, Laura 176
Lema, Tony 150
Lewis, Eddie 49
Lindsay, Maurice 90
Lineker, Gary 290, 304, 312
Linton Colliery 1–3, 9, 12
Longson, Sam 241
Lorenzo, Peter 141, 147
Lorimer, Peter 89, 95, 174, 175,
    179, 185, 186
Lumsden, Jimmy 118
Lynch, Declan 294–5, 296, 306,
    310
Lynott, Philomena 200
Lyon, Robert 17–18

McAteer, Jason 324

McCafferty, Nell 303
McCarthy, Mick 289, 304, 306,
    310–11
McCreery, David 265
McCullagh, Mike 263
McCulloch, Andy 249, 250,
    253, 255, 262
McDermott, Terry 264, 265,
    271
McDonald, Alan 313, 315
McDowell, Les 86
McFaul, Willie 265
McGee, Bert 243, 245
McGrath, Paul 283, 287–8, 294,
    297, 314, 317–18, 319, 322,
    324, 325
McGuinness, Wilf 45, 98, 104,
    107, 108–9, 112, 195–9,
    203–4, 205, 214
Mackay, Gary 293, 294
McKinstry, Leo 25
McLaughlin, Jim 280
McLoughlin, Alan 300, 314,
    315
McMahon, John 234
McMahon, Steve 304
McNeill, Billy 279, 280–1
McPherson, Dr 79
Madeley, Paul 180, 185
Manchester United 6, 36–8,
    44–52, 64–81, 90, 94,
    96–8, 100–2, 106–13,
    120–1, 122–8, 194–215,
    218–19, 257, 311–12,
    335–6
  Bobby's board appointment
    265, 266–7, 326–7,
    332
  European Cup 6, 161–72
  European football 66–8, 81
  Munich air crash 6, 69–81,
    98, 113
Manning, J. L. 144–5, 149

Mao Zedong 18
Maple Clothes 183
Marsden, Keith 49–50
Matthews, Stanley 37, 134
Meades, Jonathan 132
Mellor, Ian 'Spider' 252, 253
Middlesbrough 220–6, 228–30,
     231–2, 238–9, 241, 263
Miklos, Bela 72, 78
Milburn, Cissie *see*
     Charlton, Cissie (née
     Milburn – mother)
Milburn, Jackie 16–17, 18, 37–8,
     145, 264, 275
Milburn, Jack 'Tanner' 14–15,
     22, 26, 28, 30–1
Milburn, Jack 'Warhorse' 14
Milburn, Stan 15, 30
Millichip, Bert 240
Mills, David 224–5, 230, 232,
     238–9, 259–60, 265
miners' strike 9
Miročević, Ante 255–7, 261
Moir, Ian 121
Montague, Larry 77
Moore, Bobby 110–11, 137, 138,
     139, 141, 142, 154, 155,
     158, 189–91
Moore, Brian 243
Moran, Kevin 294, 297, 312
Morgans, Kenny 70, 102
Morgan, Willie 195–6, 211
Morris, Albert 92
Mossop, James 158–9
Mourinho, José 327
Mullen, Jimmy 247
Mullery, Alan 188
Mulligan, Paddy 280
Munich air crash 6, 69–81, 98,
     113
Murdoch, Bobby 223, 224,
     230
Murphy, Jimmy 44, 45, 47–50,
     51, 68, 75–6, 79–80, 110,
     138, 145, 214–15
Murray, Bill 87

Neill, Terry 279
Newcastle United 16–17, 37–8,
     263–5, 268–76
Nicholls, David 74
Nicholson, Jimmy 107, 110
Norman, Maurice 138

O'Donavan, Paul 258
O'Driscoll, Peadar 280, 285,
     286
O'Farrell, Frank 106, 207, 210,
     211, 213, 218–19
O'Leary, Charlie 315
O'Leary, David 288–9, 302–3,
     308
Oliver, Gavin 254
Oliver, Michael 183
O'Neill, Tony 279, 280, 286–7
O'Shea, John 289
Otto, Heini 263
Overfield, Jackie 59, 60
Owen, Syd 91, 175

Padilla, Clara 189, 190, 191
Paine, Terry 140
Paisley, Bob 258, 281–3, 284
Pawson, Tony 157
Peacock, Alan 95
Pearson, John 254–5, 261
Pearson, Mark 72
Pegg, David 45–6, 62, 70, 77,
     81
Peskett, Roy 123, 124
Peters, Martin 142–3, 154,
     334
Phelan, Terry 314, 320, 322
Phillips, Jimmy 315
Phillips, Neil 189, 192, 220
Pickering, Fred 114

Pitman Painters 17–18
pitmatic 13–14
Platt, Jim 222, 223, 238
Popović, Vladica 164
Powell, Arthur 74–5
Powell, Jeff 191
Preston North End 226–30, 231, 232–7
Price, Arnold 57
Pye, Freddie 257

Queen, Cyril 1
Quinn, Niall 286, 307, 314, 319, 325, 328, 329
Quixall, Albert 96, 97, 120

Ramsey, Alf 105, 129–32, 135–57, 188–92, 220, 225, 241, 332
Ramsey, Victoria 129, 135
Rattín, Antonio 147–8, 149
Rayment, Kenneth 78
Reaney, Paul 204
Reed, Bernadette 27
Reilly, George 269, 273
Reilly, Noel 286
Revie, Don 63, 82–95, 117–20, 121–2, 125–6, 128, 134, 138, 173, 175–9, 182, 184–6, 221, 240, 241, 331–2
Reynolds, Harry 87, 88, 92, 119, 121
Richardson, John 275
Richards, Steve 123, 124
Robb, Graham 18
Robertson, John 243
Robinson, Mary 309
Robinson, Michael 261
Robson, Bobby 304
Rose, Henry 74, 78
Routledge, Ron 37, 79
Rowan, Paul 283, 284, 323–4

Rowe, Arthur 131
Roxburgh, Andy 292–3
Roxburgh, Bob 60
Ryan, Colonel Tom 282
Ryan, Sean 285, 323

Sadler, David 166, 168, 169, 170, 200, 227, 266
St John, Ian 248
Sandbrook, Dominic 157, 158
Sanger, Eric 118
Satinoff, Willie 78
Saunders, Donald 124, 140, 141
Saunders, Wes 270
Scanlon, Albert 64–5, 70, 102
Scargill, Arthur 9, 228
Scott, Jack 55
Šekularac, Dragoslav 68–9, 76
Setters, Maurice 102, 104, 107, 108, 111, 112, 244, 248, 265, 276, 286, 292, 321, 325
Sexton, Dave 106, 195
Shackleton, Len 29
Shankly, Bill 62, 93, 94, 101, 127, 165, 220, 258
Shapiro, Marlene 103–4
Sheedy, Kevin 288, 289, 304, 317
Sheffield Wednesday 243–57, 259–62
Shepherdson, Harold 220
Shilton, Peter 211, 296
Simon, Maurice 156
Skinner, Tommy 80, 217
Smith, Eric 61, 89
Smith, Mark 250–1, 253, 258–9
Smith, Ron 260
Smith, Septimus 83–4, 85
Soccer Schools 265–6, 267, 326
Šoškić, Milutin 164–5

Souness, Graeme 224, 228, 232
Spark, Alex 234
Sprake, Gary 179, 181, 182
Springett, Ron 136
Stainrod, Simon 253–4
Stapleton, Frank 278, 290, 298, 299–300, 306, 319
Staunton, Steve 320, 328
Stein, Jock 111, 221–2, 223, 267
Stepney, Alex 111, 166, 167, 170, 195, 196, 211, 212
Stewart, Ian 274
Stiles, Nobby 74–5, 126, 139, 141, 142, 146, 153, 155, 156, 162, 164, 165, 168, 214, 227, 257, 334
Stokes, Ken 115–16
Stuart, Charlie 282, 283
Stukeley, William 19
Suggett, Colin 183, 265
Summerbee, Mike 200
Summerbell, Charles 118
Sutcliffe, Peter 13
Swift, Frank 70, 78

Taggart, Gerry 315
Tait, Thomas 1
Tapscott, Derek 65
Taylor, Ernie 80
Taylor, Frank 60–1, 124–5
Taylor, Jack 60–1, 199, 200
Taylor, Tommy 37, 46, 62, 64–5, 66, 67, 70, 75, 77, 81
Temple, Derek 114–15
Thomas, Martin 271
Thomas, Peter 285
Thompson, Eric 78
Thompson, Peter 189, 191
Tilkowski, Hans 153
Tinkler, Ray 183, 184
Toms, Tony 248, 254, 256

Townsend, Andy 299, 309, 312, 319, 322, 325
Trautmann, Bert 86
Treacy, Ray 278, 295
Trevillion, Paul 184–5
Trewick, John 265
Tuohy, Liam 280–2, 285–6
Turner, Arthur 60
Turner, Chris 245, 246, 247, 251, 270

Ure, Ian 197, 199

Viollet, Dennis 64–5, 66, 68, 70, 71–2, 214

Waddle, Chris 263–4, 269, 271, 274, 304
Waddock, Gary 300
Waterford 257–8
Watkins, Maurice 266
Webster, Colin 68, 81, 102
West, Gordon 179
Whalley, Bert 77
Whelan, Billy 45, 49, 62, 67, 70, 71, 77
Whelan, Ronnie 288, 297, 307
Whitehead, Roy 243
Whittaker, George 64, 68
Williams, Michael 156
Williamson, Cyril 118
Williams, R. H. 123
Wilson, Peter 128
Wilson, Ray 137, 139, 141–2, 144, 149, 151, 152, 153, 158, 334
Windle, Dick 124
Witcombe, Ronald 25–6
Wood, Mark 11
Wood, Ray 65, 70
World in Action 266

Ainm ....

(BLOCLITREACHA)

Dáta Breithe: ....

Seoladh ....

....

Eircód .... 📱 .... ☎ ....

Glacfaigh mé fógraí ón leabharlann trí: ríomhphoist ☐   téacs ☐

Seoladh r-phoist: ....

Lig don leabharlann ábhar margaíochta a sheoladh chugat: ☐
Roghnaigh an rogha seo más mian leat an t-eolas is déanaí a fháil
faoi imeachtaí na leabharlainne

Cuir in iúl dom má fuair mé earra ar iasacht roimhe seo: ☐
Roghnaigh an rogha seo más mian leat fógraí a fháil agus teideal á
fhorchoimeád nó á fháil ar iasacht agat má fuair tú é ar iasacht roimhe seo

Aontaím mo chuid sonraí a roinnt le líonra leabharlanna poiblí   ☐
Leabharlanna Éireann. Tuigim nach roinnfear mo chuid sonraí le
heagraíochtaí lasmuigh den líonra seo gan mo thoiliú.

Siniú: ....   Dáta: ....

Le comhlánú ag tuismitheoir nó ag caomhnóir má tá an t-iarratasóir faoi 18 mbliana d'aois

Ceadaitear fáil ar earraí do dhaoine fásta leis an mballraíocht seo, mar shampla
leabhair, dlúthdhioscaí nó físdioscaí

LIBRARIES
LEABHARLANNA

Cork City Council Comhairle Cathrach Corcaí

Tá cead ag an iarratasóir:

an tIdirlíon iomlán a úsáid ☐   Fógraí ríomhpoist ón leabharlann a ghlacadh ☐

Siniú an Tuismitheora/Chaomhnóra: ....

Seoladh: ....

Seoladh r-phoist an Tuismitheora/Chaomhnóra: ....

Fón an Tuismitheora/Chaomhnóra: ....

Name ....
(BLOCK LETTERS)

Date of Birth ....

Address ....

Eircode ....

Send me library notices by: email [ ]   text [ ]

email: ....

Allow the library to send marketing material to you: [ ]
Select this option if you would like to receive the latest information about library events

Notify me if I have previously borrowed an item: [ ]
Select this option if you would like to receive notifications when reserving or borrowing a title if you have previously borrowed it

I agree to share my details with the Libraries Ireland network of public libraries. I understand my details will not be shared with organisations outside this network without my consent. [ ]

Signature: ....   Date: ....

To be completed by a parent or guardian if applicant is under 18 years

This membership may allow access to adult items including books, CDs or DVDs

I give my permission for:

Full internet access [ ]   Library notices by email [ ]

Parent/Guardian signature: ....

Address ....

email address of Parent/Guardian ....

Contact number of Parent/Guardian ....

Cork City Council is committed to fulfilling its obligations imposed by the Data Protection Acts 1988 to 2018 and the GDPR. Our privacy statement and data protection policy is available at https://www.corkcity.ie/en/council-services/public-info/gdpr/. We request that you read these as they contain important information about how we process personal data.

LIBRARIES LEABHARLANNA

Cork City Council | Comhairle Cathrach Chorcaí

We are Cork.

World Cups 82–3, 103, 187,
    191–3, 196, 243, 265, 267,
    277, 278, 290, 312
  1966 5–6, 128, 129–32, 135,
    136, 140, 143–60, 187
  Ireland 277, 278, 290, 298–9,
    302–9, 310–11, 312–26

Wylde, Rodger 244, 247–8, 249,
    251, 252, 253

Yarwood, Mike 104
Young, Edwin 26
Younger, Tommy 91